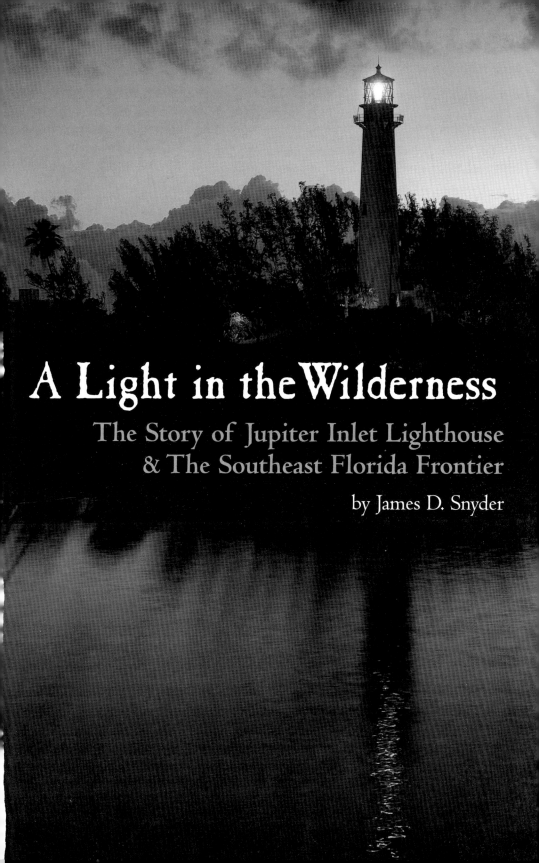

A Light in the Wilderness

The Story of Jupiter Inlet Lighthouse
& The Southeast Florida Frontier

by James D. Snyder

Published by Pharos Books, 8657 SE Merritt Way,
Jupiter, FL 33458-1007. Phone: 561-575-3430

Cover by Ron Parvu.

Inside cover photo by Jim Johnston.
Design and production by Jim Johnston.

First printing, first edition. Printed in China.

Library of Congress Control Number: 2006902971

Publisher's Cataloging-in-Publication
(Provided by Quality Books, Inc.)

Snyder, James D.
  A light in the wilderness : The story of Jupiter Inlet Lighthouse
and the Southeast Florida frontier / by James D. Snyder.
    p. cm.
  Includes bibliographical references and index.
  LCCN 2006902971
  ISBN 09675200-1-0

  1. Jupiter Inlet Light (Fla.)—History—19th century.
  2. Lighthouses—Florida—History—19th century.
  3. Atlantic Coast (Fla.)—History—19th century.
  4. Florida—History—19th century.   I. Title.

F317.P2S69 2006   975.9'3203
                         QBI06-600124

TABLE OF CONTENTS

PART I: A LIGHT

Chapter 1. Nowhere / page 3

The lonely coastline in the mid-1800s. Old Fort Jupiter and the Seminoles. Digging at Jupiter Inlet. Congress authorizes a lighthouse.

Chapter 2. Reefs / page 7

Navigating the Florida coast. The rise of shipping. Key West and its wreckers. Courts and cargo auctions. America's "richest" city.

Chapter 3. Lights!? / page 15

Early lighthouses and lightships. Low bids lead to shoddy workmanship, short towers and weak lights. Fresnel's revolutionary lens. Congress creates a Lighthouse Board. South Florida targeted for construction projects, including one at Jupiter Inlet.

Chapter 4. Meade / page 29

A young aristocrat designs lighthouses in Florida. The army's Topographical Engineers. George Meade's early projects. Where to locate the Jupiter light? Why it was the most difficult to build. Establishing the "new" Fort Jupiter. The Seminoles revolt again. The attack at Cape Florida. Meade's transfer and Raynolds' arrival.

Chapter 5. Outpost / page 55

The Seminole threat halts lighthouse plans. Building a bridge at Fort Jupiter. Another whack at the sandbar across Jupiter Inlet. A soldier's letters home. The Third Seminole War limps to an end.

Chapter 6. Progress? / page 69

"Stinging insects," Yellow Fever and bureaucratic delays. Raynolds heads West and Hartman Bache takes over key lighthouse post. Civil War clouds loom. Jupiter project endangered. Bache finagles a reprieve.

Chapter 7. Yorke / page 81

The mystery man who built Jupiter Light. Escaping the ice and into the sea. A roller coaster ride down the coast. Arrival at "Jones Hill." The tower rises. Preparing the lantern and calibrating the light signature. The search for a keeper. The crew departs and the light shines.

Timelines: 1716-1860 / page 96

PART II. A WAR

Chapter 8. Separation / page 101

A beacon in the wilderness. Florida and the "Black Republican." The state's woeful wartime economy. The Union's *Anaconda* Plan and the first blockade runners. Nassau becomes the Confederacy's general store and playground.

Chapter 9. Vigilantes / page 115

The Blockading Squadron tightens the noose. Florida concedes its coastline. "Kidnapping" the light at Jupiter. The destruction of Cape Florida Lighthouse.

Chapter 10. Gunboats / page 123

The Union holds onto Key West. Destroying salt works. A young officer's personal log. Gunboats take aim at Jupiter Inlet. The lighthouse as Rebel storehouse and lookout tower.

Chapter 11. Crane/ page 139

The *Sagamore* gets "volunteers" to chase blockade runners upriver. Henry Crane and James Armour. The number of captures escalates. Towing "prizes" to Key West. Raiding on the river and the recovery of the Jupiter light apparatus. The *Charm* and its cotton cargo. The shelling of New Smyrna. Death on the *Sagamore*.

Chapter 12. Breakup / page 157

Success dissolves Crane and his volunteers. New Smyrna revisited. Adjudication trials in Key West. The *Charm* found guilty and its cargo auctioned off. Traffic into Nassau harbor dwindles. The war winds down in South Florida.

Confederate Ships Captured / page 166

A list of rebel blockade runners sunk or captured from Jupiter Inlet to Indian River Inlet.

PART III: A SETTLEMENT

Preface

In 2003, when completing *Five Thousand Years on the Loxahatchee*, the history of Jupiter-Tequesta, Florida, I had an uneasy feeling that I'd shortchanged readers when it came to the construction and first years of Jupiter Inlet Lighthouse. Solid bedrock information was sorely lacking.

The early lighthouse data I used were mostly yellowed newspaper clippings. The problem with old press clips is that the first thing a reporter does upon getting a new assignment is go to the "morgue" (the file cabinet of old stories) and read what another reporter wrote on the same subject the last time around. This becomes the new starting point, and if it is full of inaccuracies, it gets handed down to another generation of readers — all of which is how we got ingrained with tales like George Washington chopping down the cherry tree and tossing a silver dollar across the Potomac.

The people of South Florida deserve to know a lot more than they do now. For one thing, Jupiter Lighthouse is southeast Florida's oldest public building in continuous use and the light that drew the first settlers. When the wick was first lit in 1860, the lighthouse was applauded by ship owners and their insurance companies on three continents, deplored by the wreckers of Key West, and watched warily by southern leaders. Abraham Lincoln, excoriated as the "Black Republican" by the southern press, was gaining ground in the 1860 presidential campaign and the air was acrid with talk of secession. Officials in slave-owning Florida wondered whether this new light to promote commercial shipping and safety at sea would help or harm their own cause.

And in their new tower, a half-mile inside Jupiter Inlet, three keepers wondered whether they could survive in one of America's most forlorn outposts when they would be supplied only two or three times a year by a passing Lighthouse Service tender — usually by leaving crates on the beach.

Little did they know that their beacon in the wilderness would soon become a lookout and storage depot for Confederate blockade runners headed to and from Nassau, or that the tower would also help patrolling Union gunboats track down and capture more than fifty rebel ships and several secret storage depots on land.

In a research effort that ranged from the National Archives in Washington to U.S. district court records in Key West, my biggest joy was in finding so many documents intact. Military personnel may grumble about bureaucratic paperwork, but it certainly did help reconstruct a wealth of background knowledge about when forts were manned, how lighthouses were built, and where ships were stationed.

My biggest disappointment was the fire of 1920. That's the year in which a blaze swept through the Commerce Department in Washington, destroying many original records of the old Light House Board. Thus, for example, we have only a one-sentence scrap reporting that the gunboat *Sagamore* recovered the kidnapped lighthouse parts in 1863. Likewise, we have three complete letters accusing lighthouse keeper James Armour of major malfeasance, but only a one-sentence summary exonerating him. And we might have learned more about Edward Yorke, the mystery man who built Jupiter Light.

What we *do* have in the aggregate is a new perspective on the settlement of southeast Florida and how interdependent and interconnected the early pioneers were — from Titusville at the tip of the Indian River, to Cape Florida and the Miami River. The story of Jupiter Lighthouse is *their* story as well.

Acknowledgements

The following organizations and individuals all provided help and resources for this project: the Brevard County Historical Commission and Commissioner Roz Foster; the Brevard County Public Library; Cape Canaveral Lighthouse historian Rose Wooley; the Florida Historical Society; the state of Florida's Bureau of Surveying & Mapping and historian Joe Knetsch, Ph. D.; genealogist Lynn Drake of Jupiter; FL; the Historical Museum of South Florida; the Historical Society of Palm Beach County and Research Director Debi Murray; the Historical Society of Pennsylvania, the Loxahatchee River Historical Society and Executive Director Jamie Stuve; lighthouse historian/consultant Candace Clifford; the Monroe County Public Library at Key West and historian Tom Hambright; the helpful staff of the National Archives and Records Administration, the New Smyrna Museum of History; Ponce De Leon Inlet LightHouse and Curator Ellen Henry. Thanks also to three living descendants of lighthouse keepers: Kathy Legal (James Armour), Marty Baum (Hannibal Pierce) and Raymond Swanson (Ralph Swanson and Mills O. Burnham).

My special thanks to those who took their valuable time to edit and comment on the manuscript. They are: Rodney Dillon, Roz Foster, Joe Knetsch, Debi Murray, and Rose Wooley. And from the Loxahatchee River Historical Society: Robert Boyd, Catherine Dosa and Chuck Millhauser.

Finally, my love and thanks to my wife Sue, the only person who has been at my side throughout every research trip and every part of the editing process.

PART I

A Light

MAP

OF THE

SEAT OF WAR

IN

FLORIDA

COMPILED BY ORDER OF

BV.T BRIG.R GEN.L Z . TAYLOR,

principally from the surveys and reconnaissances
of the Officers of the U.S.Army,

BY CAP.T JOHN MACKAY AND LIEU.T J.E.BLAKE

Just after the Second Seminole War, the southeastern Florida wilderness was interrupted only by a few military trails. The rough-hewn roads would one day become major highways.
(Library of Congress / Geography and Map Division)

In additi
importan
the follow

Capt.s Gu
Gunniso
Lieut. La
Capt.s J.F
G.Thoma
Capt.s Ba
J.W.Ande
Lieut. Ca

SCALE OF STATUTE MILES

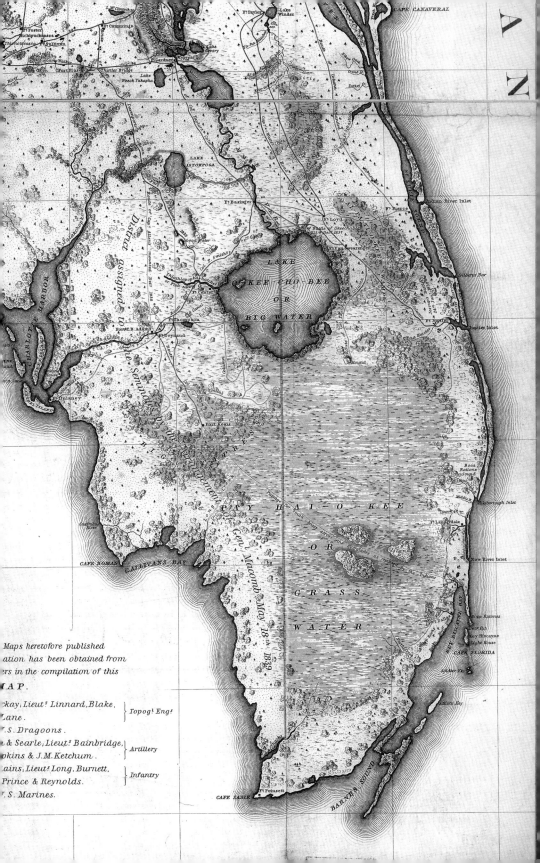

N

CAPE CANAVERAL

F? Taylor   Lake Winder

F? Foster
Fichtucknasas
Sullivan

F? Cumming

Indian River Inlet

Walker

F? Gardner

Cypress L.

Lake Weeok Takapka

Thistles Bridge

Fort Pratt

F? Pierce

LAKE ISTOKPOGA

F? Basinger

F? Loyd
Battle of Okeechobee
25 th Dec. 1837

Calberts Bar

District assigned to the Seminoles by the

LAKE
KEE-CHO-BEE
OR
BIG WATER

F? Smith's

F? Colton

F? Jupiter

Jupiter Inlet

F? Thompson

Fort M. B. Adams

F? Vleyland

CHARLOTTE HARBOR

Dulaney

Fort Keais

Boca
Ratons
Sound

Indian Cove

Middle R.

Hisborough Inlet

PESS

PAY-HAI-O-KEE

F? Lauderdale

CAPE ROMAN

SULLIVANS BAY

OR

New River Inlet

by Gen? Macomb May 18 th 1839

GRASS

KEY BISCAYNE BAY

Boca Ratones
Bear Cut
Key Biscayne
Light House

WATER

CAPE FLORIDA

Soldier Key

Elliots Key

CAPE SABLE   F? Poinsett

BARNES SOUND

Chapter 1

Nowhere

From Cape Canaveral to Key Biscayne, Florida's sandy southeast coast stretches over 250 miles. It covers seven counties that together take up nearly 10,000 square miles – bigger than the state of Vermont.

Today that corridor contains nearly seven million residents and who knows how many tourists and vacation homeowners.

In 1845, when Florida became a state, scarcely anyone lived there at all. To be sure, the Ais, Jeaga and other offshoots of the powerful Calusa Indians had walked and canoed all over the place for some 5,000 years. But by the mid-eighteenth century, the Spaniards and English, with all their guns and poxes, had wiped out the last of the indigenous Indians. After fifty or so years, a few thousand Seminole Indians would filter in from southern tier states, but by 1845, they, too, were on the verge of extermination.

At the southern end of the coast, what is now Miami consisted of an abandoned U.S. Army outpost once called Fort Dallas. Five miles away on Key Biscayne stood the crumbling, charred husk of the Cape Florida Lighthouse, the only other man-made structure of any consequence in South Florida. It had been built and lit in 1825, but had provided only flickers of safety to passing ships. Soon after its construction, reports from mariners reached Washington City that the keeper preferred to live on the mainland, allowing the lighthouse to be run by slaves when he didn't need them for other chores. In 1836 the lighthouse was torched by marauding Seminole Indians, and afterwards no one felt safe enough to venture out in that no man's land to try rebuilding it.

At the northern end of the corridor, where the salty lagoon took on two channels as it swept by Merritt Island, the only inhabitants were a few hermits who lived in bug-infested shacks made of driftwood and roofed with palmetto leaves. In 1848 the federal government would build a 60-foot lighthouse on Cape Canaveral, but it was so short that mariners often ran aground on the shoals looking for it. After a while, no one gave it much thought.

At Jupiter Inlet, in the middle of the corridor, there was absolutely no one. Unless you count ghosts. In January 1838 Major General Thomas S. Jesup and 1,600 soldiers tracked some 300 Indian warriors to an obscure riverfront about 9 miles west of Jupiter and finally wore them down in a battle that was supposed to end the Second Seminole Indian War. There, on the upper Loxahatchee River, they built a crude stockade of sorts so the troops could lick their wounds, bury their dead and await new provisions from army headquarters in Tampa.

Fort Jupiter also served as a corral in which to round up some 500 exhausted Seminole men, women and children so they could be herded off to newly-created reservations in Oklahoma.

Perhaps the first "tourist" to write about life in Jupiter was Jacob Rhett Motte, an army surgeon who had slogged through the swamps with Jesup's foot soldiers as they nicked their limbs on the razor-like sawgrass and filled their boots with swamp muck in their dirty, dreary pursuit of the elusive Indian. Motte was a Harvard-educated blueblood from genteel Charleston society who rued the day his youthful imagination was dazzled by the glitter of an officer's sword. As he recalled, after spending $300 for his own uniforms and medical instruments, "I had to find lodging, board, clothing and washing on a monthly paycheck of $54."

Motte most lamented the separation from his books, longing for "even the sight of an old almanac to refresh my eyes with something in print." His only solace, only contact with anything literary was in keeping his own journal. Here is what he wrote about Jupiter and South Florida:

It is in fact a most hideous region to live in; a perfect paradise for Indians, alligators, serpents, frogs and every other kind of loathsome reptile. The whole peninsula is alluvial, having been formed by successive encroachments on the Atlantic; and offers but feeble allurements to an agricultural population, the only land fit for cultivation being on the margin of the rivers, and inconsiderable as to extent, and barely sufficient to raise the ordinary subsistence for small families.

The only resources are ranges for cattle, wrecking and the fisheries. The sea beach is constantly enriched by the misfortunes of the enterprising, which I believe [accounts for] *the strong attraction of the Indians to the country. Such can be the only allurements to emigrant adventurers. Then why not in the name of common sense let the Indians keep it?* [1]

Indeed, the weary, wretched, nearly starved Seminoles had clustered around Fort Jupiter, beseeching General Jesup to plead with the Great Father in Washington (the role being played at the time by Martin Van Buren) to let them stay in this unhealthy swamp rather than leave the spirits of their forefathers and perhaps die on the trek to alien Oklahoma. Jesup, who would have agreed with his surgeon's journal entries, finally decided to send a young lieutenant to Washington for a decision by President Van Buren and/or his secretary of war, Joel Roberts Poinsett.

While the Indians waited, busying themselves playing ball games and mooching whiskey, Motte was stricken with a crushing headache that forced him into a crumpled heap in his soppy, bug-infested tent for two weeks. "My sickness produced at the time the feelings of perfect disgust for Florida and the life we led there," he would write later. "Oh that I could only have escaped this detested soil, thought I. That I might once more live as a human being." 2

After he recovered, Motte's only pleasure would be an occasional two-and-a-half mile row down to Jupiter Inlet, where he and fellow officers would walk the beach and "gather the beautiful shells and other marine substances thrown up by the sea."

On his last visit to the inlet, Motte was amazed to find it "completely closed up, a dry sand bar across its mouth in one night." The previous day, he wrote, "we had left it a broad, deep channel, capable of admitting the smaller vessels that sail the ocean."

That was in February 1838. On March 20 the army messenger returned to Fort Jupiter with a response from Secretary Poinsett. After spending $8 million to hound what began as 3,500 Seminoles to the ends of Florida, (or $3 million more than the government had spent to buy the state from Spain), Poinsett was damned if he was going to allow the last ragged, wretched survivors even an alligator-infested swamp that no white man wanted. He sympathized with Jesup's logic, but he stated that any leniency would contradict the recently-enacted Indian Removal Act. Poinsett also ruminated that observers abroad might conclude that the up-and-coming United States capitulated to a ragged band of savages.

Well before the presidential proclamation arrived, some 200 Seminoles had melted away after deciding not to bet their lives on the Great Father's leniency. As soon as the messenger arrived from Washington, the 300 remaining Seminoles were invited to a sort of hootenanny, with promises of whiskey to enliven the dancing. In the early morning hours, their libations having produced what Motte called "profound sleep," the snoring Indians were aroused by the poking of gun butts to find themselves surrounded by soldiers. Only then were they told that the Great Father had insisted on unconditional surrender.

By May 1838 the last of the Indian captives had been shipped west. Motte had gone off with the rest of his comrades toward Fort Lauderdale in pursuit of the 200 phantoms who now dwelled in the swamps and hammocks to the south.

In 1844 a federal land surveyor passed by the abandoned Fort Jupiter and reported it a "burned out carcass."

That same year, William Davis decided that it just didn't seem right that the Loxahatchee River would flow eastward for 14 miles, only to have its rendezvous with the sea blocked by a slender sandbar. At the time, Davis, who would one day be the keeper who re-lit the Jupiter Lighthouse after the Civil War, was a soldier at Fort Capron (just west of the Fort Pierce Inlet) who delivered the mail to Cape Florida. According to a young officer who heard about the sand bar when visiting Fort Capron, Davis persuaded five other men to pack tents and shovels and accompany him as far south as Jupiter Inlet on one of his mail runs. Wrote Lieutenant Andrew A. Humphries:

After digging for several hours, they succeeded by nightfall in starting outward a stream of water four inches in depth. Upon this they desisted from labor and went to their camp, which was some fifty feet from the ditch.

The river inside was unusually high from a freshet [overflowing of water] *in the Everglades, and a strong north wind was blowing. At night, the sleeping party were awakened by a flood of water and had to abandon their camp equipage and run for their lives, barely escaping being carried out to sea. The next day there was a channel nearly a quarter of a mile wide, and the rush of water could be traced far out into the ocean.* [3]

The inlet had remained open when Lieutenant Humphries himself visited it a few years later, prompting him to report back to Washington that the inlet entrance, "protected from the north wind by a ledge of rocks" and having "admitted vessels drawing eight feet," might just "render the harbor one of the best upon the eastern coast."

The inlet was still open in 1852 when lighthouse planners in Washington decided that Jupiter Inlet needed a beacon.

The bureaucrats had no idea what they were getting into.

Chapter 2

Reefs

So......why build a lighthouse where nobody lived?

There was no one, but there was every reason to do so. A lighthouse was wanted by everyone from the navy, which had to provide safe supply to its vital Key West base, to sea captains, insurance companies and the merchants of young, trade-starved Florida. And in the minds of visionaries, the lighthouse one day would be part of a coastal chain ensuring that no sea captain would ever be out of sight of a beacon.

Besides, the whole Florida coastline had always been a navigational nightmare. A captain heading south would sail inside the Gulf Stream, which flowed northward from two to ten miles offshore. The Stream began to get its power when the sea waters were squeezed into an eighty-mile channel between Cuba and the Florida Keys. But when it rounded Cape Florida, its speed increased to 5 or so knots an hour as the water was compressed into a 45-mile-wide stretch between Grand Bahama and the Florida Coast. In midstream off Jupiter, for example, the Gulf Stream, driven by a steady southeast wind, could push a southbound sailing ship all the way back to the islands of Georgia.

On a clear day the ship's navigator could easily discern the cobalt blue of the Gulf Stream to his port. To his starboard he could make out the light green waters around reefs and the mottled brown and pale orange of coral heads below. But by night these color coordinates were turned off. Unlike a shoreline with mountains or a populated place with lights twinkling in buildings, the Florida coast was a flat gray enigma that dissolved into the horizon.

One thing more: Florida had fickle winds that could bedevil a sailing vessel. When winds were becalmed, sailors whittled while they waited helplessly for the return of their only source of power. But too often the winds raged, battering the beams of ships towards reefs and sandbars. And if a captain tried to escape into an inlet for shelter, he was rolling the dice that he could dodge reefs to get inside and avoid sandy shoals once he did.

Ever since the Spanish settled South America, ships have sailed through the Cuba-Key West gap, around Cape Florida and into the Gulf Stream, which would propel them towards ports in Europe. As the number of galleons laden with copper, silver, gold, tobacco and indigo increased, so did the number of pirates chasing them. But the reefs claimed even more ships than pirates. No wonder that the Florida Keys were known in the 16th century as *Las Islas de los Martires*, or Martyr Islands.

But now, in the 19th century, shipping through the Florida Straits was increasing exponentially. After the United States acquired the Louisiana Territory in 1803, Gulf ports began to flourish. Cotton, lumber and farm produce were carried down the Mississippi River in flatboats, loaded onto ocean-going ships in New Orleans and sent around Cape Florida on their way to Europe, Canada and eastern U.S. ports. They joined other ships carrying logwood and cochineal from Campeche, coffee and rum from Jamaica and sugar from Cardenas and Matanzas. And headed back the other way was a steady stream of provisions and luxury goods for the planters of the Caribbean and Gulf of Mexico.

In 1819, when Spain ceded Florida to the U.S., many a Spaniard unloaded property to bargain-hunting Americans before sailing off to Cuba. In 1821 one of them sold an island just 90 miles north of Cuba to John Simonton, a well-connected New Jersey businessman, for $2,000. By then its Spanish name had become *Cayo Hueso* ("Bone" Key), but Americans were already calling it Key West. It was only a sun-bleached, two-by-four-mile outcrop of dead coral, but Simonton had himself a bargain. He had bought himself the only deep water harbor in the United States from there to Charleston.

One end of the island was already home to a couple hundred squatters who fished and sponged and recognized no landowner, or no government, for that matter. Simonton seemed scarcely to notice them as he sliced his new land into four large plots and sold off three to some equally successful entrepreneurs from New England.

But all this was secondary to his main purpose. Simonton envisioned the island as an ideal wrecking center. At the time, almost all the salvaging of stricken ships off southern Florida was done by crews from Nassau who brought their largesse to friendly English courts that would grant them 50 to 75 percent of a ship or cargo's value at auction. At the same time, Simonton, who had business contacts from New Orleans to New York, began lobbying the Monroe administration to take advantage of his deep harbor and establish America's southernmost navy base.

In 1822 Navy Secretary Smith Thompson persuaded President James Monroe to back the idea. "We are, at this time, dependent on the wreckers of New Providence for the protection of our property in case of shipwreck," Thompson wrote. Moreover, "it is intended to make [Key West] a depot for provisions and supplies for the expedition against the pirates [as] lately authorized by Congress." [1]

A home for wreckers, but not pirates? There was indeed a difference, although definitions varied from man to man.

Wreckers. Even the rescuers called themselves by that name, but at a time when there was no Coast Guard and absolutely no one living along the Florida coast, grounding a ship could be tantamount to death. It wasn't until the 1870s that the federal government began building a series of life saving stations every fifty or so miles. Before that, the shipwrecked were dependent on the good graces of small-rigged boats that were outfitted primarily for fishing, sponging and turtling. But when the "*Wreck Ashore!*" call spread through the crew's quarters – invariably at a time of gale winds and high seas – they often put their own lives in peril even to approach a ship twisting violently in the clutches of a reef. In 1842 even the shipper-friendly *Hunt's Merchants' Magazine* editorialized that "wreckers," for all the negative connotations of the name, "have never refused to listen to the calls of humanity, even when doing so has been to their loss." [2]

But ah, once the passengers and baggage had been safely accounted for, the sport could begin! Author Vincent Gilpin captured the scene surrounding a reefed ship bound for Havana with a "huge general emporium" containing everything from lace and silk to liquor and fine furniture:

On deck two crews of fifty each manned great tackles, their faces alight with joy, their mellow voices ringing out, adrip with glory, as the grand old chanties rolled across the waves, timing their pull on the cargo nets. How their eyes gleamed as each load swung out on deck, and followed every item on its way to the schooners alongside! How they laughed and joked in the intervals! How the joy of life fairly lit up the scene! It was the fun of wrecking at its best. [3]

Although some Key West lore – such as the tales of putting lanterns on cows and moving them around to confuse navigators – is probably a hangover from 18th century pirate days, some early wreckers "sailed pretty close to the wind," as one of them recalled.

Bradish W. "Hog" Johnson, for example, specialized in probing abandoned hulls. Some weeks after a stricken ship's cargo had been collected and auctioned off, Johnson's schooner would loom over the sunken vessel with a team of Bahamian divers who could last two minutes underwater purely on lung power. Diving naked, they would glide through the ghost ship, removing expensive fixtures and prying into lockers for valuables hastily left behind.

In one instance, Johnson was paid to tow a damaged cargo ship onto a shoal and pump her out so as to gauge her chances of repair. But try as he might, Johnson's powerful wrecking pumps couldn't displace the water in the hull. "Worms must have ruined her bottom," he sadly informed the owner. When another man came along and offered $200 for the hulk, the distressed owner accepted it and caught the next north-bound schooner for home.

But saints be praised! No sooner had the owner departed when it was discovered that the pumping problem had been caused by a missing plank in the hull. As luck would have it, Johnson had one exactly the same size in his ramshackle warehouse! Once the plank was hammered into the hull, the boat was raised, refitted and sold to another shipper for $5,000.

It seems that the $200 "buyer" had used Johnson's money and gotten a $50 "consulting fee" for his trouble. [4]

When the U.S. acquired Florida from Spain in 1821, it was a signal to grab the wrecking business from the English in Nassau. The Legislative Council of the Territory of Florida was so inclined, but powerless to do what was clearly the prerogative of Congress. So wreckers in Key West soon took matters in their own hands, refusing en masse to furnish fresh water and other provisions to Bahamian salvors.

In 1825 Congress did act, ruling that no vessel salvaged within the jurisdiction of the U.S. could be taken to a foreign port. It meant that all wreckers had to take salvaged property to Key West or make the arduous trip to St. Augustine. Soon, writes Dorothy Dodd in her enviable treatise on wrecking, "Every person in Key West, excepting possibly those in the navy, was interested in the business, and the territorial law placed the adjudication of salvage entirely in local hands. Sometimes," she adds, "the presiding magistrate was the judge who condemned, the auctioneer who sold, and the purchaser of the same property." With salvage awards running from 75 to 93 percent (Key Westers seemed to be out-grabbing their rivals in Nassau) no wonder that the *New York Mercantile Advertiser* would lament that "special little is therefore left for the underwriters." [5]

In 1828 Congress established a federal court at Key West covering everything south of a line extending from Indian River west to Charlotte Harbor. Its sole judge was also given special powers to license wreckers and disqualify any found to be in collusion with the master of a wrecked vessel. From that time until 1863 the court was headed by two men – James Webb, and his successor William Marvin – who between them created the case law that evolved wrecking into a well-regulated business. It all revolved around the court's power to revoke licenses. The causes, as Judge Marvin put it, could include "embezzlement of wrecked goods; voluntarily running a vessel aground under the pretense of piloting her; colluding with the master of a vessel wrecked or in distress; or corrupting him by an unlawful present or promise." [6]

The court recognized the intense competition that ruled the reefs by allowing that wreckers should be admitted to attend a stricken ship in the order in which they arrived. The first boarder was required to hand the captain a copy of his wrecking license. The latter had the right to refuse all help or to employ any other vessel he chose. But with both the seas and his passengers probably heaving as the ship wobbled atop a reef, the odds were that the captain would welcome the first to arrive. If so, the boarding captain would become the "wreck master." He could exclude other salvors as long as he had the resources to save the property. However, the typical wrecker – a fisher or sponger just hours before – probably couldn't handle a large cargo ship without help.

Under the court's guiding hand, the number of licensed vessels grew from 20 in 1835 to 57 in 1858. Most vessels, owned by New England whalers and commercial buccaneers, were fast-sailing, clean-rigged sloops and schooners, ranging from ten to a hundred tons, with an average value of about $2,500. Against that investment, the average annual salvage for all vessels during 1844-59 was $114,378. But there were also indirect profits. Because wreckers also owned wharves and warehouses, they quickly created what would today be called an "aftermarket" of commissions and fees from handling the ships and goods brought into Key West by their crews.

Under the system that evolved, half the total salvage allotted to a vessel by the court went to the wrecker-owner(s). The other half was divided among the crew. If the wrecker vessel were over 30 tons, the master received 3 shares, the mate 2, the cook 1.25 and ordinary seamen 1 each. Boys under 18 got half shares.

And so, in a typical case, the *James* was beached between Cape Florida and Jupiter in 1836 with a cargo of cotton. Captain John H. Geiger of the schooner *Hester Ann* learned about it in Key West and soon formed a consortium with the masters of the *Caroline, Amelia* and *Splendid*. When the four schooners arrived at the wreck scene, their crews became one team as they began to unload the *James*. After 16 hours, the 38 crewmen from the 4 wreckers, aided by 8 men from the stricken *James*, had off-loaded 519 bales of cotton, which, at 180 pounds each, would require a good dram of rum to relieve an aching back. For its services the court awarded the wrecking consortium $12,313.55, based on 40 percent of the cargo rescued. The crewmen got their shares in the form of cotton, which pitted them against each other in selling at auction.

When wrecked property was taken to Key West, storing and selling it meant employing another group of islanders. The captain of the wrecked vessel was required to consign the cargo to a local resident, who became its business agent. Usually that person was a merchant who also owned wharves and warehouses. The agent was entitled to five percent of all sums he spent for unloading and storage. Both salvors and ship owners had to be represented in court by lawyers, called proctors, at a standard fee of $20 plus 3 percent of the salvage value.

If salvage were awarded in kind (such as bales of cotton), the goods had to be properly valued, meaning a $10-per-day fee for the appraiser. If salvage were paid in money, the goods were sold by a U.S. marshal, who got two percent for "costs."

With a legal system now entrenched for licensing wreckers and setting salvage values, Key West attracted both capital and captains from the northeast's most established fishing fleets. By the 1850s the island city was flourishing with more than 50 wreckers, who could count on 2 or 3 ships per month hitting reefs as if on some sort of pre-ordained schedule. In the 16 years ending in 1859, the court awarded them about $1.8 million as their share of salvage value and another $1.4 million in reimbursed expenses. The $3.2 million total was based on the salvaged vessels' combined cargo value of $25.4 million. Thus, the wreckers got a combined 12.5 percent for their efforts.

The community sharing in that largesse had around 500 residents in 1838 and 2,241 by 1860. No one argued when Key West was described as America's wealthiest town on a per-capita basis. No wonder that the large Victorian homes of wreckers were known for sporting the most cosmopolitan collection of fine furniture, linens and china in the hemisphere.

Everyone was happy but insurance companies. Stunned by loss after loss, marine underwriters initially pointed to Key West's monopoly on wrecking as the chief cause. Lamented *Hunt's Merchant Magazine* in 1842:

> *The marshal advertises the goods…the auction sale comes on, and thirty to forty thousand dollars worth of goods are sold on an island containing five to six merchants, nearly a hundred miles from any inhabited land. The day of sale arrives. Who are the bidders? The aforesaid five merchants! How easily might these merchants agree not to* [compete with] *each other on their bids. And thus a whole cargo, worth thirty thousand dollars, might be divided among them at a cost of two thousand dollars each or less.* [7]

For underwriters, it always seemed a case of their agent learning about a wreck too late and arriving on the scene after all the goods had vanished. In 1838, for example, insurers didn't know that the ship *Bombay* had run up on a reef near the Tortugas until twenty days later. When their agent finally reached Key West, he found that the captain of the *Bombay* had sold her hull for $1,400 to wreckers, who bought her salvaged rigging in Key West for $3,000. They had already refitted the freed ship and sold it to a New Orleans company for $12,000.

Fishing boats from Key West converted instantly to wreckers when a passing ship piled up on the many surrounding reefs. And ships did so with amazing regularity. *(Illustration from Harpers New Monthly Magazine)*

Chapter 3

Lights!?

By the late 1840s underwriters had learned their lesson and many had stationed resident agents in Key West, as had several European nations. But they still hadn't made a dent in insurance rates. In 1849 the prevailing rate on merchantmen bound for the Florida Straits was 1.5% of the combined ship and cargo value – the same as for vessels sailing around the more treacherous, tumultuous Straits of Magellan for the hemisphere's western coast.

Before long, complaints began to center on aids to navigation – or the lack thereof. Until the middle of the nineteenth century, no complete survey had been made of the Florida reef. Nautical charts were based on Spanish works, which were often copies of slapdash efforts made by the British during their brief reign between 1763 and 1783. In 1849, after the collector of customs in Key West pointed out that three-fourths of all the vessels bound for the Florida Strait were owned by northern firms, Congress finally authorized a major effort to chart Florida's coast and reefs.

Lighthouses were in equally shabby shape. Congress had acted in 1824, but the first results were dismaying. Plans were laid for lights at Cape Florida, Key West, Sand Key, Carysfort Reef and the Dry Tortugas and all were expected to be completed by the end of the following year. However, the contractor, who sailed from Boston in August 1824, was reported lost at sea along with all his materials. The lighthouses, when eventually built, were all about 65 feet high and instantly ridiculed by captains that they weren't tall enough to be seen until one was almost on the reefs they were supposed to guard.

The only architectural exception was a lightship that was to be stationed outside the dangerous Carysfort Reef (off Key Largo). Not long after being tethered to its mooring, the lightship broke away, wandered into the Gulf Stream, got stuck on Key Biscayne and was hauled off by wreckers. Once reclaimed and repositioned, Carysfort Lightship fell into disrepute amidst charges that captains of leaky old tubs often arranged for the keeper to dim his light so they could run into the reefs and claim full insurance value.

When the Colonies became a nation in 1789 the government inherited a jumble of navigational aids. Lights and towers came in a mishmash of sizes, financed by private pocketbooks, lotteries and general taxes. The only constant factor was that the actual beams were fixed (steady) white lights that left skippers wondering where they were on black stormy nights.

On August 7, 1789, in just the ninth bill passed by the first Congress, the federal government took responsibility for all navigational aids, to be financed from the general treasury. Alexander Hamilton, the first treasury secretary, personally supervised the lights. Archives show that presidents such as Washington, Adams and Jefferson all involved themselves in selecting lighthouse construction sites and appointing keepers.

In 1820, with the number of lighthouses now up to 55, the Treasury Department assigned their supervision to the commissioner of revenue. Why? Because a collector of customs was often stationed by a lighthouse or at the harbor from which revenue cutters would sail out to meet and board an arriving ship. The inbound vessel would be denied entry unless its cargo was first inventoried and the proper import duties paid. One good result was that the cutters — seven at the turn of the nineteenth century — were outfitted with extra stores and given an extra mission. Instead of remaining snuggly at wharf side until ships hove outside the harbor, revenue cutters now spent whole winters patrolling the seas for troubled ships in need of help.

Beginning in 1820, the fate of lighthouses would be linked with that of one man for 32 years. In that year their jurisdiction was assigned — still within the Treasury Department — to one Stephen Pleasanton, who held the title of Fifth Auditor.

Pleasanton, with his craggy features and studious frown, could have served as Charles Dickens' inspiration for Ebenezer Scrooge. And Scrooge would have approved of the labels people applied to him: "zealous," "hard-working," and a "conscientious guardian of the public dollar."

Despite his mundane sounding title, Stephen Pleasanton was one of nine principal fiscal guardians for the U.S. government, and his platoon of clerks oversaw spending for a cluster of agencies such as the State Department, Patent Office and Census Bureau.

The Pleasanton era arrived just as the young government was making a major effort to bring its system of navigational aids in line with its role as an emerging sea power. By 1832 the Fifth Auditor was overseeing 256 lighthouses,

30 lightships and nearly 1,000 buoys. In the mind of the maritime world, this office-bound accountant was the de facto czar of lighthouses and the era was as much associated with his name as was the F.B.I. under J. Edgar Hoover a century later.

Pleasanton's powers were delegated broadly. Except for the appointment of keepers, made by the Treasury Secretary, the Fifth Auditor deputized the various collectors of customs to construct and maintain all navigational aids in their districts. They handled personnel matters, conducted annual inspections, and for their troubles received a 2.5 percent commission on all lighthouse disbursements. The collectors, in turn, relied heavily on private contractors for everything from building lighthouses to keeping them provisioned.

Pleasanton rode herd on this network of supervisors by mandating his personal approval of all outlays over $100. All contracts were rigidly reviewed to be sure they had gone to the lowest bidder. The Fifth Auditor's greatest achievement, in his own eyes, was his efficiency and economy, often claiming that he had returned more money to the general treasury each year than any other auditor. Indeed, in 1842 he testified proudly at a congressional hearing that he operated American lighthouses at half the cost of his English counterpart. [1]

But there was another side to the coin, of course. Each revenue collector who supervised lighthouse keepers in his district was himself a political appointee, and lighthouses soon became pawns on the chessboard of politics. Keepers came to expect that when a new political party assumed power, a replacement would show up with an "Extinguished Service Check" – a printed form about the size of a bank check. It bore the signature of the local collector of revenue and stated coldly:

> "You are suspended as keeper of _____ light station on (date)_____by_____, the bearer of this notice."

The bearer had a snug patronage job for the duration, but it also meant that most keepers were keener on attending meetings of their local political clubs than attending to the grinding routine of a lighthouse.

Even so, the system's greater shortcoming was in the design and construction of lighthouses themselves. It began with the aforementioned lack of height brought on by parsimonious construction policies.

Except for the light at Key Biscayne, in 1825, the government took no action to build lighthouses on the east coast of Florida until ten years later. What happened then typified a maritime malaise on a national scale. The next light, at Mosquito Inlet (today's Ponce Inlet) never functioned. The keeper was still awaiting his first shipment of oil when a storm sent seawater rushing over the base, sucking out the sand and collapsing the tower. Rebuilding, slowed by Indian hostilities, would wait until 1886.

When the 65-foot Cape Canaveral tower went up, engineers had recommended the strongest light available, but the one that arrived was so ineffectual that many ships ran up on the surrounding shoals looking for it.

Continuing problems with the somewhat older lights in the Florida Keys illustrated the downside of hiring contractors. In 1837 a team sent to examine the effects of the Indian attack on the Cape Florida light at Key Biscayne found that whereas the specifications had called for solid brick walls five feet thick, they were "hollow from the base upwards," meaning that "one-half of the bricks and materials required to erect a solid wall were saved to the benefit of the contractor." [2]

The inspection team also learned that the contractor's bricks originally came from demolished buildings in northern cities. The mélange assembled by masons at Cape Florida — varying greatly by strength and age — had been bought by the contractor at a yard in Boston that sold used bricks cheaply for use as ballast in ship bottoms. And yet on December 17, 1825, the district customs collector had sent the Treasury Department a letter certifying that "the lighthouse and dwelling-house on Cape Florida are finished in a workmanlike manner, agreeably to the within-written contract." [3]

Stephen Pleasanton's most dubious legacy was in the outmoded, ghostly lights that flickered in the precarious towers. Lighthouse historian F. Ross Holland Jr. wrote that "one wonders how many ships that wrecked during Pleasanton's 32-year administration would have been saved had more effective lights been available." [4]

Actually, there *was* a better light and Stephen Pleasanton was aware of it even in his landlocked office in the Treasury building. By then almost everyone in the maritime world had heard of the Frenchman Fresnel and his marvelous lens.

Augustin-Jean Fresnel was born in 1788. His father was an architect who managed major building projects for nobles in the courts of Louis XV and XVI. Besides being an ardent royalist, both father and mother were Catholics and Jansenists – followers of Cornelius Otto Jansen, who taught that God predestined everyone to eternal damnation except for a select hardworking, virtuous few.

When the republican revolution erupted in Paris with all its tumult, Fresnel whisked his family away to the quiet Norman village of Mathieu, where Augustin-Jean was raised. Frail and quiet from his earliest years, Fresnel could barely pass his reading lessons, yet showed a remarkable talent for science and math. Because of his delicate health, he couldn't qualify as an officer in Napoleon's army, the goal of most promising lads. Instead he became a civil engineer, to be employed in building roads and bridges.

Fresnel hated road-building. But worse than that, "I hate to lead men," the introverted young man would write. Every spare moment he had was spent in solitary research on scientific inquiries.

One of his interests was *light* and how it travels. At the time, the conventional view of light had been formulated by Isaac Newton 150 years before, namely that beams were really swarms of "corpuscles" moving through "ether." Newton theorized that each light corpuscle had a different mass that varied according to its color. When Newton's corpuscles exhibited themselves as rays of light, they were either refracted or reflected depending on their mass and color.

The lenses used in lighthouses at the time were *catoptric* – usually a "bull's-eye" that drew light to a central target area. However, it also dissipated a beam's power by allowing some of the light to escape from the top and bottom of the lens.

Later came the *dioptric* lens, which bent light and directed it to the desired point.

What Fresnel did in between his reluctant road building projects was to combine the two former systems into a single lens called *catadioptric*. As explained by maritime historian Dennis L. Noble, "the lens contained a central reflecting bull's-eye surrounded by a series of concentric prismatic rings and refracting prisms. In very brief terms, light is directed by prismatic rings to the central bull's-eye where it emerges as a single concentrated shaft of light traveling in one direction." [5]

Or, as Hans Christian Adamson explains in his *Keepers of the Lights*, "The effect is similar to the flow of water through a well-nozzled hose. The bull's-eye is the hose. The refracting prisms and glass rings that bend and direct the beams corresponds to the nozzle that directs a solid column in only one direction — outward." [6]

Perhaps the best thing that happened to Fresnel as a research scientist was the return of Napoleon from Elba in 1815 and another (albeit short-lived) military dictatorship. Known as a staunch royalist, Fresnel was forced from his engineering position, but suddenly found himself with time to focus on his light experiments. Although his health was failing, he seemed driven on by an even greater sense of urgency. "All the compliments I have ever received never gave me so much pleasure as the discovery of a theoretic truth or the confirmation of a calculation by experiment," he once said. [7]

In 1821, still only 33, Fresnel was named temporary secretary to the Commission for Lighthouses. Soon his lenses were installed in the most important lighthouses on the French coast. But in 1827, on Bastille Day, Fresnel's frail health failed him.

Fortunately, his technology was adopted by at least four major optical manufacturers, all clustered around Paris. Together they would go on to produce hundreds of lens systems in six *orders* ranked according to size and brightness. For example, the sixth order lens, which was earmarked for use on piers or breakwaters, weighed 220 pounds and its lamp was calculated to burn 3.15 ounces of rapeseed or colza oil per hour. At the top of the hierarchy, the first order lens, designed for major seacoast lighthouses, weighed 12,800 pounds and its lamp consumed 26 ounces of oil per hour. In terms of relative brightness, the first order outshone the sixth order by a factor of eighteen.

Stephen Pleasanton, never known to leave Washington nor inspect a lighthouse, had long heard talk of Fresnel, but it wasn't until 1830 that the Fifth Auditor troubled himself to write one of the manufacturers in Paris to find out how much the confounded things actually cost. When he learned that the price tag on a first-order lens was $5,000 and that even a third order one was $2,000, he reacted like the man who decided he wasn't going to quit driving his quaint Oldsmobile just because someone had invented a Corvette. The American standby at the time was the Winslow Lewis lens, and Pleasanton had practically developed a partnership with its inventor.

Winslow Lewis would occupy center stage in U.S. lighthouse affairs even longer than Pleasanton. Born in 1770, 15 years before Fresnel, this son of a merchant captain from Cape Cod was his counterpart's opposite in personality. At the age of 35 he had become a successful sea captain himself, hauling merchandise between Boston and Liverpool. But in 1807, when President Jefferson embargoed all trade between the U.S. and England in what would lead to the War of 1812, Lewis found himself with no way to support his wife and six children.

Although he had no formal scientific training, Lewis was well aware of the poor quality of navigational beacons in America, and he began to tinker. Always in the back of his mind was inventing a better lens and winning government contracts to install it throughout the hemisphere. In 1808 he obtained a patent for lighting binnacles, the glass cases that housed ship's compasses. Two years later he patented his "reflecting and magnifying lantern," got the Boston Marine Society to try it in Boston Harbor and came away with an enthusiastic endorsement.

Actually, Lewis' breakthrough, like Fresnel's, was a combination of devices already in operation. The new lens was of impure, slightly green glass, set in a copper rim. Even though the lens actually diminished the lamp, the lamp and reflector were judged an improvement over the most commonly used designs. The big attraction was that the Lewis lens used only half as much oil as the others.

The same year he got the patent, Lewis prevailed on the secretary of the treasury to test his device in a light at Cape Ann, Massachusetts. The local customs collector was so impressed that he wrote the secretary urging that all lighthouses be equipped with the invention.

Before long Winslow Lewis had a contract for $60,000 to install his lens in all 49 U.S. lighthouses and maintain them for not less than 7 years. Moreover, he persuaded the government to assign him a custom-built schooner, fitted with a blacksmith shop, carpenter shop and bunks for a crew of thirteen.

Lewis had found his niche. By 1815 he'd equipped all the lighthouses in his contract. Collector of Customs Henry Dearborn wrote the treasury secretary that U.S. lighthouses were "now equal, if not superior, to any in the world." [8]

During the next few years Lewis expanded the contract terms so that he was now *de facto* superintendent of lighthouses, with leeway to determine such things as the number of lamps in a light and the diameter of reflectors used in each station. Because his lamps consumed less oil, and because he was free to sell off any surplus generated, it's estimated that he netted around $12,000 a year —

more than twice the treasury secretary's annual salary – just from selling excess oil on the open market.

Complaints about Lewis' "monopoly" increased, and when his latest contract expired in 1827, another firm submitted a lower bid. But by then Lewis was into the higher stakes end of the business: building lighthouses themselves.

What caught Stephen Pleasanton's eye was how Lewis handled an $80,000 contract that had been practically pressed on him. The task involved carrying out a prominent architect's dubious design for a lighthouse to be built on the spongy Mississippi delta. Lewis took the job only on condition that he'd be paid even if the tower collapsed. As he predicted, the tower's weight was too heavy for the foundation and it toppled over midway into the project. Lewis collected the fallen materials, acquired some of his own, and rebuilt the lighthouse for just $9,750.

This was the Fifth Auditor's kind of man! Lewis' building contracts grew in number, and the inexperienced Pleasanton was soon relying on his advice for virtually all construction projects. As historian Dennis L. Noble noted: "Lewis would often say a contract for a light was too high, the bid would be rejected, and Lewis would then be awarded the contract." [9]

Lewis won so many contracts that he drew up a set of plans for the five different sets of towers that he believed would meet the needs of any site on land. He also became the leading contractor for refitting old lights.

All this led to charges of collusion, but they were never proved. Rather, Lewis was undone over the quality of his lens – and by his own nephew, no less. Isaiah William Penn Lewis, who had been a Caribbean sea captain, had quit to work for his uncle as a lighthouse inspector, and had cleaved the Lewis family by abruptly leaving to start his own competing firm. Before long he charged publicly that his uncle had copied the lens at the South Stack Lighthouse in Wales, which the latter had no doubt passed often as a captain transporting goods to Liverpool. For good measure, Lewis the nephew insisted that his uncle's reflectors were of poor quality.

Charges and counter charges were still flying in 1850 when the elder Lewis died, but to most captains and lighthouse keepers there was no debate that the one-size-fits-all Lewis lenses were nothing to celebrate. Down at Cape Florida, for example, complaints continued that the lens shone not more than 13 miles on a clear night. As sea captain Thomas J. Heler, wrote Congress, "I have been many years in the coasting trade, and I have seen the Gulf of Florida light only twice."

An officer aboard the *Illinois* added that if the light weren't improved, "it had better be dispensed with, as the navigator is apt to run aground looking for it." [10]

The shortcoming was soon made more glaring. In 1847, Congress, now beginning to hear from all too many constituents about the flip side of the Fifth Auditor's parsimonious management, had ordered that six lighthouses be built directly by military engineers. On one such project, Sankaty Head Light on Nantucket, the engineers had managed to finagle a Fresnel lens from Paris – probably as what one now might be called a "free demo" model with promise of cash sales to come if it worked. When Sankaty Head Light shone for the first time in 1850, passing ship captains were so amazed at the beam that they proclaimed it "the blazing star." The contrast was so sharp that Congress forgot about any cost differences. When the new Light House Board was created in 1852, one of its mandates was to install Fresnel lenses in every American light station as soon as possible.

By 1851 so many complaints about poor lighthouses and slipshod managers had piled up on the congressional doorstep that lawmakers named a six-member panel of military officers and distinguished citizens to recommend ways to improve the management of navigational aids. The result was a 760-page report full of biting criticism and a unanimous call for a new management system.

It's no surprise that the governing body Congress created in 1852 would resemble the panel that had done the investigating. The new Light House Board would have nine members from diverse backgrounds: two senior naval officers, one civilian engineer, one army engineer, two civilians of "high scientific attainments," two secretaries to run day-to-day affairs, and a president ex-officio.

When members of the new Light House Board looked over their realm, they must have felt a twinge of empathy for Stephen Pleasanton. Thirty years before, there had been seventy lighthouses in the entire country. By 1852 there were 331 lighthouses and 42 lightships. Yet, there was no "West Point" to develop lighthouse builders and keepers, no ready-made bureaucracy to manage them except for a cadre of hungry contractors.

So, the Board did the next best thing: it divvied up the work among existing agencies, with key personnel simply borrowed for various assignments. Ideally (though not always in practice) the U. S. Coast Survey would locate new sites for navigational aids. Officers of the Topographical Engineers, the army's elite survey and engineering branch, would be assigned to the Board for specific construction projects, then turn them over to the Treasury Department when completed. The navy ran supply ships and maintained buoys.

The new Board divided the nation into twelve lighthouse districts. Each was supervised by an inspector – always an army or navy officer – who paid and provisioned lighthouse keepers. A keeper's most crucial hour would come when a district inspector showed up for a full-dress performance review.

Collectively, all of the above personnel – mostly borrowed – would be known as the U.S. Lighthouse Service (sometimes the Lighthouse Establishment) even though it initially had no official headquarters, no employee pension system or any other trappings of a full-fledged government agency.

Within a very quick time the new Board made landmark improvements by creating a classification system for lights, assimilating the French-made Fresnel lens, issuing a rulebook for keepers and establishing a central supply depot on Staten Island. Perhaps its most welcome achievement in the eyes of mariners was publishing an annual *Light List*. Besides describing the locations and characteristics of every navigational aid in the U.S., it provided for a "Notice to Mariners" that would be published whenever the system built a light or altered its nature.

When the Light House Board carved the country into twelve districts, none were in such need of attention as the Seventh. Back then it took in the entire coastlines of South Carolina, Georgia and the peninsula of Florida from Jacksonville down to Cape Florida, around the Keys and up the west coast to Cedar Key. Already a logistical nightmare from an inspector's standpoint, the Seventh District probably had the shabbiest lighthouses as well as the most areas in need of new ones.

Fortunately, the squeakiest wheels – or in this case, dimmest lights – command the most attention. The same year it was created, the Light House Board authorized several construction and repair projects in southern Florida. Among them was $35,000 to build a lighthouse in the area of Jupiter Inlet, preferably on the pencil-thin barrier island called Jupiter Island. A specific site hadn't been picked, but insurance underwriters were already nagging Florida's elected officials about the need for a light to guide ships away from the reefs that ran between Jupiter's jutting coast and the Gulf Stream.

Part of the decision probably stemmed from reports sent back by army surveyors at the time. Jupiter Inlet, though unoccupied, had the potential to become a first-rate harbor and port. In fact, as if to underscore its importance, the Board on July 23, 1853 ordered a first order Fresnel lens for the new Jupiter light.

Building the tower needn't be too difficult if materials could be brought through the inlet and unloaded in calm waters. Indeed, an army surveyor had reported earlier that year that the inlet had "opened itself" after being closed to all but the shallowest of boats for five years.

But as the ink was drying on the congressional authorization, the sand had again drifted south across the narrow inlet. For many years hence it would form a wide bar that trapped the out-flowing river except for a foot or so of freshwater that escaped at high tide.

Stephen A. Pleasanton (ABOVE), the tight-fisted Fifth Auditor who oversaw all early lighthouses from his Treasury Department office, grew to rely all too greatly on an ambitious contractor, Winslow Lewis (RIGHT). *(Pleasanton: Library of Congress. Lewis: Smithsonian Institution.)*

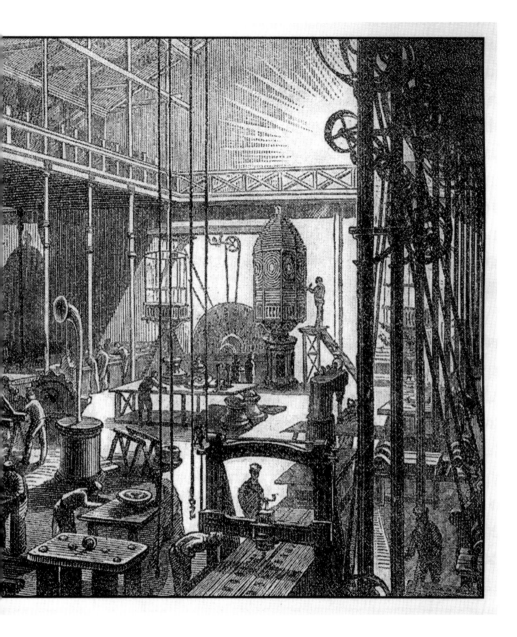

UPPER LEFT: Augustin-Jean Fresnel revolutionized lens design by magnifying a light's power many-fold. *(Smithsonian Institution)*

LEFT: A restored first-order Fresnel lens on display. *(Sue S. Snyder)*

ABOVE: The same-type lens (see far right) is readied for shipment at the L. Sautter & Co. production plant on the outskirts of Paris. *(Thomas Tag / U.S. Lighthouse Society)*

Chapter 4

Meade

If you had searched the entire U.S. army you could not have found a man more qualified or able to improve navigational aids on the Florida coast than Lieutenant George Gordon Meade. As a young topographical engineer, he had not only surveyed the reefs of lower Florida, but had already designed several lighthouses and even engineered some bold innovations. In temperament he was just the man to head Seventh District engineering for the Light House Board. As his son George would observe in the official family biography many years later, "his bearing was dignified and manly, his manners affable, his opinions were of weight among members of the corps, and he was universally liked and respected." [1]

Finally, there was another attribute that may have buoyed George Meade even more than his education and work ethic. He had *connections*.

All of the above, however, did not bode well for the newly authorized Jupiter Inlet Lighthouse project. As it was barely beginning to surface on the Seventh District "to-do" list, Meade was already trying his best to get out of steamy Florida, out of the stifling Corps of Topographical Engineers and into the more rewarding regular army chain of command, whose center was near the family home, where a lonesome young wife eagerly awaited. Meade scarcely could have had an inkling that in just a few years he would become a major general and lead the Union forces against Robert E. Lee in the Battle of Gettysburg, but he did know that he yearned to be on center stage and that it surely wasn't to be found among raccoons and mosquitoes in the mangroves of South Florida.

The first George Meade was a cosmopolitan from the day of his birth. Born in the city of Cadiz, Spain, in 1815, his father, Richard Worsam Meade, was the latest in a line of Philadelphia merchant traders whose pedigree included organizing a bank to help finance George Washington's rebel army. The family story of financial success and civic service was broken only when Richard's father apparently went on the hook for large tracts of undeveloped land, hoping to sell off plots to newly-arrived immigrants. Alas, says the stilted Victorian style of the family biography, "the large outlay," together with "the failure of certain foreign houses in the crisis of 1796, had caused his financial embarrassment and failure." Although "every consideration was shown by his creditors to one who had held so high a position in the commercial world," the grandfather of George Gordon Meade was eventually forced into bankruptcy. By 1808 he succumbed to what could only be diagnosed as acute shame and worry. [2]

By that time, his son Richard was continuing the family mercantile tradition in Cadiz, where the family biography says he had pursued "an excellent opportunity of forming advantageous commercial connections in that country." In fact, Meade would spend 17 years in Spain, not all of it in pleasant circumstances. In the early years Richard's import-export savvy produced a stately home, the company of Spain's finest grandees and even an appointment as naval agent of the United States for the port of Cadiz. In 1807 a nasty quarrel had erupted between King Charles IV and his son Ferdinand. Napoleon marched his French army into Spain "in the interest of "peace," whisked the whole royal family off to Paris for their "protection" and installed his own brother Joseph on the throne. All Spain erupted in civil war, Cadiz became a sort of city-state, and Meade suddenly became indispensable by supplying its grateful Supreme Junta with badly needed arms and merchandise. In fact, when the war ended, Cadiz and some other local governments were heavily in debt to Meade with no money to repay it.

A long wait set in. By 1817 Meade and his wife Margaret had produced ten children – two-year-old George was the youngest – and they decided that all but the father would return to Philadelphia so that the children could obtain the kind of schooling a patrician American family expected. Richard would return just as soon as his "affairs" could be straightened out.

But they never were. Ferdinand VII had assumed the throne of Spain and financial matters such as old supply contracts were suddenly stuck in limbo. Doubtless the war-torn government simply didn't have the money. Or perhaps some royal exchequer reviewed the paperwork and concluded that the fathers of Cadiz had been charged horribly inflated prices and ought to settle their own mess.

While Meade waited in his lonely merchant's manor, he seems to have been named "assignee" for the agent of a bankrupt English firm with business in Cadiz. When creditors instead pressed Meade himself for payment, he was tossed into prison by the Spanish Tribunal of Commerce. There he languished for two years until the U.S. minister to Spain finally secured a pardon from the king.

Part of Meade's release had to do with the Treaty of Paris (1819), which ceded Spanish Florida to the U.S. In exchange for the new territory, the U.S.

government agreed to assume all pending monetary claims against Spain by American citizens. Suddenly Meade's debtor was his own government – and the claim could be pressed in his own capital, just a short ride from the family home in Philadelphia!

For a few years the Meades again flourished among Philadelphia's finest, just like old times. At age eight young George was enrolled in the prestigious Mount Airy boarding-school, where military drills were mixed with Greek, Latin, arithmetic and algebra. As his son would write, "He was very popular among his school-mates, and the friendships formed at this very early stage of his career [as we shall see] lasted in many instances throughout life." [3]

Whereas Meade's grandfather had been worn down by shame, his father was being ground down by bitterness and frustration in trying to pry the entire family nest egg from an indifferent government. In 1826 he moved the family to the nation's capital so he could give every ounce of energy to working his connections there. In 1828, George was still away at his prestigious school when Richard Worsam Meade succumbed to his miseries at the age of fifty. The bitterness was still there when his grandson wrote nearly a century later:

He [Richard Worsam Meade] *had had to contemplate, year after year, the injustice through which the property, which he as a private citizen of the United States had accumulated by honest industry… had gone to the coffers of the state, never to be recovered, by means of a treaty of which his country had reaped the full benefit in the acquisition of territory. He had to strive year after year, unavailingly to attain the justice never received, and at last, reduced in fortune to what may justly be called poverty, considering the affluence in which he had lived. Broken in health and spirits, he succumbed, his death his silent protest against the injustice of his country!* [4]

The widow Meade was suddenly faced with feeding ten offspring and downsizing the lofty futures her husband had once planned for them. Young George was plucked from Mount Airy Academy and transferred to a much less expensive boarding school in Baltimore. When he graduated at 15 (able to read Cicero in Latin and Voltaire in French), his pathways to a patrician life were reduced to the only one available to a widow with no money but splendid social connections. Just as she had maneuvered her eldest son (Richard Worsam, Jr.) into the Naval Academy, she was able to get friends to recommend that President Andrew Jackson appoint her youngest son a cadet at West Point.

George Meade graduated 19th of 56 in his class, but so hated the drudgery of drills that he made up his mind early to jettison the army as soon as his two-year obligation was met. Being one of the youngest cadets, "quite small in stature at this time, and slender and delicate in appearance," family friends doubted that he could stand up to the physical demands of life in an army camp. [5]

And they were proven right. Meade's first tour of duty began in January 1836 when he was sent to Fort Brooke at Tampa Bay, which was expecting to be besieged in the midst of the Second Seminole Indian War. However, the demands of going out on constant patrol in muggy swamps soon took its toll. "The hardships of the service in a semi-tropical climate caused him to suffer repeated attacks of fever…and so debilitated him," wrote his son, "that he was…pronounced unfit to march with the army." His ticket out of Florida was to accompany a group of captured Seminoles ("not the most agreeable of traveling companions") who were being sent from Tampa Bay to a new reservation in Oklahoma.

After a routine ordnance assignment at Watertown Arsenal, Massachusetts that took him past his two-year obligation, Second Lieutenant Meade got an offer that made him bolt. His brother-in-law was chief engineer in Pensacola, Florida, building the Alabama, Florida and Georgia Railroad, and he needed an assistant. A year later, Meade was productively employed there. So was a contingent of the army's Corps of Topographical Engineers. The Corps needed a civilian engineer to join a party to survey the mouth of the Sabine River, which formed the boundary between the U.S. and the Republic of Texas. Meade spent six months at it, went to New York City to draw up the resulting maps, then again worked for the Corps as a civilian contractor in mapping the northeast boundary between the U.S. and Canada.

There seemed to be ample leisure time between these assignments, and Meade stayed for long stretches at his mother's house in Washington. "Intelligent, well-educated, vivacious, and fond of society, he was naturally welcomed in all his comings and goings by a large circle of friends," notes his loyal biographer.

During this interlude, those family connections led him to the convivial home of Congressman John Sergeant of the Meade's native Philadelphia. At the many soirees in Washington, the "constant companion of her venerable father" was eldest daughter Margaretta, who "had received her education under his immediate eye and had been reared in the refined and brilliant circle that surrounded him." The charming Mr. Meade soon had *her* eye as well and before long he asked for her hand. Alas, notes our Victorian chronicle, the "uncertainty attending his permanent occupation, together with the still unsettled condition of his mother's affairs, caused the proposed marriage to be considered with grave deliberation." [6]

At last the old man acquiesced. The marriage took place on December 31, 1840, with all of genteel Philadelphia on hand at the spacious Sergeant home. But there may have been some *quid pro quo* regarding the groom's lack of gainful employment. It seems that Congress, in a wave of parsimony, was about to deploy the Corps of Topographical Engineers on some public works projects (including a few lighthouses) on which it had formerly used private contractors. The Corps suddenly needed more engineers. Father-in-law Sergeant went to work on his contacts. So did brother-in-law Henry A. Wise, one of the most powerful Whigs in Congress, who had married another Sergeant daughter. On May 19, 1842, President James Tyler named George Gordon Meade a second lieutenant in the Corps of Topographical Engineers.

The forerunner of today's vastly larger Army Corps of Engineers, the "Topogs" were a select — some say elite — group of men. Whereas almost any career officer was expected to know his Homer and the art of penning a flowery letter along with how to march men and shoot a gun, the Topogs added an extra dimension with their skills of surveying, cartography and engineering. Evidence of their talent as a group is that when the Civil War broke out, Topog officers were eagerly sought by the armies of both sides and many were catapulted to general.

The Topogs were also elite simply due to their small number. Before the Civil War, their officer ranks seldom exceeded 35, and after 1852 perhaps one-third of them at any one time were on assignment to the Light House Board. If any Topog were attached to a new detail, chances are he'd know someone there from a previous assignment.

Presiding over this diffuse group from the War Department in Washington was Colonel John James Abert, who would be the Corps' chief officer and dominant personality from 1829 until 1861 when failing health forced him to retire. Although Abert had always welcomed new frontiers for his men to map and survey, he wasn't one bit happy about deploying his valuable men on lighthouse work.

Newly-married George Meade went off to finish up the Canadian boundary survey, but in November 1843 he was ordered to report to Topog Major Hartman Bache who was busy making surveys and building lighthouses on Delaware Bay. To Meade, headquartered in Philadelphia where he and Margaretta had set up housekeeping, it was a lovely assignment. Bache, 17 years his senior, was a great-grandson of Benjamin Franklin and swam in the cream of Philadelphia society. He had already made his mark as a lighthouse designer in some of the nation's most wild and windy seacoasts. Bache took to his new charge at once and often spent leave at Meade's home in Philadelphia. He would eventually court one of Meade's sisters and became a brother-in-law.

Their first construction project together was the Brandywine Shoal Lighthouse, about eight miles northwest of Cape May, New Jersey. Bache had done the survey work some nine years after the first tower had toppled over. Now, with an old leaky lightship proving a poor substitute for a permanent tower, Bache and his assistant were ready to employ a new technology developed by a blind brick maker in Ireland.

The novel method was the *screw-pile*. Shafts of cast iron were sunk into the ground, each with a drill bit that twisted into the hard surface 15 to 20 feet below the sand. Once secured, the shafts were connected and reinforced by horizontal iron rods, usually in a hexagon shape. Onto this was built a platform for the keeper's house and then the light a few feet above the roof line. The Brandywine project involved intricate engineering, which would cost a hefty $53,317 and not light the seacoast until 1850. Meade was gone for part of the construction because on August 12, 1845, he was ordered to Texas to join a major force preparing to fight a war with Mexico. By then he and Margaretta had three children and a wide circle of friends. But *duty* – always paramount in his priorities – called, and Meade responded by leaving the day after receiving his orders without attempting even a quick stop in Philadelphia. A letter, written August 15 from what was then called "Washington City," opens,

To Mrs. George G. Meade:
I trust you have not placed any fond hopes on seeing me come back from this place. I found on my arrival here this morning that there was nothing to be done but to proceed to the destination assigned me....
In the meantime, keep up your spirits and take care of your health and that of

the children. No one can tell how my heart was rent at parting with you; but I believe it is for the best that we should be parted, if I am to go, for the terrible agony I endured at the very sight of you and my dear children, it would be impossible to describe. However, there is no use in fretting over what cannot be helped, and there only remains for us to pray God to protect us and bring us together in his good pleasure. [7]

By then, Lieutenant Meade was thirty. "His constitution," says his son and biographer, "greatly strengthened and improved within the ten years which had elapsed since his experience in Florida, was now, comparatively speaking, robust." Although at first he seemed to expect that French or English mediators would defuse Mexican-American bluster and send him home, Meade saw plenty of combat under Brigadier General Zachary Taylor and won his share of accolades.

It is well that he was fit, because beginning in March 1847 Meade would be back in his least favorite place, southern Florida, surveying its reefs. There was no Light House Board. Congress, growing more disenchanted with the Treasury Department's lowest-contract-bidder style of lighthouse construction, had decided to assign the army a half-dozen new projects to see if it could do better. Since most were in Florida, the Topographical Engineers were told to see where best to put them.

Until then, several military surveyors had mapped parts of southern Florida, but few had spent more time or covered a greater area than George Meade. He spent at least 14 months walking sandy seashores and another 10 back in Philadelphia preparing his maps and lighthouse designs.

By August 1849 Meade had spent the previous eight months with Bache putting finishing touches on the new Brandywine Light at Cape May when another call came from Florida, and at the rainiest, buggiest time of the year. Once again, Seminoles had worried the command at Fort Brooke on Tampa Bay. Sending off a thousand or so Florida Indians out west in 1838 hadn't really settled the Second Seminole War, and now a few of the roughly 300 who had fled into the Everglades were marauding against white farmers and actually murdering some.

Meade had even more reason to rue this particular assignment because he and Major General David Twiggs, now the commander at Ft. Brooke, had come to dislike one another while fighting with Zach Taylor near the Rio Grande in Texas. The cause isn't known, but one can imagine it starting with Meade showing an aristocrat's disdain for a rough-hewn Georgia Cracker who was called "the Bengal Tiger" and who was known to "cuss a man right out of his boots." And it may be that the general took Meade's urbanity to be the Cracker's deadliest sin – effeminacy.

Indeed, when another Meade biographer, Richard Bache, first met the young officer during this period, he did a double take.

> *He wore his hair down to the nape of the neck…and that being the fashion, did not, of course attract my attention; but what did attract and fix it was the new experience to me of a man with long ringlets, looking as to his head like a cavalier of the time of Charles I. He was, in a word, a dandy…without being particularly good looking in face. In figure…he was tall and slender and graceful with an air of higher breeding."* [8]

Whatever the case, Twiggs needed Meade's surveying skills. The army was planning to re-open the chain of forts that had linked its Florida supply lines during the previous war and the general wanted the smoothest topography possible for his network of wagon trails. He also wanted the coast surveyed from Tampa Bay all the way around to the Indian River Inlet to identify sites for new forts.

One day the major general, looking up at the new arrival standing rigidly in front of his desk, asked what men and materials he needed to do his job.

"Two men and a mule," said Meade.

That's all he got, but Twiggs was impressed with Meade's grit. Several days later, he told his adjutant: "Meade is doing good work and putting on no staff airs. Order the quartermaster to send him a proper outfit and make him comfortable."

Meade later thanked the aide, assuming it was *his* idea, only to be pleasantly surprised when told it came from the general himself. Later, when inspecting one of the lieutenant's proposed sites for a stockade on the Peace River, Twiggs was so pleased with the selection that he named it Fort Meade. [9]

From January 1850 through April 1851 Meade split his time between a full life at home and Hartman's Bache's complex construction project at Cape May, New Jersey. Presumably he was there to see it finally lit on October 28, 1850, but he was certainly busy incorporating the Brandywine experience into his own lighthouse design. Meade was again headed to Florida – this time to rescue a tough lighthouse project that had gone sour. The reef off Key Largo had probably caused more wrecks than anywhere in the Florida Straits, and Washington had been trying to replace the decrepit, disreputable lightship there for a dozen years.

In 1848 Congress had authorized a screw-pile platform that would stand in some five feet of water. Much to the surprise of engineers, once the iron screws chewed through brittle Florida coral they failed to hit the limestone bedrock, but instead churned about in soft sand. Makeshift solutions hadn't worked, and now the project's on-site engineer had up and died before finishing the job.

Meade, the only screw-pile expert other than Hartman Bache, was sent into the breech and thus began a stay in Florida that led from one lighthouse project to the next. He would stay with the troublesome Carysfort Reef platform, an ordeal extended by the sudden failure of Congress to fund needed materials, until its lighting on March 10, 1852.

No doubt what kept him going were dreams of a pleasant sabbatical full of warm baths, romps with his children and the company of his adored mother, who had moved in with the family to spend her old age. Ten days later after Carysfort was lit, Margaret Meade died. On November 25 the family got another blow when Margaretta's father also passed away. It was an especially painful blow because the old congressman had become his son-in-law's greatest supporter.

Meade would go on to build lighthouses in Sand Key, Key West and other places, but perhaps he had been jolted by a personal reminder that life is fragile and that time spent apart can't be replaced.

And one thing more. There was a downside to the small, "elite" nature of the Topogs. While special to some, it was an obscure corner of the army to the many who dreamed of blazing their careers with battlefield glories. And with only 35 or so officers, men advanced at glacial speed. After all, even the legendary chief Abert was a mere colonel, and the Corps had only two majors. Finally, the Topogs were full of *brevet* officers — a term meaning that the tight-fisted War Department had acquiesced to a promotion in rank, but not a raise in pay.

Creation of the new Light House Board in August 1852 may have tipped the scales for Meade. He could no longer convince himself that he was merely in Florida on a temporary assignment that would soon end and propel him back to home and family. He was now a first lieutenant, but in the bargain, also the engineering chief of the newly created Seventh Lighthouse District.

The Light House Board's engineering secretary and *de facto* chief operating officer was Captain Edmund F. Hardcastle. Sometime in the early fall of 1853 Hardcastle must have received a letter from First Lieutenant Meade that made him sit up straight. No copy has surfaced, but Meade had obviously worked behind the scenes to get orders transferring him to another post in the War Department.

What we do have is Hardcastle's initial response in October lamenting that the Board is "greatly disappointed" at the news and would meet on the matter forthwith. The next day a perfunctory letter goes out directing Meade to inventory the public property under his charge so that it can be turned over to a successor.

We know nothing more until early December when the Board writes the War Department. It doesn't mince words:

The withdrawal of Lt. Meade from Light House service would delay the completion of these very important works which Congress has provided for an aid to navigation on this dangerous coast, which the Board hoped would be [under the] *superintendence of that officer, be completed in the coming season.*

Lt. Meade's reports on the aids required for safe navigation of the Florida coast show him to be particularly qualified for the discharge of duties entrusted to him and are the reasons why the Board first applied for the services of this officer. His familiarity with the coast reefs of Florida, and the study and attention he has given to the subject of Light House structure for this locality, make it no disparagement to others to say that he can carry on and complete the works under his charge more economically and judicially than any other officer [of] *the Engineers who might relieve him.* [10]

By early 1854 there is no more mention of the subject from either party. One can imagine the young officer being summoned to Washington at Christmas time and finding himself in the baronial office of a three-star general with the fireplace ablaze. After some chit-chat about friends they had in common, the general would say gently that the army had perhaps acted too quickly on his request for a transfer, and that such a fine young officer wouldn't want to risk jeopardizing his career by pressing the issue.

When the Jupiter Inlet light was first authorized, the powers in

Washington had every expectation that it would be up and shining in short order. To understand why it would take seven years, one must see things through the eyes of the Seventh District engineer.

First, Jupiter Inlet was just one of several projects in Florida under his direction. At the outset of 1854, Lieutenant Meade had just activated the new Sand Key light nine miles west of Key West and faced the usual annoying breakdowns in its shakedown year. Forty-three miles west of Key West, out in turbulent waters where the Gulf meets the Atlantic, Meade was charged with somehow putting up a new beacon on Rebecca Shoal. Up the west coast, off Cedar Key, he was probing the best location for what would become Sea Horse Key light. Back at Key Biscayne, with only a deserted, charred lighthouse, Meade was charged with a total restoration that included raising the much-criticized tower by some forty feet.

Second, in April, 1854, Meade's mentor, Hartman Bache, was ordered to head the Twelfth Lighthouse District in Oregon and California. There he would not only build several towers on the rocky coast, but capture their likenesses in many memorable watercolors, still sold in gift shops today. The Light House Board's way of filling the gap left in Bache's Fourth District (New Jersey and Delaware) was to put Meade in charge of two districts and double the reasons to bind him to the Corps.

Actually, it's arguable that Meade himself was part of the bargaining that led to the decision. It came coupled with someone's brilliant idea that the Corps could maximize its efficiency by using the same construction/repair crews year-around. In the summer, everyone dreaded going to South Florida with its miserable heat, insect invasions and constant threat of Yellow Fever (which no one had yet linked to the mosquito). Now they could feel the briny breezes of Chesapeake Bay in summer and visit Florida from January to late May.

For George Meade, now the father of four, being allowed to be at the Fourth and Seventh District offices in Philadelphia headquarters more or less half the year — and to see more of his family — was probably an attractive trade-off for a man who just had spent the better part of two years grinding screw-piles into Carysfort Reef.

Third, Meade was increasingly aware that Jupiter Inlet could well be his greatest challenge. In terms of supporting towns and supply transport, it was the most remote. And if Jupiter always seemed to be listed last in Meade's progress reports, there was a plausible excuse: the Powers That Be hadn't even decided on a site. On February 6, 1854, we have a letter from the Florida attorney general's office, affirming a Light House Board inquiry as to whether the governor was empowered to cede some land around Jupiter Inlet for a lighthouse.

The wait for mail, of course, ate up lots of time in 1854. In May the Board's naval secretary, Lieutenant Thornton A. Jenkins, wrote Meade that "the proper site for this light will be somewhere in the neighborhood of half way between Jupiter Inlet and Gilbert's Bar, the entire distance between these two being about twelve miles." He asked Meade to search for at least forty acres that would accommodate the project's needs. [11]

If approved, it would have put the lighthouse smack dab in the middle of today's elite town of Jupiter Island, perhaps imposing a world-class obstacle on its posh fairways. But no, Meade was informed by another letter on August 15 that the General Land Office in Washington had done further research and learned that "the whole of the island between Gilbert's Bar and Jupiter Inlet has been taken up and probably belongs to a Mr. E. [Eusebio] Gomez." [12]

By then Meade had waded in with his own recommendation. He had already surveyed the area and pinpointed a place called "Jones Hill," said to be a natural parabolic dune that was safely located around three quarters of a mile behind the mouth of the inlet. It also stood conveniently at the confluence of the Jupiter and Indian Rivers. By November the state attorney general had told the Light House Board Jones Hill would be just fine, and the state had ceded a fifty-acre plot to the federal government. On November 21, 1854, President Franklin Pierce had signed off on the acquisition. [13]

Official optimism was the order of the day, even before the specific site was pinpointed. On August 5 the Board had sent Meade the first $500 from the Jupiter Inlet's $35,000 appropriation as a token to cover whatever advance work was needed. As early as February, the Board's Jenkins showed he was well aware that it would be impossible to bring a heavy, brick-laden ocean vessel into Jupiter Inlet. He wrote about "getting a [shallow draft] vessel to help you," to be financed from general appropriations so that it could be used in other Florida projects. On September 12 of the same year Engineering Secretary Hardcastle wrote Meade seeking his estimates on what would be needed to acquire "the best illuminating apparatus." In December he ordered Meade to go to New York and "buy a vessel of light draft" – presumably an old, cheap one because it was to be sold "after the materials are landed."

By the end of January 1855 George Meade was already in Key West restarting his many other lighthouse projects and with every apparent expectation of activating the new one at Jupiter. Indeed, a report to Congress by the Light House Board at about the same time reported that "the necessary materials have been manufactured and prepared for shipment to the site." [14]

"Prepared for shipment" should have meant that 500 tons of brick, cast iron, steam engines and tools were piled up on the long pier at Staten Island, New York. Although probably covered by then with a veneer of ice and snow, January would be the right time for loading crews and materials on a large motorized schooner for the beginning of "the season" in South Florida.

Others who shipped from Staten Island pier would have been happy to see the lighthouse tender off. The Lighthouse Service had more or less commandeered much of the sprawling wharf as its primary east coast depot after being evicted by the authorities of lower Manhattan several months earlier. Stocking all that oil and materials for dozens of building projects presented a constant fire threat. The worst nightmare was that the lenses might magnify the sun rays exponentially and burst the whole wharf in flames. Now, with several of the new-fangled, ultra-powerful Fresnel lenses piled up, the dock master made sure they were kept crated or wrapped with cloth covers at all times.

But as winter wore on in Florida, no materials arrived for Jupiter Inlet. One reason is that merely reducing a vessel's draft had by no means solved the logistics problem. In the following report to Congress, also intended to grease the skids for another $5,000, the Light House Board described the extent of the challenge:

The great difficulty to overcome in the construction of this work is getting the materials to the site. To effect this it will be necessary…to send the materials, estimated at between four and five hundred tons in bulk, in a vessel to the Indian River, where they must be lightered into the Indian River Inlet, as it is impossible to obtain seagoing vessels here to carry any burden with a draught of only five feet, which is the limit of depth on the Indian River bar that is deemed safe to depend on.

After the difficult operation of lightering a vessel over a rough bar is accomplished, then there remains thirty-five miles of narrow, tortuous, and shallow navigation, where no greater depth than twenty inches can be relied on. This involves the use of scow-boats, the burden of which is limited by the shallow water and the narrow and crooked channel; so that, estimating the bulk of the materials at five hundred tons, and the capacity of a scow boat…at ten tons, we have fifty trips of three boats – going and coming – thirty-five miles. It will be clearly seen that this operation will consume a great deal of time and, in consequences, involves inordinate expense." [15]

Coincidentally, the army was already working out the logistics for a similar task. Officers at Fort Capron, just opposite Indian River Inlet, were planning to re-staff old Fort Jupiter as an Indian-scouting outpost. Although they never got involved in the lighthouse project (the fort had just been vacated just before lighthouse materials actually arrived in 1859), the army faced the same supply obstacles because it had to keep soldiers fed and healthy at Fort Jupiter.

Although the broad, twenty-mile stretch of Indian River from Fort Pierce south to Sewell's Point hasn't changed greatly from 1855, the rest of the waterway looked little like the straight, deep channel cut by Army contractors at the turn of the century. As soon as a navigator crossed Sewell's Point and what's now St. Lucie Inlet, he entered the tangled, twisted realm of Jupiter Narrows.

When a Fort Capron lieutenant, Ambrose P. Hill, was sent off to assess the supply route, he paid special attention to the six-mile obstacle course most folks simply called "The Narrows." Hill described this tangle of mangrove islands as "exceedingly tortuous, of good depth, of strong current setting either way with the wind" until reaching the wider Hobe Sound. Back in the 1840s, Lieutenant Joseph C. Ives, an army cartographer, had written of "lofty mangroves, full sixty feet in height, whose branches nearly meet from the opposite sides of the stream." [16]

Six miles downriver, The Narrows ended abruptly at a large, broad oyster bed that allowed passage only of boats drawing less than three feet at high tide. Lieutenant Ives then describes Hobe Sound, the remaining eight-mile run to Jupiter Inlet, as

…skirted on the west by high hills covered with oak scrub, while the beach that borders the opposite side is a thick hammock that extends four and a half miles to the south. Where the hammock ends, there is a narrow place in the sound, occasioned by a sharp point of mangroves which puts out from the west shore from near the base of a hill, sixty feet in height, that rises rapidly from the water. This place is called Couch's Bar, and the greatest depth of water upon it is about three feet. [17]

Couch's Bar, which would soon trip up many a Civil War blockade runner, had been named for Darien Nash Couch, a U.S. Coast Survey lieutenant, just as other South Florida landmarks got their names from members of early survey teams. In fact, when our 1855 army scout, Lieutenant Hill, finally emerged into Jupiter River and headed west past the mound that would one day support the lighthouse, he knew it only as "Jones Hill," named for Alfred H. Jones, another early surveyor. And as he approached the site of Old Fort Jupiter on Pennock Point, he would also know the tributary that flowed by it as Jones Creek. [18]

Residents of modern Pennock Point in Jupiter have long known the site of Old Fort Jupiter by the number of musket balls and belt buckles imbedded near the eastward-facing shore. Lieutenant Hill makes it plain why the old site was unsuitable ("bare of timber") for a stockade and cabins and where he would put the new one. He simply went east across the mouth of Jones Creek, today the mouth of the much wider C-18 Canal. In Hill's words:

> *The eastern fork of the Jupiter* [Loxahatchee] *River and Jones Creek is half a mile nearer Jupiter Bar, the pine land is more elevated and continues* [for] *some five miles back. The timber comes down to the water's edge, and the water is of sufficient depth for small boats closer in shore.*
>
> *In selecting a position for a post if regard be had for convenience of timber, for vicinity of hard wood, good soils for gardening and anchorage, loading and unloading boats, I deem the Eastern fork the preferable to Old Fort Jupiter, or any location in its vicinity. At any position the dependence on fresh water must be upon wells. Jupiter Bar is now entirely closed, and the water fresh, but this may not continue.* [19]

Lieutenant Hill's biggest challenge was finding boats able to send men and supplies without taking forever. Still tethered at the dilapidated dock at Old Fort Jupiter were four Mackinac boats, three of them full of wood rot. Mackinacs were rugged-but-boxy tubs originally built to haul loggers to camps around the Great Lakes. Lieutenant Hill clearly wrinkled his nose at these remnants from Old Fort Jupiter days:

> *To transport supplies from* [Fort Capron] *to Jupiter, nearly fifty miles, 'twould be necessary that the boats should be strong and tight. In a head wind Mackinac boats must lay by in the open river, and for six months of the year the prevailing wind is southeast dead-ahead. Under the most favorable circumstances, a Mackinac boat could not make the trip in under four days —* [it] *might be twenty. It would take fifteen Mackinac boat loads to transport a three month's supply to Jupiter.* [20]

Hill asked for exactly what Jupiter's first settlers would themselves select one day: "a small sloop, after the pattern of the old surf boats used [in the Mexican War], not drawing over three feet loaded."

From the reels of military microfilm at the National Archives one learns that the new Fort Jupiter was staked out and occupied in February 1855 by 3 officers and 38 privates. The routine monthly "muster report" for that month adds only one comment: a request for more blankets.

Perhaps malarial chills were already setting in. In any case, the number of sick on the muster rolls increased with the heat. On May 19 an army surgeon visited the post and wrote the commander at Fort Capron to report two cases of "scorbutus" (scurvy). They "probably originated from the want of a proper diet," he said, "and as it is likely that other cases of a similar nature may occur....I would request that you have vegetables issued to the troops at this post three times a week until the tendency to scorbutus disappears." [21]

Meanwhile, George Meade was busy in Key West but increasingly frustrated that the season was grinding on without his most ambitious project moving an inch. In addition to his supply ship, he had been expecting the delicate first order Fresnel lens to arrive from Paris via Staten Island. In late June Meade received a letter from L. Sautter & Co., the French manufacturer, apologizing for a "mistake" in which the Jupiter lens had been uncrated and used as an exhibit in the *Exposition Universelle de Paris*, the World's Fair of its day. Sautter apparently wasn't too remorseful: the "Jupiter" lens won a gold medal at the *Palais d'Industrie* and remained there, wowing crowds, well into the fall.

In late October, after Meade had long since returned from Florida, he got a notice that must have made him utter a patrician's epithet about bureaucratic bungling. Read the letter: "Please find a bill of lading for 39 cases containing the first order lens, fixed, varied by flashes, 3.5 degrees, shipped to you by Philadelphia Steam Propeller Co., from New York for Jupiter Inlet, Florida, Lighthouse." The lens, now priced around $12,000, was heading to Key Biscayne. [22]

But Meade never gave up on Jupiter. As the winter of 1855-56 approached, the records show him ordering "600 or 700 gallons winter oil in strong iron-bound casks....[each to be] stenciled *Jupiter Inlet*." Again, materials were assembled on the docks at Staten Island and some were even sent to Key Biscayne, which seems to have been designated the temporary depot for supplies earmarked for Jupiter Inlet. [23]

But, there they would stay.

In December 1855, well before he left for another "season," Meade must have gotten word from army friends in Washington that many of the Florida garrisons were breaking camp and heading towards Big Cypress Swamp. One of them was the small contingent at Fort Jupiter, transferred December 8 to a Caloosahatchee River camp "with a view to ulterior operations in the Indian country." [24]

Why? Indian "uprisings" or white encroachment — depending on one's skin color.

To begin with, the Second Seminole Indian War had never really settled much except to leave the Seminoles with fewer warriors. The 300 or so who had melted into the Everglades in 1838 had done their best to live in obscurity. For over ten years, the people of Chief Billy Bowlegs (whites had corrupted his English surname, *Boleck*) had lived peacefully, their only outside contact a trading post on the shores of Charlotte Harbor. But in July 1849 a band of five outlaw youths went off the reservation and killed some settlers near Fort Pierce. They then doubled back and killed two men at the trading post at Charlotte Harbor. Because the two events happened so quickly and so far apart, white settlers decided that Indians in general were on the warpath. Hysteria gripped the pioneer community and some 1,400 federal troops were sent off to Florida. But Billy Bowlegs was already taking his own action. His warriors quickly hunted down three of the outlaws and turned them over to the army. When a fourth was captured and tried to escape, Bowlegs' men killed him and sent the army his severed hand as evidence. The fifth remained a fugitive but did no more harm. [25]

Calm returned for a while, but in 1850 Congress stoked the fire again when it passed the Swamp and Overflowed Land Act. Essentially, the new law turned over to the states all federal land that was covered with water for at least part of the year. The intent was to drain wetlands for farm production, but a byproduct was that government surveyors called "selecting agents" were suddenly crisscrossing the 20 million acres that had changed hands in Florida. And in the Everglades they found "black gold" so fertile they compared it to the banks of the Nile River.

Seminoles believed that people belonged to the land — not the other way around. When they objected to survey parties on their "reservation" (they'd never signed a treaty to that effect), Washington's response was to bring Billy

Bowlegs to Washington for some high-level partying, followed by some serious parlaying. The government would give each Florida Seminole a few thousand dollars if they'd just agree to join their kinfolk out west.

Bowlegs had received the VIP treatment in Washington before and had always refused when the subject of the westward move came around. Within a few months, more forts were built in a rough semi-circle around Big Cypress Swamp. The resulting tension had to have its bursting point, and it came in December 1855. A small patrol led by Lieutenant George Hartsuff rode into one of Billy's villages and found it deserted. The Indian version says they ransacked it. The army version says that before departing, some soldiers merely cut a few branches from Chief Billy's favorite banana tree and peeled themselves a few tasty snacks for the trip back.

Whatever the truth, the village incursion proved the tipping point. A war party of about thirty Seminoles attacked the army patrol on the way home, killing four soldiers and seriously wounding another four, including Hartsuff. Suddenly it seemed to South Florida settlers that Indians were everywhere: two men tending a coontie flour mill killed near Fort Dallas (Miami); five soldiers murdered near Fort Denaud on the Caloosahatchee River; two soldiers from the fort killed while out on patrol; two oystermen ambushed and killed on their boat in Charlotte Harbor; three men killed leading a wagon train of military supplies near the Peace River.

In no case did Indians strike north or east of Sarasota and only once did they fight what could be called a "battle." But the uprising would quickly become the "Third Seminole Indian War" for two reasons. First, white settlers were largely isolated, poorly informed and easily prone to sensational newspaper accounts portraying the state afire. Second, an aroused Seminole didn't exactly practice white conventions. By mutilating bodies, shooting horses and holding frenzied "scalp dances," the Indians only magnified the white settler's worst fears and stereotypes.

After six months of hit and run guerrilla tactics, the army got a break. In mid-June a detachment of 19 men chased a group of warriors who had attacked a family farm along the Peace River and killed several in a prolonged shootout. They were surprised to find among the dead one Oscen Tustenuggee, who had not only led the war party, but the main Seminole war faction. No one knew it at the time, but the skirmish probably marked the war's turning point. From then on it would be a case of weary, hungry Indians scurrying from hammock to makeshift village in the Everglades as bands of army troops gradually closed in and confiscated everything they'd leave behind.

By then, however, it was too late to think of starting any major new lighthouse projects in Florida. As early as January 7, 1856, just after Meade had arrived at Key West, he was writing the head of the naval base for permission to arm his work crews against possible Indian attacks. He had good reason: his archipelago of lighthouses wrapped around the southern tip of Florida, with both Key Largo and Key West an equidistant hundred miles from the heart of Big Cypress Swamp on the mainland.

And who knew just where else Indians might be? One of the first tales any green army recruit heard around the campfire was of the "massacre" at Cape Florida Light just twenty years before. On July 24, 1836, with keeper John Dubose away in Key West on family business, the light at Key Biscayne was left in charge of John W. Thompson and an elderly man named Aaron Carter — probably Thompson's slave. That afternoon at 4 p.m., as Thompson was walking from the keeper's house to the detached kitchen, he saw "a large body of Indians within twenty yards of me, back of the kitchen." He ran for the lighthouse, calling for Carter to come quickly, just as a volley of rifle balls tore through his shirt and hat.

But let's re-start the story from the Indian perspective. William Cooley, one of the first settlers along the New River (Fort Lauderdale), was respected enough to get elected justice of the peace. In 1835 a group of white men allegedly killed Alibama, the much revered chief of a nearby Indian community. As justice of the peace, Cooley took the accused into custody and had them tried in Key West. When charges were dismissed for lack of evidence, the Indians around New River were outraged. They charged that Cooley had withheld vital evidence.

In January 1836, when Cooley was away salvaging a wrecked ship, Indians attacked his homestead, shooting down his wife, infant and eleven-year-old daughter. Then they clubbed his nine-year-old son to death.

When Cooley returned to his destroyed home, he wound up fleeing with some sixty other defenseless settlers, first to Key Biscayne, and then to the better protected Indian Key. A year later, with the Indian threat seemingly diminished, Cooley returned to Key Biscayne and became its lighthouse keeper.

In a few months Cooley was replaced by Dubose, and it may well be that the Indians raided the Cape Florida light because they were after Cooley. But once they fired on Thompson, there was no time to sort out the truth. Thompson and Carter had no sooner slammed the wooden lighthouse door when it was perforated by rifle balls in several places. Thompson snatched his three muskets, already loaded, climbed to a second-floor window and scattered the Indians below with three quick shots.

The assistant keeper kept the Indians pinned in the surrounding bushes until well after nightfall, but then darkness gave the advantage to the assailants. Indians snuck out in the blackness and set fire to the door of the light tower. The flames soon spread and then ignited a 225-gallon tank of oil in the vestibule. All at once the lower tower was a roaring inferno.

It happened just as Thompson and Carter reached the top of the wooden staircase, Thompson panting under the weight of a gunpowder keg he'd brought to keep his muskets cracking. Smoke and flames shot up at them as they flung open the hinged trap door and rolled onto the iron galley floor. It was there that Thompson had intended to make a last stand until the gunpowder ran out. But the heat was already unbearable. "The lantern was now full of flame" with "lamps and glasses bursting and flying in all directions...my flesh roasting." Carter was quickly hit several times and soon was lying in a heap on the scalding iron surface. Thompson had taken the first of what would be six rifle balls in his feet and could hardly stand to shoot.

At that point "I decided to put an end to my horrible suffering," Thompson recalled. He picked up the keg of gunpowder and heaved it down the scuttle. "It instantly exploded and shook the tower from top to bottom."

But it did not, as he put it, "have the desired effect of blowing me to eternity." By sending the wooden staircase crashing to the bottom, it had saved him from being overwhelmed by swarms of Indians and mutilated alive. The assailants, thinking the two keepers dead, looted the keeper's house, loaded up two canoes with booty and shoved off down the bay.

Thompson, now barely alive, escaped further roasting from the red-hot grille below his feet only by crawling atop the dead Carter's charred body.

Just then the wind shifted and he noticed the fire beginning to abate.

It was scarcely something to cheer about:

I was almost as bad off as before; a burning fever on me, my feet shot to pieces, no clothes to cover me, nothing to eat or drink, a hot sun overhead, a dead man by my side, no friend near nor any to expect, and placed between seventy and eighty feet from the earth with no chance of getting down. My situation was truly horrible. ²⁶

But the change of wind brought a change of luck. A passing navy ship, the *Motto*, seven miles offshore, had spotted the tower ablaze on the night of July 23, but strong currents prevented a crew from landing and reaching the smoldering lighthouse until 5 p.m. the next day. Thompson was barely alive but still able to call down to the men below. Even then, no one at the base could fathom a way to reach him. They finally did so by firing twine from their muskets. Thompson eventually caught several pieces and tied them end to end. Then, securing the end to the gallery railing, he dropped the twine so that it reached the ground. The sailors below tied a stout rope to the twine, which Thompson then reeled up and fastened to the gallery rail. Soon two sailors, old hands at climbing a rigging, shinnied up and brought him down.

Thompson survived, but would be crippled for life. His story was seared into the minds of all lighthouse keepers in Florida. And it certainly explains why, on January 19, 1856, George Meade received approval from the Light House Board to continue storing the materials for Jupiter Inlet at Key Biscayne "and postpone for the present the commencement of this work."

The war also meant the end of George Gordon Meade in Florida. By late March all lighthouse operations in South Florida had abruptly ceased and Meade was on his way back to Philadelphia. Hysteria had gripped the southern U.S., as evidenced by the front page of the *Florida Peninsular* in Tampa on March 29, 1856:

LATEST INDIAN NEWS!!
Important from Washington!!
Reward for Living Indians!!

Captain Casey, the Agent for Indians Affairs in Florida, is authorized to offer a *per capita* reward for living Indians who may be captured, or induced to come in, for emigration to the West. The following rates will be paid, by him. For Indians delivered at Ft. Brooks or Ft. Myers, viz:

For each Warrior, from $250.00 to $500.00.
For each woman, from $150.00 to $200.00.
For each Boy over 10 years, $100.00 to $200.00.

But this was far too mild for the publisher of *The Peninsular,* who further fanned the flames in the following editorial:

We will rejoice to see the Indians removed from our State by the means here indicated, yet we fear this policy, dictated by humane sympathy and justifiable when dealing with a rational foe, is reprehensible in this instance. Yet, we regard this as an important move, which (as we predict) will not end the race of the "red man" in Florida, [but] *will soon prove its impracticality, and* [will] *induce Government to offer a reward for every Indian captured dead or alive!*

This may sound harsh, but antecedents of this bloody race justify such a course. What has the Seminole done to cause us to deal with him with such lenity? He has never spared the tomahawk or scalping knife when an opportunity offered. He has smitten us upon the left cheek and we have turned the right, and we have been the recipients of his deathful blows. And now, with all the philanthropy of a saint, our government has exhibited its nether extremity, and, after the folly of this maneuver is shown, we think the acme of bad policy will have been reached... If the Indians have determined to remain in Florida, they will not be taken alive.

Given the intensity of feeling on both sides, it was no wonder that Washington would forgo all lighthouse activities in Florida until safer conditions prevailed. And it may also be that Meade's early return caused Topog Chief Abert to begin ruminating something like this: "On one hand, we have this highly experienced, trustworthy lighthouse designer and project engineer. He is ambitious – even impatient – for promotion and already resigned in frustration once before. On the other hand, his projects in Florida have been idled by war; and in the Chesapeake Bay area nearly all of his major projects have been completed. What can we do to challenge his skills and at the same time justify a promotion?"

The Great Lakes, of course! Five huge lakes plagued by tempestuous winter storms cried out for even more lighthouses and buoys than the South Florida coast. Thus, on April 30, 1856, Abert received a *pro forma* letter that he himself had probably instigated:

Sir,
I have the honor to acknowledge the receipt this day, of the orders of the Bureau of Top. Engineers dated Washington April 29, 1856 & of special orders No. 43,

Washington, April 24th, by which I am directed to report to Detroit, Michigan to be the officer in charge of the Survey of the Lakes as soon as relieved of my present L.H. [lighthouse] duties by 1st Lieutenant W. F. Raynolds, Topographical Engineers. [27]

It was George Meade's last letter as a lieutenant (he became a captain in May) and the last thing he would ever have to do with Florida and its much postponed Jupiter Inlet Lighthouse. He would go on to survey some 6,000 miles of shoreline in the Great Lakes region and to be snatched up by the Union when the Civil War broke out. In just seven years he would be a major general, leading 130,000 Union troops against General Robert E. Lee, his fellow West Point graduate and Topog colleague, in the Battle of Gettysburg.

TOP: The legendary Colonel John James Abert headed the lighthouse-building Corps of Topographical Engineers for 47 years prior to the Civil War. *(U.S. Army)*

MIDDLE: George G. Meade as a captain, just after designing Jupiter Lighthouse. *(State of Florida Archives).*

MIDDLE RIGHT: Meade's mentor and brother-in-law, Hartman Bache, succeeded him as engineer of the Seventh Lighthouse District and oversaw completion of the Jupiter Lighthouse. *(Brevet Generals of the American Civil War)*

BELOW: Major General David Twiggs, the salty commander of Fort Brooke near Tampa, came to respect the urbane Meade for his surveying and survival skills. *(National Archives and Records Administration)*

RIGHT: The screw-pile design for the Sand Key Lighthouse *(National Archives and Records Administration)* and early photo of the same design employed at Sombrero Key Lighthouse off Marathon Key *(Naval Institute Press)*. "Screw-pile" literally meant drilling iron pilings into the bedrock and tying them together with rods.

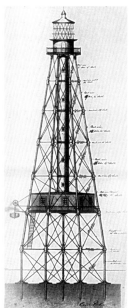

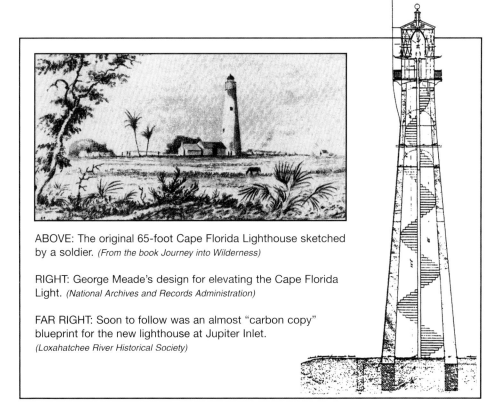

ABOVE: The original 65-foot Cape Florida Lighthouse sketched by a soldier. *(From the book Journey into Wilderness)*

RIGHT: George Meade's design for elevating the Cape Florida Light. *(National Archives and Records Administration)*

FAR RIGHT: Soon to follow was an almost "carbon copy" blueprint for the new lighthouse at Jupiter Inlet. *(Loxahatchee River Historical Society)*

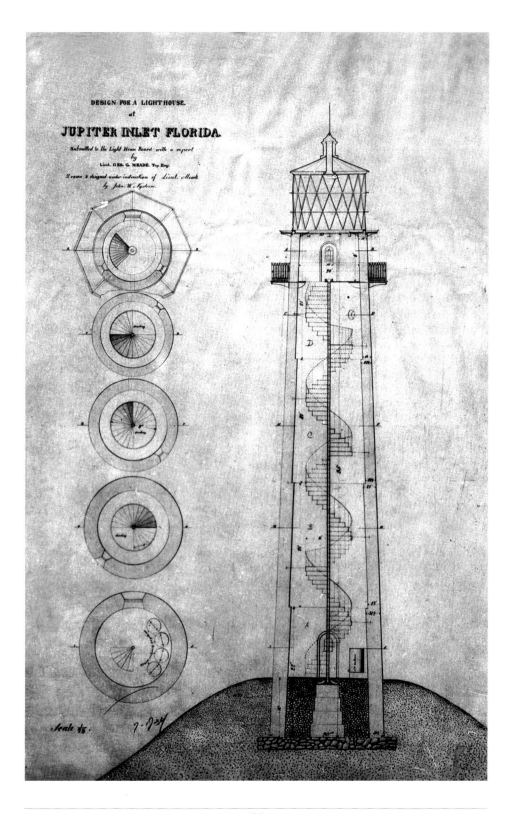

Chapter 5

Outpost

Meade's successor was destined for fame in his own right. In 1859 William F. Raynolds would lead an expedition – some say the most important one since Lewis and Clark – to explore the tributaries of the Yellowstone River and the headwaters of the Missouri. It was Raynolds who charted 600 miles of the Yellowstone for steamboat navigation and identified several wagon trails that were to lead pioneers through the mountain passes of the northwest.

In the spring of 1856 he was just another dutiful lieutenant bouncing between survey and construction assignments as one of the interchangeable parts serving Colonel Abert's Topographical Engineers. Although the rigidly official correspondence between Raynolds and Meade gives no hint of it, the two had surely bonded when surveying the northeast boundaries and serving before that under Mexican War generals Zachary Taylor and Winfield Scott.

Although the war had precluded Florida operations in the spring and summer of 1856, the frugal Colonel Abert made sure Raynolds had no idle time on his hands. In addition to Meade's districts (Chesapeake Bay, the Fourth) and Florida (the Seventh), Abert gave the newcomer the Fifth, covering most of the New Jersey coast. He would have his hands full enough just completing the 167-foot Absecon Light in Atlantic City, which Meade had designed.

Whereas Jupiter Inlet always seemed to be at the end of Meade's priority list, it was number one in the reports filed by Raynolds – but only if the Seminole war ended and he could get to Florida. Although Congress appropriated another $19,523 for "the continuation and completion" of the Jupiter light in August, the Light House Board's John G. Parke wrote Raynolds the next month: "I have to inform you that the active operation which it is the intention of the War Department to [bring] against the hostile Seminoles during the ensuing winter will render the position of a working party site of the proposed lighthouse one of danger. It is therefore deemed expedient to postpone the prosecution of this work until the hostilities have ceased." [1]

The Corps even deemed Key Biscayne too risky for continuing to store the 39 cases containing the expensive Fresnel illuminating apparatus. The following spring (1857) a north-bound tender stopped by to pick it up, with the Light

House Board's Thornton Jenkins telling Raynolds "It might be used at some [other] lighthouse of the first order now authorized, and when the Indian war is over, a new one made to replace it." [2]

Egmont Key was well within the protection of army headquarters at Fort Brooke (Tampa), so plans went ahead to start a new tower there. And so, on October 16, 1857 the Board's new engineering secretary, William Franklin wrote Raynolds: "I have been…instructed to authorize you to make use of the materials which have been collected at Jupiter Inlet in the construction of the Egmont Key tower and to require you to keep an account of such materials so that the appropriation for Jupiter Inlet Lighthouse may be afterward reimbursed if possible."

Each lighthouse project had its own appropriations account, and robbing Peter to pay Paul was a common practice, so this one raised no eyebrows as long as accounts were eventually squared. But it did create a puzzle for historians decades later. Today it's probably impossible to determine just where Jupiter's "first" lens wound up.

Jupiter Inlet may have been quiet in 1857, but that wasn't the case two miles west of it. The plan to beef up the army's presence in Florida alluded to in the letter to Raynolds meant that the abandoned Fort Jupiter would have a new garrison. This one, Company D of the Fourth Artillery, under Captain Joseph Roberts, had a head start over its predecessor in the form of a map and ten-page narrative of how best to traverse the wilderness to get from one post to another. Based on several surveys and scouting reports in previous years, it had been assembled adroitly in 1856 by Lieutenant J. C. Ives, the man who gave us our first description of Jupiter Narrows. Ives, by the way, was a Topog engineer who had never left his Washington office to visit Florida. [3]

The narrative accompanying the map offers the first written account of many of modern Jupiter's early environs. Here, for example, is a description of pristine Lake Worth before a soul lived on it:

Lake Worth is a pretty sheet of water, about twenty miles long and three quarters of a mile in width; bounded on the west by pine barren, and on the east by the sand hills of the beach, which are sometimes twelve or fifteen feet in height, and covered with cabbage trees, wild figs, mangroves, saw palmetto, etc., with here and there a variety of the cactus.

In the centre of the lake, a mile and a half from the head, is an island, bearing a tree resembling the wold fig in appearance, with a fruit like the olive in shape and size, of a yellow color when ripe, and used by the Indians as food. A delicate running vine is also here found, yielding a vegetable about three quarters of an inch long, with a flavor similar to that of the cucumber.

Opposite to the middle of the island is a Haulover, only eighty yards across, descending twelve feet to the sea, at an angle of forty-five degrees. Two miles and a half beyond is another Haulover, one hundred yards width. Below, along the eastern border of the lake, are long strips of cultivatable ground about two hundred yards wide, separated from the beach by ponds and wet prairie. These were formerly tilled by the Indians, who had large villages in the neighborhood. The soil is light, but very rich, being almost entirely vegetable mould. Rock occasionally makes its appearance on the surface, and heaps of sea shells are strewn here and there. The country on the west side would afford fine grazing.

Six miles from the last Haulover, on the west side of the Lake, is Chachi's Landing [today's West Palm Beach]. A broad trail, half a mile in length, formerly led from this place over a spruce scrub towards the villages of the Indians whose gardens were upon the opposite side of Lake Worth, which they reached by hauling their canoes over the trail. The last fields were five miles from the foot of the Lake. [4]

Making sure those Indian villages weren't reoccupied was one of the garrison's priorities. But Indian-hunting excursions constantly went off in all directions as soon as the company settled in and shored up the outpost on Jones Creek. Captain Roberts' first muster report, dated March 15, 1857, showed three officers and 71 enlisted men. It had taken the men and seven wagons six days to reach Fort Jupiter on well-worn trails, but it was already clear to Roberts that Jupiter was the end of the line for wagons. Soon after arriving he sent the empty wagons off to Fort Capron and dispatched thirty men to Fort Dallas to bring back six Whitehall boats. The Whitehalls, first built in lower New York, were 15-foot rowboats with sharp bows for cutting through grassy creeks and wide beams for maximum cargo storage. For the next year they would ferry supplies from Fort Capron and Fort Dallas.

Roberts had originally intended to occupy Fort Jupiter only until he could build a new "base of operations" on Lake Worth and nearer the vacated Indian villages. But after heading his new Whitehalls down the labyrinthine Jupiter Creek, he gave up trying to find a navigable entrance to the lake. Suddenly Fort Jupiter began to look a lot better. Roberts' big worry was that the post had been reported to be very unhealthy by the Company that had departed in 1855, but now the captain decided it had probably been because of the "extremely low state of the Jupiter River whereby the flats were exposed to the action of the hot sun, and the malaise was induced by draining of fiords in the neighborhood when the summer was somewhat advanced." Anyway, he added, it would only take a day or two to find another location if the men became sick. [5]

During the ensuing year, the camp would have four successive commanders: Roberts, then a Captain Truman Seymour (taking over in August), then a troupe of Florida Mounted Volunteers headed by Captain Oscar Hart, and finally a Lieutenant Charles H. Webber, who left little trace of himself. Despite the several scouting expeditions, no Indians – or even recently abandoned camps – were ever sighted. In short, the garrisons in 1857-58 made no mark on military history. But they *did* leave behind some rare correspondence that shows what it was like to live on the confluence of the Jupiter River and Jones Creek before the Civil War.

For one thing, we now have a plausible candidate for Jupiter's first pioneer. As soon as Roberts and Company D unpacked, they were greeted by a "Mr. Stone" who, said the captain, "has a garden on the south bank of the Jupiter River near the Inlet." Thirty years later, when the newly married Harry and Susan DuBois built a house in what is now DuBois Park, they had heard vaguely that the spot had once been called "Stone's Point" after an odd character who once grew bananas there. [6]

They had it right on both counts. David Stone, 49 years old when Roberts arrived, had been born in Massachusetts and had spent most of his adult life beachcombing from Cape Canaveral to Jupiter Inlet. He was undoubtedly helpful to the soldiers in finding ways into Lake Worth, but it would seem from the post commanders' reports that he pestered them for supplies and favors to the point where they probably ducked behind trees when they saw him coming. More about Mr. Stone in a moment. [7]

So what did three officers do to keep seventy men from terminal boredom when they weren't off scouting? Like camp commanders everywhere, they kept them hammering and sawing. In Captain Roberts' case the pet projects seem to have been hewing a log cabin for the officers and a building a bridge across Jones Creek. The latter may be difficult to envision because today's "Jones Creek" is known only as a small tributary leading into the wide C-18 Canal (which in turn meets the Loxahatchee, known equally then as Jupiter River). Back then "Jones Creek" meant the whole length of today's south fork. In 1857 it was shallow enough so that men could almost wade across except for a stretch of perhaps forty or fifty feet in the middle. To span that stretch, Roberts and his men built a bridge of pine logs cut from the hammock behind the outpost.

We know of it only as seen through the eyes of Oscar Hart, the volunteer corps commander, who arrived at Fort Jupiter for the first time on November 20, 1857. Heavy rains had accompanied his wagon train ever since leaving Fort Capron on the 12th, and when the wet, weary soldiers finally approached the fort from a trail to its west, they found the bridge swept away. Reported Hart:

The bottom foundation logs had, however, been pieced together and could not float off. And upon that base I [meaning his soggy soldiers] *laid a large and heavy string of cross timbers, having no augur to pin them together in sufficient quantity to build upon the foundation above the water's level, and by this means I succeeded in pressing and in keeping the logs firm and from being swept away by the current. From marks upon the trees and the height of the water above the old bridge, the river was about four feet higher than it was when the bridge was first made. At the end of four days of steady heavy work, we had rebuilt the bridge, crossed the wagons and that night* [November 20] *reached Fort Jupiter.* [8]

Oscar Hart's pet project — perhaps obsession — was to cut through the sand barrier that kept Jupiter Inlet closed to the sea. Apparently the regular army garrison had tried it unsuccessfully in 1855 and Hart was determined to show that his Florida Mounted Volunteers were men enough to get the job done. Just two days after the long, wet march from Fort Capron and the arduous bridge repair task — and on a Sunday, no less — taskmaster Hart took "thirty of my best men" down to the Inlet. He then sighted up the most direct line from Inlet to Ocean — not where the Inlet flowed naturally a quarter mile south, but exactly where barges and engineers in 1921 would cut the channel that exists today. As Hart tells it,

[By] *working in bands of five each, and each band working seven and a half minutes, and instantly relieved at the moment the period expired, one band kept at work incessantly and all had the opportunity to become rested by the time when their turn came up again. We continued opening a canal which had formerly been commissioned and left unfinished, and by sunset had opened a passage for this water from the river.* [It] *ran about four-fifths of the way across the ocean* [but] *then the salt water rose from the bottom of the canal, it being lower than the low water mark on the beach. Of course it was a failure, and we returned to the Fort dispirited and disheartened.* [9]

One can imagine the groans next morning when the same thirty "best men" were rousted from their tents and told to get marching back to Jupiter Inlet. Hart had apparently re-thought the whole scheme the night before and decided that "there may be a better point for the connection of the River and Ocean about four hundred yards south of the point marked" [see his hand-drawn map]. There, "at what appears to be the end of the River and the <u>natural</u> outlet for its waters," Hart ordered the men to start digging again. This time,

…laboring (each band five minutes & each instantly relieved on the expiration of their time), at the end of two days incessant work, we had the happiness to see the waters of the River flowing into the ocean and with a rapidity that satisfied us we had this time labored successfully. We returned to our post, and on the morning of the 26th I accompanied Capt. Kilburn [a visiting army inspector from Tampa] and others to the place & found the opening some sixty or seventy feet wide, with the prospect of widening, but discovered, unfortunately, that a ledge of rocks extended from the south bank northward into the opening. With the hope of securing a channel which would be free from this obstacle, I again set to work with my men, and at the expiration of two days more, succeeded in cutting away the north bank (the loose sand from which was washed out & onto the south bank) to the width of eighty or ninety yards, and the satisfaction to find that the rocks did not extend probably more than fifty feet from the south bank into the opening of the channel. [The] loose sand, as it washed onto the south bank, widened and extended that bank, covering the rocks to some extent and gradually the water swept more to…deepen the channel on the North. [10]

Triumph! "So forcibly did the water from the River flow," wrote Hart," that it drove back the high waves and marked a distinct track for several hundred yards out in the Ocean."

Triumph? Had this realized the dream of allowing ocean vessels to enter a safe, deep harbor? Quite the contrary! "The River has fallen between two and three feet, and I fear is too shoal to be navigated by vessels of any size," he observed in the same report.

Gone with the deep water harbor dream was any last hope of bringing a heavy-laden ship of bricks directly to the site selected for the Jupiter Inlet Lighthouse. And gone, while we're at it, were the entrepreneurial dreams of Jupiter's first resident, David Stone. Tradition has it, passed on by Harry and Susan DuBois, that Mr. Stone had discovered a chest of Spanish gold coins and merchandise on the beach a short time before the soldiers reoccupied the second Fort Jupiter. He'd probably found several washed-up coins while walking the shoreline, as have many Jupiter beachcombers since. In any case, Stone had enough of them to forget all about growing bananas. He took the coins to New York, cashed them in, and bought a wide-beamed schooner to pursue another dream. He would cut pine and cypress logs in Jupiter and haul them down to the Keys, where he'd make a fortune selling them to lumber-starved builders. The story goes that he had the schooner all loaded up with logs when something happened to lower the River so rapidly that his heavy boat was stranded. Dejected and destitute, he abandoned it and walked up the beach, existing on rum and turtle eggs, until he reached Cape Canaveral and caught a ship headed north.

Fort Commander Hart's letters show that Mr. Stone repeatedly pestered him about "loaning" him a private to accompany him on the long walk up the beach. Hart did so and was later reprimanded by his superiors for letting a soldier help on someone's private business.

Maybe Hart had felt he owed Mr. Stone a favor.

Despite occasional bursts of activity, there was plenty of time for soldiers to write home, and we should be grateful that at least one officer's letters to his mother survive. Again, they aren't significant except to show an early glimpse of life on the Loxahatchee River.

Theodore Talbot was an explorer and army officer who would distinguish himself in several campaigns from Florida to Oregon. A collection of his letters in the Library of Congress includes two letters that he wrote his mother and sister in Washington, D.C., while serving under Roberts' successor, Captain Seymour. They are mostly chitchat about family and friends back home, but historically exquisite in that the first page of the letter to his mother (dated August 20, 1857) which opens with a lovely sketch of the cabin and view that he shared with Captain Seymour and an orderly (see page **65**). A few vignettes:

We get up frequent and very severe storms in Florida, but in the manner of hail cannot pretend to enter the competition with the specimens presented in your diagrams [of hail stones in a recent storm in Washington]. *It is fortunate that we cannot, for although we have no windows to break, yet our frail roofs, which afford but feeble protection against a heavy rain, would not withstand for many minutes such a shower of grapeshot.*

About his quarters:

I have been alone here for a week past, [Captain] *Seymour having gone to Ft. Capron to see his wife. I am very well satisfied with this place. On the first page I have given you a little pen and ink sketch looking from my quarters to the Eastward down*

Jupiter River and, at the bottom of the page, the mansion in which I reside. Seymour has one room and I the other in the little log house. Our dining room is an al fresco arrangement under the shadow of its porch. If it should happen to rain at mealtime, our frugal repast is deferred until the weather changes. The little palmetto hut on the left is the kitchen and bedroom of our attendant. [11]

Talbot passes on some scuttlebutt that the camp's only physician just received orders to report to "H Company" on the Indian River, "which would seem to imply that we are not considered fixtures at Jupiter, but may be packed off somewhere else in a short while." Then he went back to describing his surroundings to his mother.

We have set to much building with logs and palmettos to make shelters for ourselves and be as comfortable as circumstances permit while we do stay. We are also commencing a garden on the generous principle that if we don't see its fruits, somebody else will. We think that if we can only get some planks to make floors, doors, etc., we could establish ourselves most luxuriously. The quartermaster department, however, permits no such extravagances, and our only hope is that some lumber vessel may be wrecked on the coast outside...." [12]

And anticipating a mother's concern for her son's health, he writes:

Although Florida is not generally considered a health resort in the summer season, I find that the climate has agreed with me very well. Therefore, I believe that I am looking very well and I certainly feel so. The mosquitoes are not quite so bad as they were, which is a real blessing. Although the monster cockroaches eat my books, boots, shirts and whatever else they can get a hold of, and the scorpions keep me somewhat in dread (I shook one out of my pantaloons the other morning), still there are but minor troubles compared to mosquitoes. I keep some pet lizards to look after the small insects such as fleas and flies, and find them very useful, and indefatigable for their exertions. [13]

Actually, Talbot's description of Fort Jupiter's healthy climate either may have been for a worried mother's eyes or the overly optimistic assessment of an officer living in a cabin with a separate kitchen and an orderly to keep it tidy. He wrote, after all, in the muggy month of August, when it was common to find the word "miasma" in the reports of field commanders from lonely outposts. Indeed, as early as June, Captain Roberts was writing about "transporting supplies, mails and the sick [to Fort Capron] who I am obliged to send to that post for medical attendance in consequence of not having a medical officer here." In September an assistant surgeon was sent down from Fort Capron to investigate conditions. He reported back that of 64 men at the post, "all the officers and thirty enlisted men were unable to do duty, in consequence of having been attacked by intermittent...fevers." These included "some ten or fifteen men" who had already been treated at Fort Capron and returned to duty at Fort Jupiter. It was doubtless due to a malarious atmosphere," said the doctor (who had no idea what caused it). His assessment:

The medical topography of Fort Jupiter is very unfavorable to health. The post is surrounded on three sides by a fresh water lagoon filled with a rank growth of bushes and other vegetation peculiar to the climate. The unhealthiness of the post is owing, doubtless, to the decomposition and decay of this immense amount of vegetable matter. [14]

The assistant surgeon, citing similar opinions by his counterparts in 1855, concluded that "with a view to the preservation of the health and lives of the men, I have respectfully to recommend that they be temporarily removed to Fort Capron until such time...as the advancing season and improved health of the men warrant."

It would appear that army medics repeatedly suspected the cause of malaria had something to do with the musty smell of exposed mangrove roots at low tide. Whatever the case, health concerns – not Indians – led to the departure of Company D and to the arrival of the Florida Mounted Volunteers in November as a probably more expendable replacement. On February 1, 1858, after a stay of not quite three months, Oscar Hart and his volunteers moved on to another location.

The last contingent at Fort Jupiter, headed by Lieutenant Charles Webber, consisted of a mere twenty men. Webber's commanding officer at Fort Capron was Captain Abner Doubleday (who, it seems, had already assured himself immortality by inventing a game called baseball in 1839). By March 11, 1858, Doubleday was writing headquarters in Tampa that "eight or ten" of the Jupiter garrison were already "sick with intermittent fever" and predicting that "the place will continue to be unhealthy throughout the summer." The captain blamed it mostly on the low level of fresh water in the Loxahatchee (no thanks to Oscar Hart) and the "vegetative decay" on the shoreline. Low water, he added, was allowing the sandbar at the inlet to mount to the point where he believed "the inlet will soon be closed." [15]

Doubleday's frustration with Jupiter stemmed in part from trying to keep it supplied. Fort Capron was charged with provisioning Fort Lloyd, Fort Micklen and a garrison at Cape Canaveral Lighthouse as well as Jupiter. Wagon trains routinely bogged down in swampy trails. Army boats were so leaky and undependable that Doubleday had to coax William Davis, the fort's nearby neighbor, to give up his turtling for a few weeks and use his broad-beamed Mackinaw, *Katie*, to haul supplies down to Jupiter. Davis got a handsome $3 per day for his efforts, but soon the call of the sea beckoned again. When others balked at the job, Doubleday gave up and recalled the men from Jupiter. No one ever occupied Fort Jupiter again. [16]

The Third Seminole Indian War staggered to a messy, inglorious end just like the second one. In March 1858 an exhausted Billy Bowlegs was coaxed out of the Big Cypress Swamp to hear another offer to emigrate west. Although his people still hadn't recovered from having their main camp discovered and destroyed by soldiers the previous fall (500 bushels of pumpkins, 100 of rice, 50 of corn all lost) his answer to their entreaties might still have been no except for a new factor.

Out in Oklahoma the Seminoles had been in a reservation dominated by Creeks, whom they regarded as a worse oppressor than the Great Father. Washington had recently tried to fix the problem by giving the western Seminoles their own reservation and creating a $500,000 trust fund. But half of the money was to be withheld until the Florida Seminoles could be persuaded to emigrate and claim their share. So, when army officers waved the flag of truce and implored Billy Bowlegs to leave the swamp for one more peace proposal, they had on hand several chiefs from Oklahoma to tell him about the life of peace and plenty that could be his for the taking.

In May, Bowlegs and 156 followers agreed to go to Fort Egmont near Tampa and board a steamer heading west. Even though stubborn Sam Jones and his band of 150 or so would remain (and become the forefathers of today's Seminole and Micosukee communities) the army was all too ready to declare victory and go home.

Summed up on a balance sheet, the government had paid roughly $10,000 for each of the Seminoles it had moved west (something like $500,000 in today's dollars). Or by another yardstick, the cost was one dead soldier for every two Seminoles who emigrated. But it would be hardly noticed compared to the cost of another conflict that would erupt just three years later.

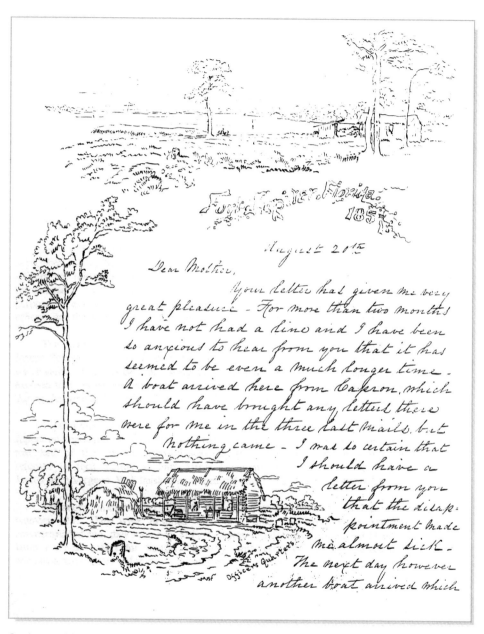

On August 20, 1857, Lieutenant Theodore Talbot began a letter to his mother with the only known sketch of the relocated Fort Jupiter and the surrounding Loxahatchee River. *(State of Florida / Bureau of Surveying & Mapping)*

LEFT: William Raynolds became engineer for Florida lighthouse construction when George Meade left to survey the Great Lakes. In two years, Raynolds would depart on a mission to survey the Yellowstone River watershed. *(U.S. Army Military History Institute)*

CENTER: Captain Joseph Roberts commanded Fort Jupiter in 1857, mainly to scout for signs of Seminole habitation. *(U.S. Army Military History Institute)*

BELOW: Some six miles north of Jupiter, the broad Indian River became a twisted, shallow labyrinth of mangrove islands. "Jupiter Narrows," from Seminole War days to the construction of Jupiter Lighthouse, to the later paddlewheel steamer era, confounded all but experienced pilots. *(Skip Gladwin Collection / Photo by Seth Shear)*

Abner Doubleday, later to be immortalized for inventing the game of baseball, commanded Fort Capron during the difficult days of supplying the new Fort Jupiter. *(U.S. Army Military History Institute)*

Chapter 6

Progress?

The interminable war had again stymied almost all lighthouse work in South Florida and on June 1, 1858 William Raynolds reported that he'd just "closed operations" there for the season. In August, back in Philadelphia, he wrote the Light House Board asking if it still wanted to pursue the much-delayed project at Jupiter Inlet. On September 7 Engineering Secretary William B. Franklin replied that "the Board at its meeting yesterday decided that the construction of the Jupiter Inlet Lighthouse should be commenced this fall, and I have been instructed to require you to take the necessary steps to proceed with the work as soon as operations can safely be undertaken at that point."

Franklin noted that the balance available was $19,587.45 and added that "a lantern [lens] will be furnished without expense to the appropriation" (the Jupiter account already having paid for the one that got diverted elsewhere). [1]

The new order meant that Raynolds would have to hasten his preparations for the coming season because he now had double the men and materials to procure — one set for Jupiter Inlet and one for the nearly-completed light at Egmont Key in Tampa Bay. The key to success was the Seventh District's new tender, *Delaware*, a large, 138-ton schooner-steamer that (exact dimensions aren't known) probably measured around 140 feet in length. The problem was that the *Delaware* was then busy delivering supplies from Tampa to Bradenton. It was needed back at the Philadelphia Navy Yard ASAP for its annual maintenance work and then some. In order to haul tons of bricks to Jupiter, the *Delaware* would have to manage to get through Indian River Inlet so that it could be in waters calm enough to begin lightering its materials onto the shallow draft scows. That meant getting retrofitted at the Philadelphia Navy Yard so that it would draw, say, nine or ten feet instead of the usual sixteen.

A lighter, leaner *Delaware* meant less hauling capacity, so Raynolds was authorized to charter a larger schooner, the *Lenox*, to ferry mail, men and perishable provisions between Indian River, Jupiter Inlet, Cape Florida and Key West while the work was underway. [2]

By December, 1858 the piles of materials were mounting on the dock in

Philadelphia when Raynolds wrote the Board a letter that almost read like "Oh, by the way…" He asked if a specific site had been selected for the Jupiter tower. Well, it hadn't. The Board had picked out "Jones Hill," the natural, 45-foot dune that was easy to agree on, but how big should the lighthouse reservation be? The Board's Franklin replied, in essence, that the Board didn't really care as long as Raynolds made the surrounding area about fifty acres. [3]

On December 28 Raynolds wrote that "working parties" for Jupiter and Egmont had departed on the revamped *Delaware*. On February 1 he wrote that he'd arrived in Jupiter and had personally "examined the means of getting materials to the site." A month later oarsmen left a passing ship and delivered this letter to Raynolds, wading out from the beach at Jupiter:

The Board hopes that you will be able to complete the Jupiter Inlet Lighthouse in one season, but is confident that whatever course you may take in this matter will be justified by the emergencies of the case.

The fact that the expenses of the construction will be so much increased by stopping the work for another season will be good reason for using every exertion to complete it during the season.

The amount now in the treasury belonging to appropriation for the Jupiter Inlet Lighthouse:

Amount in your hands, Dec. 31, 1858	*9,587.45*
As your estimate is:	*5,868.86*
[total available]	*15,456.31*
[total spent thus far]	*27,890.00*
[deficit]	*12,413.69*

There is an estimated deficiency of $12,413.69 to be made up in case another season is necessary to complete the work.

The Board hopes and does not doubt that the most strenuous exertions will be made by you to keep the work going until its completion.

[As to whether it will be] necessary on account of the sickness of the climate to stop work during the summer months, it is the impression of the Board that that part of the coast is healthy and that the work might go on during the whole summer without danger to the health of the party. Of this fact, however, you will be the best judge. [4]

At last, the brass had turned on the financial spigot and ordered the

Seventh District engineer to make it happen ASAP!

Then — yet again — the Jupiter project was suddenly trumped by higher priorities elsewhere. Just as the foundation and first layers of brickwork were creating the beginnings of a cylinder on Jones Hill, Congress was appropriating $40,000 for a special expedition to chart rivers and wagon trails throughout the Northwest Territories. It required a leader with surveying and engineering skills — and someone young enough to withstand the same rigors that had challenged Lewis and Clark in 1805. On April 6, 1859, 39-year-old William Raynolds learned that Topog czar J. J. Abert had picked him for the job. [5]

In May, as Raynolds inventoried the "public property" he would leave his successor (a requirement of all military project directors upon their transfer), it was as if work crews could sense the distraction. Health had already begun to be an issue as the days warmed, and now Raynolds was reporting that "swarms of stinging insects" were making further work near impossible.

The oft-used term *malaise* hardly describes the debilitation caused by malaria, and the attempts to cure it back then show how much it vexed people in South Florida. Witness just one article from the *Florida Peninsular* (Tampa) on August 25, 1855 telling readers how to beat "Yellow Fever" (and imagine a twenty-man work crew in the wilderness with half of the men trying to comply):

Dissolve in a wine glass of H2O a tablespoon of common salt. Pour the same into a tumbler, adding the juice of a whole lemon and two wine glasses of castor oil. The whole [is] to be taken at 1 dose by an adult. Then a hot mustard foot bath with a handful of salt in the water — the patient to be well wrapped in blankets until perspiration takes place freely. On removal to bed, the patient's feet [are] to be wrapped in blankets. Afterwards, apply mustard plaster to the abdomen, legs and soles of the feet. If the headache is very acute, apply mustard plaster to the head and temples. After the fever has broken, take 40 grains of quinine and 40 drops of elixir of vitriol, to a quart of water. Dose: a wine glass-full 3 times a day. Barley water, lemonade and ice water may be used in moderation.

Hot bath? Ice water? In South Florida?

On July 11 the tender *Delaware* arrived in Philadelphia with the Jupiter Inlet crews while piles of bricks on Jones Hill awaited their return in another year. [6]

Out of fifty or so Topog officers, why pick Raynolds for the western frontier? The answer may have more to do with Raynold's boss than himself. It's probable that Abert, with his usual cool, calculating mind, had concluded that he hadn't long to live. At 71, he was well past retirement age and served, as had the FBI's J. Edgar Hoover, because no one could think of the Topographical Engineers without him. Although he wouldn't officially leave the Corps until September 1861 (and die two years later), Abert knew his energies were waning. While not bringing himself to quit just then, he needed to have nearby a potential successor who shared his breadth of experience and knowledge of ongoing projects.

Who else but Hartman Bache? Now 61 and one of only two majors in the Corps, Bache was busy building lighthouses in Oregon and California, where mail took a month to reach. Abert needed him nearer but had no budget for an office-bound assistant chief. The solution: send Raynolds on a challenging mission and put Bache in charge of his Fourth, Fifth and Seventh lighthouse districts. Bache would already be overseeing nearly half of the nation's lights and buoys.

Besides, Bache's political savvy would be needed for a reason neither man could foresee in the summer of '59.

The Civil War "officially" ignited on April 12, 1861, when Confederate shore batteries fired on Fort Sumter, South Carolina. But as John B. Gordon, a Confederate major general, would recall in his very balanced *Reminisces of the Civil War*: "Long before a single gun was fired, public sentiment, North and South, had been lashed into a foaming sea of passion; and every timber in the framework was bending and ready to break from the heavy groundswell of tremendous agitation."

If so, when did military men and politicians in Washington first sense that a cataclysmic clash of cultures was coming? When did they begin choosing sides in their own minds? At what point did, say, a top official with a southern upbringing subtly begin to sabotage budgets and projects that could bolster the federal government's strength in his homeland?

Such questions may certainly be asked of the men upon whom Hartman Bache depended for lighthouse decisions in the fall of 1859. He had already made it clear by his actions that the Seventh District would go all out to finish the accursed Jupiter Light in the next season.

Indeed, the Light House Board itself was getting heat from the insurance industry about the lack of a beacon near the treacherous Jupiter reefs. In November, Captain William P. Pickering, who had recently become inspector for the Seventh District, was in Key West when he received a letter from one R. N. Welch, "agent for American and European insurance companies," claiming that "several ships are ashore north of Cape Florida, and in great peril." Pickering quickly sailed off in a lighthouse tender to investigate. While not sharing the insurance man's alarm, he certainly indicated a need for a light station at Jupiter Inlet. As he wrote Captain Raphael Semmes, the Light House Board's naval secretary:

I passed five wrecks between Cape Florida and Jupiter Inlet, but none unattended by wreckers except the most northerly, bark Mary Coe *from Mobile, bound for Havre* [France] *with a load of cotton. This vessel had laid bows on* [run aground] *ten miles south of Jupiter and was logged with two feet of water under her at low tide. I took from the beach her mate and five men. Her captain had left on a fishing smack some eight or ten days previous.*

At Jupiter Inlet I received intelligence [from a construction worker left there as watchman?] *that the coast was clear of wrecks from that point some distance to the northward of Cape Canaveral. I therefore returned to Key West to present my tour of inspection to the southward and up the west coast.* [7]

Back in Philadelphia, Bache was well into the provisioning process for Jupiter Inlet, hoping for a quick getaway in early December before the harbor iced up for the winter. The tenders *Delaware* and *Lenox* were repaired and ready to go. Bache's only problem seemed to be a misunderstanding with Captain Raphael Semmes, the Light House Board's naval secretary. Semmes had apparently registered surprise that Bache was now $6,200 over what was available in the Jupiter spending account. In a letter of November 11, Bache pointed out that his predecessor, Raynolds, had warned of a probable $12,000-plus shortfall the previous February. He added that the current red ink wouldn't be nearly as much if the Board had spread the recent cost of repairing the two tenders among other light stations, "as they are employed upon lighthouse service generally." [8]

Bache probably thought this a minor misunderstanding – until three days later when Captain Semmes stunned him with a reply letter. It ordered that all work on Jupiter Inlet Lighthouse be suspended. Anything in a sub-account earmarked for "Seaman's Wages" (which wouldn't be needed to pay the Jupiter crew) were ordered to be transferred to another project.

The letter explained that only $30,000 or so remained in appropriations for all lighthouse projects and that outstanding bills already exceed that amount.

"But even if this fund were in a condition to be drawn upon," Semmes added, "the Secretary of the Treasury would not permit the transfer, it being an inviolable rule with him whenever a special appropriation is exhausted, to suspend the work." [9]

Well now, just who was this Captain Semmes and what was he up to? Raphael Semmes, naval secretary of the Light House Board, was then 49. As stern and austere and with a frame as spare as the legendary Horatio Nelson, he had settled his family in Alabama soon after graduating from the naval academy. As soon as Alabama seceded from the Union on January 11, 1861, Semmes would quickly abandon his post in Washington and be commissioned a ship's captain in the new Confederate navy. He would soon gain international notoriety as the captain of the *Alabama*, plundering and sinking no less than 65 Union ships before being brought down himself in a famous gun duel with the *U.S.S. Kearsarge* off the French coast in 1864.

Who was the rigidly frugal secretary of the treasury? He was the portly, gregarious Howell Cobb, former governor of Georgia and speaker of the House of Representatives until tapped by his old friend James Buchanan for the treasury post in 1857. In the fall of 1858, Illinois senatorial candidates Abraham Lincoln and Stephen Douglas had unwittingly polarized America in their series of debates on slavery and Cobb's secessionist political allies were already urging him to resign. He continued to serve "out of my friendship for Old Buck" (Buchanan), but soon after Lincoln's election the next year, he was gone. Cobb would soon resurface as president of the Confederacy's first provisional Congress, and then as a general in the Confederate Army.

Did either Semmes or Cobb actually connive to stop a lone lighthouse at unpopulated Jupiter Inlet? Maybe not, but their combined demeanor was typical of how the coming North-South rupture was beginning to affect routine administrative decisions all over the country.

Bache, who knew something about bureaucratic gamesmanship, decided that the best way to get around Semmes and Cobb was to make them look silly. His reply of November 14, 1859, begins by again reminding Semmes that the Board, after being told almost a year before that the project would run some $12,000 in the hole, continued to approve various repairs and provisions for the coming season in Florida. To be sure, he was a dutiful subordinate and would obey the order. But, of course shutting down everything cold at the Philadelphia Navy Yard would also involve some costs.

The Delaware *has 25,000 bricks on board, 12,000 of which were shipped last summer as ballast on sending her into the Chesapeake. The* Lenox *has about 12,000 on board. The provisions are purchased, and many articles such as beef and pork are already on board the schooners. The bricks, with the exception of the 12,000 put on board the* Delaware *last summer and then paid for, the maker may possibly take back. But the cost of returning them at $2 per* [hundredweight]*, besides the loss of breakage, must be borne by the government. Whether any part of the provisions can be got rid of except by sale or auction, I have not had time since the receipt of the letter of the Board to ascertain.*

As there is nothing doing in the [lighthouse] *districts calling for the employment of the schooners* Delaware *and* Lenox*, it is recommended to lay them up in charge of a ship keeper. It will of course occur to the Board that repair will be required on them when again called for service.*

May I ask to be instructed in regard to the two men in charge of the work and Jupiter property at Jupiter Inlet? They were left on the 1st of July with a supply of provisions for four months, a period now two weeks expired.

Immediately on the receipt of the letter of the Board, [I] *telegraphed as follows: "Should like to see the Board about Jupiter Inlet Light House. Shall I go on?" While I write, the answer is handed to me at 2:45 pm. I will leave* [for Washington] *tomorrow, in the meantime suspending all measures.* [10]

No record of a meeting between Bache and the Light House Board has surfaced to date (if indeed the full Board convened). But Bache must have lost his appeal, because he sends a telegram December 3 in response to another letter in which the Board said it was having second thoughts about its decision. Could he still reassemble all the men and materials and depart for Jupiter Inlet before year-end?

Bache's return telegram states: "The last of the store and materials was sold yesterday. The vessels are dismantled and laid up and all hands discharged." He adds, his frustration showing through, that all of the off-loaded provisions, sold off at fire-sale prices, netted a measly $600.

Later the same day Bache elaborates in a letter. Yes, he could probably re-load everything, but "who can say that when all is ready, the vessels may not be deterred by the ice?" Was the Board ready to take the chance that ice might block the fully-loaded ships and that Jupiter Light would wait still another year? [11]

By this time the Jupiter project is an embarrassing boondoggle — especially with insurance industry lobbyists watching impatiently. Two more weeks go by with no word from Washington. Then Bache gets a letter dated December 17:

> *The Light House Board directs that you make arrangements with all possible expedition to recommence the work at Jupiter Inlet, Florida.*
>
> *It is hoped that your materials and supplies can be put on board and your vessels be at sea before the Delaware [River] is filled with ice. But should you think the risk of being detained by the cold weather is too great, you are authorized to send the vessels to Baltimore to be fitted out there.*
>
> *The money for your wants will be forthcoming upon receipt of your special requisition C for continuing and completing the lighthouse at Jupiter Inlet.* [12]

It would seem that Semmes has been overruled. Perhaps Bache has more friends in high places than he does.

Each December day becomes progressively colder, but the men at the Philadelphia Navy Yard keep themselves warm in their frenzy of hauling and hoisting. Bache asks Washington for $8,221 for the season's work, then tacks on $959 for a "centre column, gallery and watchroom floor plates" – all for "necessary changes in the tower called for by the novel character of the revolving machinery of the lighting apparatus...." [13]

Then he complains in a memo that "the allowance of provisions established for employees of the Light House Establishment is insufficient for men constantly engaged in labor." Bache, who knows far more about feeding work crews than any desk jockey in Washington, whacks several bushels from the government-issue supply of potatoes, beans and rice. He uses the $281 in savings to buy five extra barrels of pork and beef ($18.90 each), 200 lbs. of sugar (at $.29 per lb.), 150 lbs. of coffee (at $.15); 327 lbs. of cheese (at $.15), 300 lbs. of lard (at $.16) and 140 lbs. of butter (at $.30). [14]

By December 23 Bache is able to report the re-loading of 20,000 bricks on each of the tenders. Also aboard are 250 barrels of cement and 10 barrels of lime. As soon as a small shipment of "lumber and woodwork, hardware and sundries" arrives, Bache adds, the vessels will be ready to proceed to their destination." [15]

_____

It is time to sail – and not a moment too soon. The ground around the wharfs is already under an inch or two of hardened snow and a typical day's high temperature is scarcely above freezing. The shallow shoreline of the Delaware River is now crusty with ice, leaving only a slim channel in its deepest parts. Still,

Bache presses his luck and grants the work crews a three-day Christmas weekend, the last time they will see their families for six or so months. On Tuesday the 27th the men – probably the standard twenty for a lighthouse project – struggle up the gangplank beneath their heavy duffle bags and sea chests.

By next morning the ships will be off and Hartman Bache will return to his office in Philadelphia to begin planning the summer's work in Districts Four and Five. His only communications with the Jupiter Inlet work party will be twice a month via mail hauled by contract shippers that stop at Philadelphia, Charleston and Key West. In between, they will send out a rowed longboat to drop and pick up parcels at places like Ft. Pierce, but only if seas permit. In short, counting on deliveries twice a month from Jupiter is a crapshoot.

This lighthouse tower (not Jupiter Light) was raised in 1859 with hoists and scaffolding much like buildings are today. *(U.S. Army Corps of Engineers)*

E

Jupiter Inlet Lt. House Works
February 7th 1860.

Major Hartman Bache,
Corps Topographical Engineers
Philadelphia.

Sir:

    I have the honor to make the following report of the work under my charge.

    Since January 24th I have received three scows loaded with materials from Indian River, containing 19,000 bricks, 8 bbls. cement, all the materials for dwelling house, and about two months provisions.

    The tower is up 41 feet on the outside, the 3rd window frame set, and will be filled in to that height to morrow evening, and ready to commence on the cylinder which is now 35 feet high. Work was stopped on the tower on the 2nd 3rd and 4th inst. on account of a heavy N.E. gale with rain.

    The carpenter is progressing with the dwelling now, which has also been stopped for want of materials, one room (S.E. 2nd Story) is finished and plastered, and he is now putting in dormer windows in N.E. room.

    The Lantern is all put together, cleaned, painted and ready to take down when required; and the blacksmith and helper are now

On February 7, 1860, barely a month after his arrival at Jupiter Inlet, construction supervisor Edward A. Yorke reported significant progress on the lighthouse to his engineering supervisor in Philadelphia.
(National Archives and Records Administration)

78

ABOVE: Raphael Semmes, naval secretary of the Light House Board, would soon become the dashing captain of the Confederate warship *Alabama* that sunk 64 Union ships before meeting its demise off the French coast. *(Naval Historical Center / Department of the Navy)*

ABOVE RIGHT: The *Shubrick*, about the same size as the *Delaware* tender that served the Jupiter Lighthouse project, was the first lighthouse supply ship equipped with armor to ward off possible Indian attacks. *(Columbia River Maritime Museum)*

RIGHT: Workers pause for a photo during construction of the Ponce Inlet (Florida) Lighthouse tower in 1886. *(U.S. Lighthouse Society)*

Chapter 7

Yorke

It is now time to introduce the man who would lead the trip and who was most directly responsible for completing the long-planned lighthouse at Jupiter Inlet. Ironically, the information known about him personally is in inverse proportion to his importance.

His name was Edward A. Yorke and his official job title was "Clerk of Works." But he was much more. Yorke had captained the tender *Delaware* on its February 1859 trip to Jupiter Inlet. He must have performed admirably or he wouldn't still be in charge of the 1860 expedition. Yorke must have been a remarkably talented man to be able to captain a large, heavy schooner on wintry seas, supervise a variety of workmen in building a 108-foot tower, and then personally calibrate the intricate Fresnel lens.

Surely Yorke had managed other lighthouse projects, but his name has not yet surfaced in any of their historical documents. Although he must have been primarily a ship's captain, his name does not appear in the personnel records of the U.S. Navy, Revenue Cutter Service or Topographical Engineers. Was he a private contractor? Perhaps. One of two clues to his identity is the 1860 Census, which lists a 46-year-old Edward A. Yorke living in Philadelphia and owning real estate valued at $3,000. The second clue lies in some old Philadelphia street directories housed in the Historical Society of Pennsylvania. During 1858 through 1863 a "sea captain" and "shipmaster" of the same name is listed at 1339 South Fifth Street.

Since the Fifth Street address is just a five block stroll from the docks and navy yard, it's a good bet he's our man. But one comes to know more about him only through his letters to his supervisors up north. Despite the rigid constraints of military form, Yorke comes across as articulate, dutiful, efficient, punctual, unflappable and — above all — resourceful and courageous in overcoming nasty surprises.

Yorke would begin facing adversity on day one of his journey in the form of numbing cold and howling winds from the northeast. At 10:15 a.m. on December 28th, the *Delaware* and its sister ship left Philadelphia Navy Yard, each pulled by a tugboat, their thick belches of black smoke showing how heavily they were laboring. After more than eight hours, the towed ships reached Reedy Island, a maritime stopover some twenty miles south of Wilmington, Delaware, and managed to maneuver into its icy piers around midnight.

The next morning, when Yorke roused his men to begin chipping the night's ice from the windows and deck, he was surprised to see the owner of the two tugboats walking up the pier towards the *Delaware's* wheelhouse. Once inside, he announced bad news. Both tugs had used so much coal chugging to Reedy Island that they scarcely had enough to get back to Philadelphia. The tugs would take the tenders no further. That was it. No pleas or offers of money could sway him. [1]

Yorke emerged from his wheelhouse and concluded that the northeast gale was stronger than the day before, only this time with snow. There on Reedy Island the lighthouse tenders remained all day while Yorke and T. D. Beard, the captain of the *Lenox*, went from the harbormaster's shed to local pubs searching in vain for a willing tugboat owner to get them to sea.

Adding to the dilemma was that every minute the two schooners remained in their berths the greater the probability they would be imprisoned by ice. The next day, December 30, Yorke was of a mind to make a run for the sea, but decided first to lower one of his men to the waterline and take a quick survey of the damage the *Delaware* might have incurred plowing through fifty miles of ice and frozen flotsam. The news was grim: the wooden planks had been badly cut, in some cases ripping away the pitch and exposing the oakum (a hemp fiber used to pack the seams).

It called for some ingenuity. Aboard the *Lenox* were stacks of white pine boards, probably earmarked for the keeper's house at Jupiter Inlet. Yorke ordered them to be sawed in two-foot lengths. Next, his carpenters fashioned a makeshift scaffold, fastened ropes to their waists and lowered themselves almost to the waterline. There, in the numbing sub-freezing morning, they nailed over 300 feet of pine lengthwise to the bow and to the foresides most apt to smack into ice. [2]

The rest of the day was spent swinging picks against the ice that had locked the schooners to their piers. During the day the steamer *State of Georgia* inched by and reported that the ice was even heavier south down to the Buoy of the Middle, which was one of the last markers before entering the Atlantic. Meanwhile, each watery gash made with the whack of a pick at pier side seemed to fill with ice before the men's eyes.

In the early evening the tug *John F. Starr* chugged into view and Yorke offered her captain a dollar a mile to take each schooner to sea. "Not accepted," Yorke tersely noted.

Saturday, December 31. Suddenly the weather is calm and moderate. Yorke rouses the men and perhaps uses that bit of good news to exhort them to one more day of hacking at ice. That afternoon, crews from both ships decide to focus their combined strength at cutting the *Lenox* from her berth. "Finally got her out of the ice," Yorke reports, but "during the night intensely cold" – again undoing much of the day's work.

On Sunday, New Year's Day, 1860, Yorke decides that it's time to try a breakout, come hell or high water.

Thermometer 13 degrees. At 4 a.m. called all hands and commenced to break the ice to get the schooner out. At 6:30 every appearance of being frozen in for the winter if we remain another day.

[As] the payroll of the whole party amounts to about $40 a day, I [decided] to employ the steamer J.L. Pusey *to cut us out again and tow us beyond the heavy ice down the Bay.* [The captain] *first demanded ice boat rates, which were 40 cents* [per ton of cargo] *to the Buoy of the Middle, but I induced him to take us for $1 per mile each as far as I should require him to tow us.*

Later Yorke adds, "I gave the *J. L. Pusey* an order for $62 for towage of the two schooners 31 miles, which was as well earned as ever a towage was."

It's noteworthy that the Seventh District office in Philadelphia would learn of Yorke's progress within three or four days – almost "real time" in 1860. The reason: the tugboat owners demanded a government voucher for instant payment, which was promptly brought to Philadelphia along with Yorke's correspondence.

The rest of the January 1 log reads like a stream-of-consciousness novel as each hour brought a new challenge.

The Lenox, *being oak, is cut, but* [it seems] *as if nothing can hurt her. We got down to the Buoy of the Middle about 1:30 p.m. after about as severe a time as I want to see. The brig* Ellen Bernard *got as far as Bombay Hook with a tow boat and* [then] *stuck fast. The last we saw of her she was trying to get back to Reedy Island. I could also venture to say that we are the only vessels who will get to sea that left the wharf since Monday morning, the last.*

The Delaware *is pretty much of a wreck about her bow,* [the] *bowsprit* [and] Genoa [sail] *from running into the* Lenox. *I put her* [the Lenox] *ahead, being oak, to*

83

take the worst of the ice, and whenever she stopped in the ice we gave her a knock. However, no serious damage is done that I can see.

At 2:30 p.m. I discharged the tug boat and made all sail. As we passed, the Joe Hagger, *a schooner, was taking the crew off the brig* Mayflower, *sunk by the ice.*

I have just had the opportunity to look at the starboard side of the Delaware *when she heaves over and I am sorry to say that the upper edge of the metal is completely cut off, and we shall probably lose the upper* [sheath] *of copper before we get to Florida, and the planks are badly cut. If it was not so intensely cold I would try again and do something in* [Lewes, Delaware] *but I am afraid to stop for fear of being frozen in.* [3]

Yorke had his last marker in sight – Hartman Bache's screw-pile Brandywine Light off Cape May, New Jersey – when he suddenly got cold feet. In late afternoon he veered into a nook just short of the breakwater and carpenters tried desperately to re-nail the plate of copper that ice had torn loose from the bow. But the calm of the little cove only meant that ice formed more quickly. Before the sun rose the next morning the ships left the Delaware River for the sea and soon thought of ice no more. [4]

With a strong nor'easter at their backs, the men of the *Delaware* and *Lenox* found themselves on a five-day roller coaster ride down the Atlantic coast. When they finally came opposite Jupiter Inlet, Yorke was frustrated because he had no chance of putting workers and supplies ashore in the rough seas. His only option was ordering Captain Beard on to Cape Florida to pick up some bricks and cement stored there from the previous year. The *Delaware* would tack across to a small sheltered bay in the Bahamas and wait for the winds to subside.

That same night the wind did slack off, and Yorke had his crew up by 5 a.m. on Sunday the 8th. It took the day to tack across the Bahamas Channel and fight the Gulf Stream. It wasn't until 2:30 a.m. that they anchored just off Jupiter Inlet.

"At daylight," Yorke reported, "we commenced landing the working party, luggage and provisions." At 11 a.m. all were on the beach, where the crew was joyously greeted by the two men who had been left at Jupiter as watchmen. The only adverse news they reported was that the Inlet had fallen one foot since December 1 and could make the tenders' job more precarious.

Within an hour the *Delaware* was off to Cape Florida to rendezvous with the *Lenox*. It was just in time because the wind had already begun to blow again. Had the tender arrived at Jupiter in the afternoon, it would have been too late.

Once the *Delaware* reached Cape Florida, Yorke reckoned he'd need a week to repair the schooner and caulk the scows that would haul bricks down the Indian River. He added some questions and requests in a letter to Hartman Bache in Philadelphia:

I shall require 300 to 400 feet [of] white pine to supply the place of that quantity used in sheathing the schooners in the Delaware River. Also, 12 sheets [of] yellow metal and 10 lbs. sheathing nails to repair the Delaware.

Please take into consideration whether it will not be advisable to frame a small oil house and send all the necessary materials for building, or whether I shall risk having bricks and cement enough left to build it [after the tower is finished]. *One thing is certain: that I shall not have any suitable lumber here, after all the other work is done, to build a durable house.* [5]

Yorke never specified just how many men were on the job and what each did, but one gets an idea from his inventory of equipment. Picture a hillside with all manner of unpacked crates and tools strewn about. Among them were a steam engine, several oil tanks, three 20-foot ladders, a chest of blacksmith tools, a portable forge, 4 wheelbarrows, 4 brick hods, 3 sand sieves (for mixing concrete), a hoisting winch, scaffolding materials, and 4 sets of wheels and axles for lugging heavy materials uphill. Piled in another place were heavy lighthouse parts brought down from Philadelphia: 10 watchroom galley plates, 10 granite stanchions, the iron watchroom floor, door frames, a cornice piece for the dwelling and heavy clock weights. [6]

One thing missing from this scene is an accurate picture of the original "hill" and the lighthouse foundation. None of the reports by Yorke or the lighthouse engineers in Philadelphia ever describe it. Conventional wisdom today assumes that the surveyors found a natural 45-foot hill and built the foundation thereupon. Yet, the bottom twenty or so feet of the lighthouse is buried today. Would the builders have gone to the hilltop, dug out a twenty-foot deep, circular hole and then started laying the brick cylinders? It would involve a heap of work and excavation equipment that the crew lacked.

Well then, might they have found a 25-foot hill, put up the 20 foot foundation, and then thrown up dirt around it? Maybe. But where would they find all the dirt and clear all the thick vegetation necessary to get at it?

There's another possibility. Why wouldn't the Jeaga Indians, who had lived at Jupiter Inlet for more than 5,000 years before Europeans and their diseases wiped them out in the mid-1700s, have prized the choice land at the confluence of two rivers just as highly as their white successors? They might even have chosen it for a special burial or ceremonial site. A clue to that effect comes from a newspaper article written in 1884 by Francis R. Stebbins, a Michigan furniture maker who spent ten winters enjoying the Indian River and telling his frozen northern neighbors about how much fun he was having. One day in February Stebbins and his chartered sailboat captain had been fishing inside Jupiter Inlet when they decided to glide over to the lighthouse (then 24 years old) and have a climb. He then writes something that never shows up in the records of the Light House Board or its Seventh District:

From the top of the lighthouse this afternoon we had the most complete birds-eye view of a large "sacred enclosure," and mound of the prehistoric race. The lighthouse is built on one side of the top of the enclosure, and we could take in the whole work at a glance. This embankment enclosure is 6 rods through on the base [a rod is 16.5 feet] *and 25 feet high, and is built in the form of a horse-shoe; the open part resting on the river. In the center of the bend of the enclosure is a round mound, some 60 or more feet in diameter, and 12 or 15 feet high, the whole bend forming a grand amphitheater, full 40 rods across, where the central mound is located. I do not know if this work has ever been described in scientific works, but if not it is well worth investigation.* [7]

If Stebbins is correct, it certainly would have made the construction job easier. If the double cylinder wall were begun in the back inside of this "horseshoe," the masons could easily walk back and forth within the one open side. Since three-quarters of the circle was already rung by mounds, they would only need to cover up the open side when finished.

As this is written, an Indian pottery shard, confirmed to be around 3,000 years old, was dug up not far from the lighthouse hill. Other discoveries may well show the lighthouse to be sitting amidst an archeological treasure trove.

———————————

One of the first tasks in January 1860 might seem "backward" at first blush, but not to Edward Yorke. He needed to know the exact size of the lantern (the outer enclosure at the top of the tower) so that he could determine that the surrounding watchroom and gallery (walkway) would be sized correctly to support it. So, even though the brick tower itself was scarcely a dozen feet high at the time, Yorke had his men unpack the bulky lantern and set it upright on a piece of level ground. When they did, Yorke discovered that the crew had to clean and re-mark all the bolts and screws; rust and salt air had worn off all the written directions. 8

Another early distraction involved the *Lenox*. The sister ship had managed to glide over the bar at Indian River Inlet into calm waters and send a scow down to Jupiter Inlet with the first load of bricks. The next day Yorke was expecting a second scow, but instead got a message from Captain Beard that on January 16 the *Lenox* had settled aground at low tide. Yorke sent the empty scow back up river in hopes that by taking on another load of bricks, the *Lenox* could be lightened enough to float. It did. 9

By January 24 the outside cylinder stood 36 feet high and the inside one 29 feet. From there on it was up, up and away. On February 7 Yorke wrote Bache's assistant, G. Castor Smith:

We are getting along finely, and everything works well since the 24th [of January]. The scows have brought down 19,000 bricks, 88 barrels of cement, and all the materials for the dwelling house and two months provisions for the party. The tower is 41 feet on the outside, the [inside] cylinder 35 feet, and we are ready to commence on the cylinder again. The 3rd tower window is set. One dormer window is in and the [?] plastered, and looks very well.

From the 2nd to the 5th of this month it has been blowing a gale of wind from S.E. and with frequent showers. Therefore, we have done but little in that time, but we are now underway again and the scows [off] to Indian River for another load.

The lantern is all put together, cleaned, painted and ready to [be installed?] when required, and the blacksmith and helper are now putting down the roof plates of the lantern into firm sections.

The Lenox *will be discharged and leave Indian River on or before the 10th … and proceed to Cape Florida for winter overhaul.* 10

In the same letter Yorke grumbles that "to this date I have not heard from Philadelphia since leaving there. There is no regularity in the mail in New Smyrna."

Yorke finally got a letter from Hartman Bache dated February 23 stating that a third tender, the schooner *Elisha T. Smith* had departed Philadelphia with more materials for Jupiter. He also had instructions about the oil house. Both the Board and Bache had balked at Yorke's idea of building a wooden structure. It just wouldn't do for storing flammable fuels. The new structure, 12 by 10 feet and 8 feet high, was to be made from bricks and plaster left over from the tower.

On March 10 Yorke reported the tower "sixty feet high inside and out." Northerly winds and high water had sped the scows on their last two journeys down Indian River. The fourth and last tower windowpane would soon be set. "The carpenters are progressing with the dwelling [and it] will be ready for occupants by the 10th of April," he added. [11]

On March 20, Yorke again reported to Philadelphia. After enclosing the payroll figures (as do most of his letters from Jupiter) the clerk of works already begins to anticipate completion.

The tower is 67 feet high on the outside, 64 feet on the cylinder, with bricks and cement enough at the site to finish the tower. I can therefore report, if the weather continues fair, that the brackets [that underpin the gallery floor] *will be set on or about the last of this month.*

Eight of the brackets are here now and the scows leave tomorrow morning for another load from the Lenox. *The* Lenox *will then proceed to Cape Florida for the last of the materials required on these works. Any time after the 15th of April the* Lenox *will be ready to return north.*

The hardware, lumber, paint, etc. have all come safely to hand.

The Schnr. E. T. Smith [the third tender] *must have had as quick dispatch as he could wish; she passed here on the evening of the 4th and left Cape Florida early on the morning of the ninth* [of March.]

There is nothing at Cape Florida now but some bricks, 29 bbls cement and the frame of the oil house. The illuminating apparatus and castings are all on board the Lenox *and will be delivered here in the next scows from Indian River. Therefore, I think we are safely past the probability of any accident delaying the completion of this light house this season. Unless some unforeseen difficulty occurs, the party will be ready to leave here about the 15th of May.* [12]

In a personal letter to assistant engineer Smith, who may have been a close friend, Yorke allowed himself to crow a bit. "On the 16th and 17th," he said, "we had as heavy a gale from the southward as I ever saw and the rain fell in torrents all the time. The dwelling was perfectly tight, except one or two little places about the lower windows, which I think we have repaired now. The windows of the tower did not show damage."

He added: "I think if Major Bache would notify the Lt. House Board to send a keeper here at once, he would learn a great deal more from seeing the apparatus put up than he will ever have a chance hereafter." [13]

One reason for the increased correspondence between Yorke and G. Castor Smith is that Hartman Bache had been seized by a serious malady (perhaps flu?) that confined him to bed, his aides standing outside his bedroom door relaying the contents of correspondence and straining to hear as he rasped out instructions. The exchanges include these tidbits: [14]

March 30. Bache directs Yorke (presumably once enroute back to Philadelphia) to stop at the Cape Canaveral lighthouse site, do a soil survey and pick up a Fresnel third-order lens stored there. [15]

March 30. Smith responds to the Board's request for a description of the tower. He replies that "it is proposed to paint the lantern [the top cylinder enclosing the lens] red on the outside, with the tower to be left the natural color of the bricks." He adds that "the keepers' dwelling is not of frame [as was originally intended], but is built of coquina rock and is one story and a half high, with a piazza all around. The outside walls are [unintelligible] from the piazza roof to the top, and the woodwork painted white." [16]

March 31. Yorke tells the bedridden Bache the tower now stands 78 feet, 6 inches. A derrick will now be erected to maneuver the heavy granite brackets in place. The keepers' dwelling will be ready to occupy on April 15. All the iron work and boxes of illuminating apparatus are being hauled on the scows from Indian River Inlet. The *Lenox* will soon head home with "a portion of the working party." After building the watchroom there will be about 9,000 bricks and 30 barrels of cement, "which will be ample for the oil house." [17]

April 1. Yorke reports to Smith in Philadelphia that the scows have delivered the illuminating apparatus and iron work. "Everything is marked so plainly that there can be no mistake," he says. "At present I cannot see anything to keep the party here after the 20th May, or at the very latest, the 1st June." [18]

April 7. G. Castor Smith forwards the letters from Yorke to the Light House Board. Among other things, the clerk of works wants to know "what arrangement will be made for taking care of the Lt. House buildings and public property at Jupiter Inlet Light station until a keeper can be placed in charge of it." Smith acknowledges the budget-conscious Board's instructions to "send the schooner *Lenox* home as soon as her services can be dispensed with"…and to "reduce the working party size as soon as the service will admit." If a keeper can't be found in time, the Board wants "one or two of the present employees left in charge of the property." [19]

April 10. Smith tells Yorke that the Superintendent of Lights at St. Augustine has been asked to nominate keeper candidates. Yorke is instructed to leave various tools – a wheelbarrow, shovel, spade, etc. – on hand for the new keeper. And: "You will paint the outside of the lantern, watchroom, gallery plates and railing and outside lantern base plates red, the inside of the lantern white." [20]

April 12. Smith informs the Board that he's received thirty copies of the "Notice to Mariners" that will be published in coastal newspapers. It describes the location and "signature" (flashing pattern) of the Jupiter Inlet Light and will be added to the handbooks of sea captains sailing in South Florida waters. In short, once a Notice to Mariners is published, it's too late for any changes or delays. [21]

The entire exchange of letters between Jupiter, Philadelphia and Washington has included several requests for added expenditures – ship repairs, provisions, another tender, etc. The cost of the Jupiter Inlet Lighthouse is now approaching $60,000, making it one of the government's most expensive navigational aids for its time.

This explains why, despite the project's rapid progress, the Board's engineering secretary is constantly asking when Bache and Yorke will finish the job and send the men home. Yet, the Board's preoccupation with economy does seem peevish at times. In one example, the Board's engineering secretary, William F. Smith, asks Hartman Bache to justify why he's ordered shingles for Jupiter at $33 per thousand when ordinary cedar shingles can be bought in the northeast for anywhere from $19 to $23. So Bache, who would in two years become chief of all Topographical Engineers, is reduced to writing a treatise explaining that the $33 shingles are 30 inches by 8 compared to 26 by 6 for the others. The new type not only cost less per square foot, but cedar shingles would risk blowing off a roof "in latitudes subject to northers" [and hurricanes]. [22]

But none of this fazes Yorke, who stays focused on his mission. In a letter to Bache dated April 22 he writes:

I have the honor to report the lantern in the Lighthouse, the iron stairway completed to within 4 steps of the watchman's floor, those last requiring some alterations on account of the character of the pedestal seat, but which does not interfere with the progress of the work.

The blacksmith will commence riveting the roof of the lantern tomorrow, and unless some unforeseen difficulty occurs, the lantern will be ready to receive the [Fresnel illuminating] *apparatus on the 1st of May. And on the 20th of May the lighthouse will be ready for inspection and the working party ready to come north.*

The foundation of the oil house is built, but further progress stopped for want of bricks. The Lenox has been at Indian River since the 14th [of April] *but strong southerly winds have retarded the scows. The bricklayers are employed stopping the holes in the cylinder* [that were] *made for scaffolding....*

I would respectfully inquire whether the [steam] *engine is included in the articles to be stored here. If required for further service in the 7th District, it can be used another season without any repairs.* 23

Yorke and crew did everything to meet their timetable. On April 30 he wrote that "the works are so nearly to a close that I will send half the working party home in the *Lenox*" with the rest to depart no later than May 20.

All the iron work connected with the new arrangement of the pedestal seat is in place. The rotary machine has been geared and works well. We are now glazing the [lantern?]. *It will require three days for the carpenter to line the floor and watchroom. After he has finished and the tower thoroughly cleansed, I will put up the lens and clockwork.* 24

On May 12, the Seventh District's G. Castor Smith wrote the Board that the *Lenox* had arrived in Philadelphia with nine workmen and "a large quantity of tools." After storing the tools at James Scrimshaw & Sails warehouse, the workmen will be paid off and discharged the next day and "the schooner *Lenox* dismantled at once."

The last task for Yorke and his remaining nine or ten men was to install the illuminating apparatus. On May 11 he wrote: "Cleaned the clockwork and put it up. Attached the weights – 1/3 off – and found it to run very regular."

On May 15, Yorke hit a snag. The apparatus revolved so that it flashed every thirty seconds. Zounds! The description Bache sent to the Board – and the "signature" the Board published in the "Notice to Mariners" – called for a flash every *sixty* seconds. This could confuse ship captains because Yorke knew that the signature of Carrysfort Reef light, off Key Largo, was also every thirty seconds. The best he could do was "attempt to force [the machinery] to revolve in four minutes" [which, he doesn't fully explain] would produce the once-a-minute flash.

Yorke speculated in his report that "there must be some mistake in the time of flashing," and indeed there probably was. Later, Bache's assistant, G. Castor Smith, reckoned that a mix-up may have occurred because the original Fresnel lens had been sent back to Philadelphia during the Seminole scare. Smith wondered if it hadn't been sent by William Raynolds to Montauk, New York, but Raynolds was somewhere on the Yellowstone River and couldn't shed light on the matter. So Jupiter will never know when its first lens was made or where it wound up. [25]

Nor will it know who its first lighthouse keeper was (or were), albeit temporary. The lighthouse supervisor in St. Augustine apparently hadn't been able to lure a career man to wild and lonely Jupiter. Yorke, instructed to leave two men behind should the official keeper not arrive, wrote Bache that the caretakers would be machinist Walter F. Woolfkill (or Wolfkiel) and a Charles Smith. However, it is curious to note that when the U.S. Census was taken in Brevard County on June 20, 1860, two brothers named Charles and William Patterson (ages 25 and 26), listed themselves as "Keepers of Light House." Under "Birthplace," both listed Scotland, which produced many lighthouse experts for nineteenth century America – perhaps even Yorke himself.

The last letter from Jupiter Inlet's "clerk of works" was dated May 22 from Cape Canaveral – mostly a list of expenses and accompanying equipment. On May 30 engineer G. Castor Smith notified the Light House Board of "the arrival of the lighthouse schooner *Delaware* this a.m. from Jupiter Inlet Light House." Added Smith: "She left Jupiter Inlet on the 19th and Cape Canaveral on the 22nd [to pick up the third-order lens] and arrived here at the wharf at 10 a.m. She brought the workmen except two who are left in charge of the property, the light keeper not having arrived." [26]

The crew would be discharged the next day. Except for a few names that surfaced in reports – Beard, Woolfkill, Smith, Myers, Owens, the Patterson brothers – none except Captain Edward A. Yorke would leave a trace of himself in the National Archives. Yet all must have been bound together by the satisfaction that they had, in just five months, hacked through tons of ice to disgorge their ship from winter's clutches, braved high seas to reach Florida, braced against gale winds so fierce they couldn't work, fended off malaria and transported expensive equipment many times down the tricky Indian River. And all without harming a man or losing a brick.

All this may even have been routine for Yorke. But he must have felt great pride and confidence that the tower he and his men built at Jupiter Inlet would light the way for the settlement of South Florida.

In July, Seventh District Inspector Pickering and a Fresnel lens specialist visited the two watchmen at their lonely tower. After a final tinkering, Jupiter Inlet Light was officially lit for seamen on July 10, 1860. On a clear night it would shine across the reefs, across the Gulf Stream, nearly twenty miles into the Bahamas Channel.

Perhaps the earliest photo of Jupiter Lighthouse extant, taken by assistant keeper Melville Spencer in the late 1870s. Originally the tower was left in natural brick. Only the lantern above was painted red. *(State of Florida Archives)*

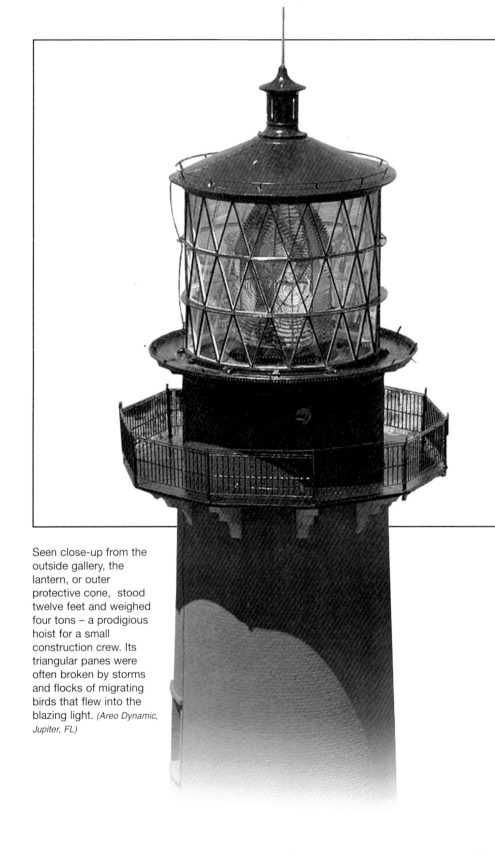

Seen close-up from the outside gallery, the lantern, or outer protective cone, stood twelve feet and weighed four tons – a prodigious hoist for a small construction crew. Its triangular panes were often broken by storms and flocks of migrating birds that flew into the blazing light. *(Areo Dynamic, Jupiter, FL)*

TOP: Early keepers carried fuel up 105 steps each night, with no handrails to steady them. *(Author photo)*

MIDDLE LEFT: Looking up at the wick (now a 1,000 watt bulb). As the apparatus and its lenses rotated, the wick remained stationary. *(Jim Johnston)*

MIDDLE RIGHT: In the watchroom at the top, the base of the illuminating apparatus turned on chariot wheels, caused by an attached cable and 300-pound weight. *(Jim Johnston)*

RIGHT: Double walls aided air circulation and allowed recesses for storing heavy butts (barrels) of lard, used for fuel. *(Jim Johnston)*

Timelines: 1716-1860

1716 – Boston Lighthouse illuminated – the first serving the continental U.S.

1789 – Congress creates a Lighthouse Establishment to build and maintain all beacons and buoys in U.S. waterways.

1819 – Spain cedes Florida to the U.S. for $5 million.

1820 – "Care and superintendence of the Lighthouse Establishment" assigned to the Fifth Auditor of the Treasury.

1822 – French physicist Augustin Fresnel begins work on a revolutionary lens.

1825 – Construction of Cape Florida Lighthouse on Key Biscayne.

1828 – U.S. District Court for Southern Florida established in Key West.

1836 – July 23. A band of Seminole Indians attacks and burns Cape Florida lighthouse.

1838 – Second Seminole Indian War. Battle of Loxahatchee River. Establishment of Fort Jupiter.

1841 – First French-made Fresnel lens installed in U.S. at Navesink Lighthouse, Atlantic Highlands, N.J.

1844 – Unsuccessful efforts to dig through the sandbar covering Jupiter Inlet.

1845 – Navy sends special commission to Europe to study ways to improve the U.S. lighthouse system. Its recommendations for reform go unheeded.

1847 – Construction of six lighthouses assigned to Army Corps of Topographical Engineers. George Meade begins work in Florida.

1850 – First screw-pile lighthouse built at Brandywine Shoal in Delaware River.

1852 – Amidst more reports of lax lighthouse administration, Congress creates a nine-member Light House Board empowered to create 12 lighthouse districts.

1852 – Carysfort Reef Lighthouse is first tall tower on the dangerous stretch of reefs between Cape Florida and Key West.

1853 – Congress appropriates $35,000 to build a lighthouse at Jupiter Inlet.

1855 – February. The army builds a new Fort Jupiter on Jones Creek.

1855 – December. Third Seminole Indian War breaks out.

1856 – April. George Meade transferred to Great Lakes lighthouse district. Replaced by William Raynolds.

1858 – May. Third Seminole War grinds down; chief Billy Bowlegs and followers agree to move to a western reservation.

1858 – September. Hartman Bache becomes chief engineer of Lighthouse District Seven and its Jupiter Inlet project.

1860 – November 7. Republican Abraham Lincoln elected president.

1860 – January 9. Tenders *Delaware* and *Lenox* arrive off Jupiter Inlet and lighthouse construction begins.

1860 – July 10. Jupiter Inlet Lighthouse illuminated for first time.

PART II
A WAR

JOHNSON'S

FLORIDA

PUBLISHED BY

A.J.JOHNSON, NEW YORK.

Scale of Miles

A map of southern Florida. Visible labels include:

Counties: CHUA, MARION, SUMTER, ORANGE, POLK, HILLSBOROUGH, BREVARD, MANATEE, MONROE, VOLUSIA, DADE

Ocean: ATLANTIC OCEAN

Towns and places: GAINESVILLE, PILATKA, Micanopy, Orange Sp., Palatka, Flemington, OCALA, Silver Sp., L. Butler, Volusia, Coxters Land., New Smyrna, Tsati, ENTERPRISE, Pineberg, Eustis, Melonville, Harney, SUMTERVILLE, L. Apopka, Spring Hill, L. Jesup, Jernigan, Christmas L., Mosquito Inlet Bar, Mosquito Inlet, False Cape, C. Canaveral, L. Poinsett, L. Winder, L. Washington, Cypress L., Kissimmee L., L. Gentry, Cypress Swamp, Sebastian, Malabar, Ft. Meade, Ft. Clinch, Ft. Arbuckle, Ft. Kissimmee, Indian River Inlet, Gabron, Ft. Pierce, BREVARD, L. Istokpoga, Ft. Crawford, Ft. Basschger, Ft. Lloyd, Taylors Battle, Ft. Van Swearingen, Ft. McRae, Ft. Jupiter, BIG PRAIRIE, Ft. Center, LAKE OKEECHOBEE, Punta Gorda, Caloosahatchee R., Ft. Adams, Ft. Hart, Ft. Thompson, Ft. Denaud, Ft. Myers, Ft. Dulaney, Ft. Simon, Lake Worth, Ft. Doane, Ft. Shackleford, Ft. Keas, Hillsboro Inlet, Ft. Lauderdale, New River In., MONROE, THE EVERGLADES, C. Rozano, Gullivan Bay, The Thousand Islands, BAHIA, CONTE or KEAS, Gards Pt., C. Florida, Soldier K., Elliots Key, Key Biscayne, White Bluff, Indian, Spider Pt., Carysfort Reef Lt. Ho., Palm Pt., Ft. Poinsett, Cape Sable, Key Largo

Latitude markings (right margin): 28, 26

5   3

Chapter 8

Separation

In its first years Jupiter Inlet Lighthouse weathered serious onslaughts, but not from the bad weather and bad engineering that had crippled other towers in Florida. The biggest danger to survival at Jupiter was isolation.

The isolation of Jupiter Light was stark even by a lighthouse keeper's standards. Albert Einstein once mused that the government ought to place young intellectuals as lighthouse keepers because the loneliness of the job was ideal for "people who wish to think out problems." In fact, lighthouses were mostly tended by older sailors or fishermen who had decided to "swallow the anchor" and continue their romance with the sea within the secure confines of a watchroom. Even then, the constant grind of the up-and-down trips to clean, polish and re-fuel the light took a hard toll — and for what? A head keeper drew about $600 a year and his assistants $300, or roughly what an average farmer might earn. Sometimes they had to pay rent on their quarters and at the end of it all there was no pension (which explains why wives often went on trudging up and down tower stairways after their husbands had given up the ghost).

The keeper in our mind's eye is the old bearded salt, pipe between clenched teeth, leaning into an icy nor'easter from his lonely perch on a rocky seacoast. Yet, if our self-reliant stereotype ran out of pipe tobacco, he could probably walk to a village store just a few miles down the road. At Jupiter Inlet there was nothing.

No, *worse* than nothing. During the Seminole wars, the area was at least dotted by military forts and intermittingly crisscrossed by a succession of surveyors, soldiers and mailmen. But by 1860 the forts were abandoned and the mail ships had no reason to put out a launch at Jupiter Inlet. Moreover, Congress had unwittingly retarded future settlement there in 1855 when it created a 9,077 acre military reservation stretching from old Fort Jupiter to the inlet and including the lighthouse property. It wouldn't be until 1884, long after the fort had been abandoned, that the government finally opened the reservation open for homestead claims.

Anyone standing on the lighthouse reservation could look to the west and know that there was total wilderness for 175 miles until Tampa Bay. To the south one would have to walk a hundred miles to reach a settlement called Miami, a grubby group of palmetto stores and shacks clustered around the decaying Fort Dallas.

Looking northward, one might at least hope for occasional contact with the few pioneers whose palmetto shacks dotted the Indian River. Jupiter was then in southern Brevard County, which extended down to Hillsboro Inlet. In June of 1860, as the last of Edward Yorke's workmen were polishing the Jupiter lens for its first lighting, U.S. census takers walked up and down Brevard's 90-mile length and counted a mere 269 souls.

Not only was our Jupiter lighthouse keeper less likely to find neighbors or stores to replace his staples, he was hard pressed to get them in the first place. Jupiter Inlet was the most difficult of all Florida stations to supply. Captains of tenders knew that to reach the lighthouse directly, they had to offload at Indian River Inlet and use one of Yorke's leftover brick-hauling barges to bring crates of fuel and foodstuffs 35 miles downriver. What captain wanted to risk riding his anchor like a bronco buster for several days while waiting for the barge to go down and back? The result was that tenders called sporadically at Jupiter Inlet and usually chose to leave crates of fuel and foodstuffs on the beach at the high tide mark and signal the keeper to jump in his skiff and retrieve them if he wanted to survive the next few months.

So it's no wonder that few would-be keepers answered the call or lasted very long. No one knows just when the Scottish Patterson brothers left. Lighthouse Service records show a Thomas Twiner as head keeper on June 12, 1860, along with an assistant named Peter Pomar. Both were listed as "removed" (dismissed) by January 21, 1861, when Joseph Papy took over. [1]

Was the personnel turnover due to politics, personalities or provisioning problems? The answers have gone up in smoke – literally. The Lighthouse Service letters of this era had been stored in the Commerce Department headquarters building in Washington when a fire broke out in 1920 and destroyed nearly all of them. However, it was standard operating procedure in the mid-1800s for an administrative aide to prepare a separate one or two sentence summary of every incoming letter so the boss could know whether to read or pass it on. Unexplainably, the summaries were stored elsewhere, and they give us a fleeting glimpse of a light station that didn't exactly function like clockwork in the summer and fall of 1860.

August 1. Reports arrival of light keepers. Inquires as to their compensation.

August 23. Keeper requests pay for additional services.

September 3. Hartman Bache receives letter reporting "working machinery out of order."

October 27. Bache (after an apparent investigation) reports "non-exhibition of light & deplorable state of affairs."

November 6. Inspector Pickering notes "light has been out owing to want of oil." (Subsequent reports cite "leaking oil casks.")

November 26. Another keeper and assistant are "nominated" (although records do not list anyone new assuming the positions in that period).

November 26. Supervision of Jupiter Light transferred from St. Augustine to Key West (probably because its tenders could call at Jupiter Inlet more often). [2]

By the fall of 1860, the political passions and egos that had been simmering for so many months would erupt into a reckless bravado. It seems that the farther from Washington, the epicenter of conflict, the more truculent one could afford to behave. And nowhere more so than in Florida, a southern backwater of 140,000 residents, just 15 years into statehood. The slaveholding, states-rights majority had already united behind the Democratic Party and its solidarity only grew as the "radical" and "fanatical" Republican Party began to emerge as a rival to reckon with. Floridians widely believed that abolitionist John Brown's raid on the Harper's Ferry arsenal in 1859 was secretly engineered by the Republicans, and already calls were coming to strengthen the state militia.

In April, a month before the Republicans would nominate a former Illinois legislator named Abraham Lincoln to head their election ticket, the more powerful Democrats met in Charleston and wound up ham-handedly cleaving themselves in two. Candidate Stephen Douglas maintained that each new U.S. territory should have the right to decide whether or not to sanction slavery. Southern Democrats saw slavery as part of the "property rights" expressly guaranteed by the Constitution. A majority of 17 states actually supported the South's position, but when the other 15-state bloc succeeded in getting its view published as a "minority platform," delegates from eight southern states walked out. Before long the "northern" Democratic Party had nominated Douglas and the "southern" Democrats had chosen John Breckinridge of Kentucky.

Suddenly, Lincoln, the "Black Republican," loomed as an ominous threat. As the alarmed *Florida Peninsular* editorialized on August 25,

Many persons are disposed to deride the assertion that the election of Lincoln…will be disunion and to assume that the threat coming from our fellow citizens of the Southern States is only intended to frighten the weak-nerved and weak minded voters of the North. We must say to all such that there is danger of disunion, in the event of his election, from the results that are sure to follow this event. As President of the United States, he will have a controlling influence over the affairs of every state…which power will have been conferred upon him wholly by the people of the Northern States. In his Cabinet there will not be one representative from the South, and in his Councils there cannot be introduced one measure which will confer upon the Southern States those benefits which they are entitled to as citizens of a common country and common destiny.

This dichotomy will extend even to the delivery of mail, said the *Peninsular.*

A man who accepts from him an appointment as postmaster will be required to deliver to all persons all papers and books which may be sent to his office for distribution. The Southern people will not do this, and cannot in consequence hold office under him. The Postmaster General will be compelled to appoint and send Northern men of his own party into the Southern States, and thus bring them into collision with the Southern people, who in their resentment of this gross outrage upon their rights, will be sure to order them to leave. If they do not leave, they will compel them, and thus come into collision with the general government and the army, who at the command of the President, will be compelled to spill the blood of American citizens. [3]

On November 7, 1860, Breckinridge and the Southern Democrats swept Florida with 8,543 votes. The Constitutional Unionists, a latecomer party formed by centrist politicians in hopes of avoiding secession, drew a surprising 5,437 votes. Stephen Douglas, the "northern" Democrat, got 367.

Abraham Lincoln won not one single vote in the whole state of Florida.

———————————————

But Florida, of course, was no mirror of the nation. In the months before

Lincoln took office, the South reacted as though a gauntlet had been thrown at its feet. "Secede!" urged the *St. Augustine Examiner* the next day. Echoed *The Florida Peninsular*:

> *Sovereigns of Florida! Will you submit to a Black Republican administration? Will you become pensioners of Black Republican bounty for the right to hold and protect your property? Will you sacrifice your HONOR and sell your birthright for a mess of postage? If yea, then you will receive the GRATITUDE of Abolitionism for your depravity and take your stand in the scale of respectability and intelligence. If nay, then you will have acted a noble part by taking a stand for liberty – by declaring the superiority of the white to the black race – by declaring that you will have no intercourse, as brethren, with those* [Unionists] *until they respect your sacred rights....*

As Governor Madison Starke Perry was notifying other southern governors that Florida would follow them into secession, only one voice of opposition could be heard in the state. Richard Keith Call, an ex-governor and defender of the Union, had tried his best to dissuade his fellow citizens in a published "Address to the People of Florida." Historian John E. Johns writes that on January 10, 1861, the day that Florida seceded from the United States, Call was walking the streets of Tallahassee when he was met by a group of celebrating secessionists.

"Well, Governor," they shouted, "we have done it!"

"And what have you done?" asked the old man, waving his walking cane over his head. "You have opened the gates of Hell, from which shall flow the curses of the damned to sink you to perdition!" 4

Let us take inventory of what awaited Florida.

During the 1850s the state had seen a steady influx of land-seeking farmers from the ring of southern states above it. Railroads, wagon trails and sawmills had been carved out of the northern tier and the number of cotton plantations increased rapidly. Despite the fact that Florida had only three towns with more than 2,000 population – Pensacola, Key West and St. Augustine – the value of real and personal property rose from $22.8 million in 1850 to $82.5 million a decade later.

Now witness what happened to the state in the first year or so after the War Between the States broke out.

Recruitment. When Florida issued its first call for volunteers in April 1861, enthusiastic young men elbowed one another to be first at the recruiter's table. Towns sponsored parades to cheer their heroes as they marched off in crisply pressed uniforms with shiny brass buttons. By the end of 1861 the call had reached 5,000 troops. The state legislature's $100,000 appropriation for arms, tents, clothing, etc., as already exhausted, mainly because nearly all such requisitions had to be bought at inflated prices in places like Charleston and New Orleans. Soon volunteers were asked to furnish their own uniforms and equipment, which inspired bake sales and lotteries by public-spirited local communities. But in time these efforts gave way to special taxes, which led to hostility when the state published lists of tax dodgers. Only the Ladies Aid societies soldiered onward, sewing socks and uniforms in hopes of making their young men presentable on the battlefield.

Weapons. The Ladies Aid, however, couldn't make guns. By the summer of 1861 Florida was able to send armed men to battle sites only by combining two companies into one while the others festered in training camps. Later that summer Governor Perry, staring at an order to send troops to Virginia, wrote the governor of North Carolina that unarmed recruits from Florida were about to march through that state. He hoped that locals would take pity on them and prevail on their governor to issue them weapons. But North Carolina had its own problems. When the still-unarmed troops reached Virginia, the Confederate Army refused to accept them.

Industry. Florida's most prevalent "industry" consisted of saw mills, mostly housed on private plantations. The only "manufacturing center" was Monticello, in the north center of the state, with a shoe factory, woolen mill and the Bailey Cotton Mill with its 65 employees and a value of $40,000. A couple of towns eastward was the Madison Shoe Factory, where 26 slaves turned out some 11,000 pairs of footwear a year.

That was about it for the state's "war machine."

Transportation. Principal towns were linked mostly by little more than cleared passages for horses and wagons. Only six railroads existed in 1860, with a combined 400 miles of track. The Florida Railroad, the state's largest, had 39 cars all told, including just 2 for passengers. By the end of 1861 it had lost its $160,000-a-year mail-carrying contract from the U.S. Post Office Department and was begging the state to take over ownership.

Taxation and revenue. Florida's counties were lazy, lax tax collectors and would only become worse. In late 1861 the newly-elected governor, John Milton, was excoriated for refusing to tell the General Assembly how much was in the state treasury. In a hastily-called secret meeting of "discreet men" among the legislators, he confided that the treasury had only $21,000 in cash and that troop payroll demands already exceeded it. The state budget, around $150,000 in 1860, would zoom to over $500,000 in succeeding war years. Fledgling Florida was soon issuing a series of increasingly dubious bonds that would tally nearly $700,000 by 1863 and $1.8 million by the war's end.

Banking and finance. In 1861 the aggregate paid-in capital of Florida's three state-chartered banks was $350,000. State and Confederate bonds were used increasingly as common currency. Because state bonds were backed by the ability to award land grants in lieu of cash, they quickly became worth more than those of the "parent" Confederate States of America (CSA). But because the "cheaper" Confederate money was now the official national tender, people in Florida would use it to pay their local taxes and bills, further depleting their treasury's "real" money. In "street" terms, calico, which usually cost 10 to 30 cents a yard when exchanged for Florida bonds, now sold for around $6 per yard in Confederate money. Rum, which cost around 20 cents a gallon "in specie" (Florida bonds), went for $60 a gallon in Confederate treasury notes.

Courts. Immediately all cases involving claims for debts were suspended until 1862. So were claims by citizens of the United States who didn't sign papers recognizing the Confederacy's independence. While this bought the CSA time to establish its own court system, it also brought day-to-day justice to a halt. The subsequent onrush of Union troops and disruptive raids by gunboats kept the whole system from ever achieving a respectable routine.

The collective impact of all the above was economic chaos. Every time the legislature tried to stick a finger in the dike by banning the hoarding of or speculation in various commodities, another gush of entrepreneurial ingenuity would spring from another crevice. For example, the 1861 legislature banned the export of beef, pork, corn, salt or "provisions of any kind" except for use by the state or Confederate forces. The maximum profit from any such sales was set at 33 percent under penalty of a $1,000 fine and a year in prison. All it did was drive up prices. If a seller was accustomed to clearing, say, $10 on a $20 sale, he simply charged $31 so that his usual profit would fall below the legal limit.

A microcosm of Florida's economic challenges and shortcomings can be seen in the production of salt. In peacetime, no one thought twice about getting enough sodium chloride. Almost every plantation produced its own. In low-lying pine forest or swamp lands one usually found brine by digging an eight-foot well and using a steam engine to pump the water into large iron kettles. It was then boiled off much like making cane sugar, the usual yield being one kettle of salt for eight of brine. In coastal Florida, however, the most common way to make salt was simply to go down and collect the brine that lapped up against thousands of miles of inlets and bays. During the summer months, when natural evaporation was at its highest, most plantations would bring a wagon train full of slaves and iron pots down to the shoreline and boil themselves enough salt to last the year.

But when war broke out, horses and wagons were in short supply. Already-rough roads were now dangerous. Cutters from Union gunboats might cruise up an estuary looking for saltworks to destroy. The combined effect was life-threatening. The 9 million residents of the 11 Confederate states each consumed a pound of salt a month, creating a combined need of 110 million pounds a year. But that was just the beginning. Salt was by far the most common way of preserving beef, mutton and pork (the Confederate Army ate its way through 500,000 hogs a year). North Carolina fishermen preserved millions of herring and shad in brine. Beef cattle needed salt in their rations and their hides later were preserved in salt while enroute to shoe and harness makers. The cavalry needed salt for its horses and even farmers used salt to kill weeds and enhance crop growth.

Salt was the essence of human life *and* commerce. "Make salt! Make salt!" editorialized the *Florida Sentinel* in Tallahassee. "Let all make salt who never made [it] before; those who have made [it] now only make more. Your bread [wheat] crop is now pretty sure of making. Your next care should be to save your bacon!" [5]

But as well-intentioned citizens and their wagon teams fanned out to the shoreline to do their patriotic duty, they consumed great amounts of animal fodder and forced up the price of hay, oats and corn. By the end of 1861 many farmers were using cash savings to buy feed from the few who had it.

Governor John Milton's worst fear was that a few entrepreneurial buccaneers would attempt to buy up vast tracts of estuarine coastline, then charge people cutthroat rates for using the lands to make salt. Although the records of land transactions don't show any such flurry of activity, the combination of high demand, difficult transport and fear of worsening shortages gradually drove up the price of salt from around $3 a bushel in 1861 to $20 by the time the war ended.

What made the governor even angrier was a sub-plot in the salt saga. Most salt workers had been excused from conscription in order to encourage production. But the salt ponds proved to be a refuge for all manner of louts and laggards who used salt as a way to dodge the recruiters. Worse, at payday a great many salt workers refused State of Florida notes, causing Governor Milton to rail against "these cowards who refuse their benefactor."

Of all the things the Union could do to harm far-away Florida, the most telling was Lincoln's decision to blockade populous southern ports soon after the firing on Fort Sumter in April 1861. It was part of a master strategy named "Anaconda," and the strangling snake imagery summed up how the North intended to win the war. Anaconda was a three-pronged plan to prevail with a minimum of bloodshed. From the west, the Confederacy would be sealed off at the Mississippi. From the North, a wall of troops would keep the South pinned well into its own territory. From the Southeast and all around the rim of the Gulf to Texas, navy gunboats would block all efforts of the Confederacy to trade its cotton and dwindling cash for supplies of any kind.

Lincoln wanted the South to wind down and wear out, not lose 258,000 men on the battlefield.

At first, Anaconda's ambitions were ahead of its abilities. In the early months of the war, sleek and swift Southern sloops created a wealth of sea lore that endures today as they brazenly outmaneuvered the large, lumbering Federal gunboats and made off to the Bahamas with cotton to trade for arms and provisions. Blockade running could also be as profitable as it was exciting. It was said that if a steamer could survive just two round-trips bringing war materials to Charleston and returning to Nassau with cotton, the Yankees could have her after that. A clear profit of $300,000 for a round-trip was common and one captain with 16 successful trips estimated his overall profits at 800 percent. [6]

In the usually torpid Bahamian capital, the impact of blockade running was, in the words of historian Thelma Peters, "the same as the prince's kiss had on Sleeping Beauty." Nassau, with about 11,000 mostly indolent, indifferent residents, became host to a reckless, wealthy and extravagant crowd that cut deals by day and frolicked by night. Their glittery hangout was the Royal Victoria Hotel, where the crowd of real-life Rhett Butlers, English ship captains, luscious ladies, newspaper correspondents, Confederate agents and high-stakes gamblers would give balls for returning ship crews and dote on their favorite captains. And no wonder. Bounties for a first class steamer that returned safely were typically a thousand English pounds for the captain, £500 for the chief engineer on down to £50 for ordinary seamen. [7]

All this was happening in the colony of a nation that was supposed to be neutral. First off, many Bahamians were descendants of the Loyalists who shoved off from American shores after the Revolutionary War. Secondly, most of Nassau's pre-war trade with the U.S. had been through southern ports. But mostly, the southerners were seen, not as rebel criminals, but brave and gallant underdogs. And what opportunities they brought for making money! Dashing English naval officers took leaves of absences so they could come to Nassau where the action was. And from all over the Bahamas, shirtless islanders scrambled aboard anything that floated to come to Nassau and work the docks, loading cargo and shoveling coal. At night, their singing and gambling on the docks was a rhythmic undercurrent as whites danced and dined at the Royal Victoria.

As Queen Victoria stoutly proclaimed England's neutrality in the far-off "American conflict," Nassau's wharves were stacked with bales of cotton. On a typical day *The Bahama Herald* counted 26 ships in Nassau harbor, including three warily received vessels from the United States. The northerners (and their spies) were free to watch waiting blockade runners taking on guns, ammunition, Confederate uniforms, salt, medicines and liquor. Some captains even bought and traded on their personal account items such as corsets, musical instruments and expensive furniture.

Nassau offered Confederate captains practical appeal as well. The sleek, shallow-draft blockade runners glided sleekly into shallow Nassau harbor, while the deeper-draft Federal warships did not. The two busiest Confederate destinations, Charleston and Wilmington, were a relatively convenient 600 or so miles away.

But the biggest attraction was *coal*. A typical steamer needed 170 tons for a round trip and Nassau was piled high with English bituminous and even anthracite from Pennsylvania. A captain's strategy called for using the cheaper, lower-grade bituminous to get across the ocean, then switching to the more efficient anthracite for a burst of speed around the blockade. [8]

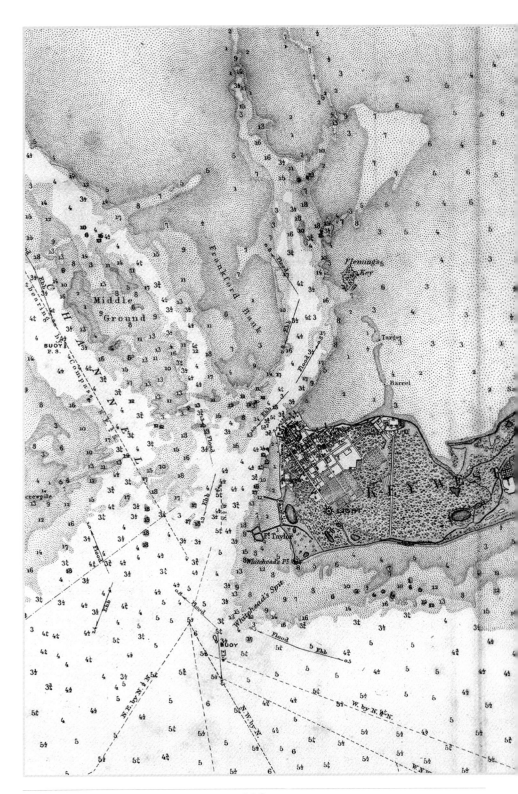

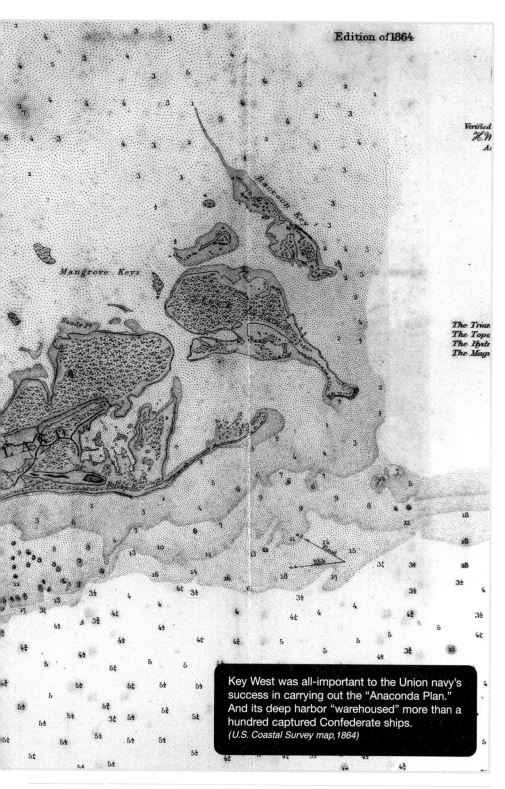

Edition of 1864

Verified
H. W
A

The Trian
The Topo
The Hydr
The Magn

Key West was all-important to the Union navy's success in carrying out the "Anaconda Plan." And its deep harbor "warehoused" more than a hundred captured Confederate ships.
(U.S. Coastal Survey map, 1864)

Chapter 9

Vigilantes

As the South Atlantic Blockading Squadron steadily added more ships and savvy, it was able to command the coast from Norfolk to Key West to Apalachicola. It forced Florida into a fateful decision only six months into the war.

Florida couldn't defend its coastline. None of it.

A prime example was Fort Clinch, near the railroad and steamship center of Fernandina, in the state's northeastern tip. It was considered the richest potential Union target in eastern Florida, but when Confederate Brigadier General John B. Grayson went there to size up its defenses in August 1861, he wrote his secretary of war a letter of despair.

The batteries are incorrectly put up and not finished. The enemy can land where they please. Guns and chassis are lying on the beach. There is not an officer to put up the guns or an officer to superintend their instruction when put up. [1]

Grayson begged for arms. Governor Milton complained that "Florida has never received a musket from the Confederate States." Milton wrote President Jefferson Davis, warning that "Florida citizens have almost despaired of protection from the Confederate Government [and] will lose confidence in it." [2]

But no aid came. Instead, more Florida men and resources were snatched away to help withstand the push of General Ulysses S. Grant into the rich farmlands of Tennessee and Mississippi. In fact, Secretary of War Judah P. Benjamin soon gave in to advisors who had been insisting that the whole of Florida and Texas be abandoned, leaving defenses only at New Orleans, Mobile and Pensacola Bay.

The only "strategy" left to Florida was to pull back from the coastline and hope the Union navy would find it logistically impossible to capture and hold anything in the interior. Indeed, farmers and businessmen had already begun relocating even before the state government made *retrenchment* official policy.

But what about lighthouses? They couldn't be moved like slaves and wagons. They might be used to spot blockaders at sea, but the Confederacy chose to see the other side of the coin. A Confederate Light House Board had been established in the spring of 1861 and one of its first orders was to begin extinguishing lights as coastal defenses collapsed. At Cape Hatteras, retreating troops hauled off the lens. At Bogue Banks Light, North Carolina, the local collector of customs, who doubled as superintendent of lights, spent $19 on blankets to wrap and store the lens in nearby Beaufort (Confederate defenders would later destroy the tower because it obstructed their cannon fire from adjacent Fort Macon). St. Augustine removed its Fresnel lens, and at Cape Canaveral, keeper Mills O. Burnham, after receiving an order from the Confederate secretary of the navy, packed his lenses in wooden crates and buried them in an orange grove on the Banana River. [3]

Jupiter Inlet was an oddity. The lighthouse there was too isolated for Confederates to seize or defend. Its head keeper, Joseph Papy, although professing solidarity with the southern cause, continued to shine Jupiter Light and draw his paycheck from the United States government via a supply tender from Key West.

Perhaps Papy's background will shine some light on his predicament. Born José Francisco Papy in 1823, "Joe" Papy was the grandson of immigrants from the Mediterranean isle of Minorca who came to Florida in 1765 to work in the ill-fated farming colony of Andrew Turnbull. Turnbull, a Scottish-born physician who married the daughter of a prominent Greek merchant, received a 100,000-acre grant near today's New Smyrna from King George III and decided that he wanted no slaves. Instead, he would bring politically disenfranchised peasants from Italy, Greece and Minorca to farm it for five years in exchange for pledges of their own land when it all panned out.

After a few years of back-breaking work and broken promises, the immigrants spread across the state in search of paying jobs. Two generations later, more American than Minorcan, Joe Papy lived in Key West with his American-born wife and three daughters. His big break came when in 1859, at age 36, he agreed to become keeper of the stark and lonely Sombrero Key Lighthouse. By January 1861 he had recently transferred to Sand Key Lighthouse at $550 a year when one can imagine the Seventh District's hard-pressed superintendent of lights coming to him with a proposition. Thomas Twiner, the keeper at Jupiter Inlet had just been dismissed (a letter explaining why went up in the 1920 fire, but a good guess is that Florida had just declared secession on January 10 and Twiner was ready to hand over the lighthouse to the rebels).

116

Would Papy take the job? Would a $50-per-year raise help his decision? The inspector might have added that if Papy could survive at Sombrero Key, a 153-foot metal tower standing in the open sea (north of today's Marathon), he might find terra firma at Jupiter Inlet a treat by comparison.

By then Papy had planted his roots in the Lighthouse Service and was comfortable in Union-run Key West. But once in Jupiter, where Yankees were as rare as Eskimos, it's easy to understand why he would at least pay lip service to the Confederacy. Especially when having to work side by side with the two strange ducks who came aboard as assistant keepers. One was Augustus Oswald Lang, a 30-year-old German immigrant – some say a former gardener to the King of Prussia – who had lived near Key West and served in a U.S. army company there. The other assistant was 32-year-old Francis A. Ivey, a veteran of the Third Seminole Indian War who seemed to create violence wherever he went. In a few years he would join the U.S. Cavalry where he would stab one of his fellow soldiers to death in a quarrel and murder another in an ambush. 4

What makes this mix of personnel so strange is that by August 1861, both assistants at Jupiter Lighthouse, both employed by the Union government, were ardent Confederates. It's futile to guess why because a century-and-a-half later all we have is a thick patina of legend and misinformation. All that's certain is that Lang and Ivey repeatedly demanded that their head keeper stop shining the beacon across the Inlet and into the Bahamas Channel. Joseph Papy insisted that he had a higher calling than a war – namely keeping ships of all nations safe at sea. Besides, he said, he had received no orders to do otherwise.

Augustus Lang finally walked off the job in frustration. He headed straight up the Indian River intent on contacting an outspoken local patriot. When he reached tiny St. Lucie Village about a mile south of the crumbling Fort Capron, Lang called at the home of James E. Paine, a salt maker, profitable canner of fresh oysters (and after the war, a local judge and postmaster). Paine, a loyal Southerner eager to help the cause, had recently joined up with Paul Arnau of St. Augustine, who seems to have been Confederate collector of customs there and perhaps the lighthouse superintendent as well. It was Arnau who, with a group of fellow patriots, had ordered the keeper at Cape Canaveral to pack up his lens and leave. Now Arnau was on a mission to extinguish the lights at Jupiter Inlet and Cape Florida.

With Lang and another man named John Whitton, Paine and Arnau soon headed downriver to Jupiter Inlet. The date was August 15, 1861. Tradition has the four vigilantes sneaking up the iron staircase at night and hauling off the startled Papy from his watchroom. But clattering one's way up a nearly vertical staircase to surprise an armed man who could fire down on the top of your head and/or slam a heavy trapdoor shut on your fingers isn't something Augustus Lang would have advised. Rather, Papy probably looked up from his painting or planting one afternoon in broad daylight and had ample time to ponder the approach of a small boat with the disgruntled Lang and three strangers.

After some stiff introductions, Papy asked by what authority they had come. As Paine would recall in a later letter to the Confederate secretary of the treasury, "I informed him that we came as citizens of the Confederate States to discharge a duty to our country, that he had refused to do, and that we would [certainly] meet with the approbation of our government." 5

Papy inventoried the pistols and ammunition belts on his callers' hips and knew he had no chance to resist. Assistant Francis Ivey also did so and quickly decided to join the conspirators. The head keeper was then invited to take his own small sloop, outfit it with a few provisions, and depart *post haste* in the direction of Key West. Before Papy's stern had crossed the inlet bar, some of the raiding party had mounted the 105 stairs and gone to work unscrewing parts of the Fresnel apparatus. "At Jupiter we destroyed no property whatever," Paine would write the governor of Florida.

The light being a revolving one and of very costly make, we took away only enough of the machinery to make it unserviceable. There is a quantity of property belonging to the light consisting of tools, machinery, paint, oil, etc. which we have secured under lock and key. 6

Later we will learn where the dismantled parts were stashed and how they were recovered. Meanwhile, the Confederate patriots, with their newest enlistee, turned their attentions to a much more difficult objective a hundred miles down the coast. The keepers at Cape Florida Light were known to be heavily armed, clearly pro-Union, and under orders to defend the tower with their lives. Moreover, the raiders were resolved to destroy the apparatus. As Paine reasoned, "the Light being within the immediate protection of Key West and almost indispensable at this time to the enemy's fleet, as well as knowing it to be useless for us to try and hold it, we determined to damage it so that it will be of no possible use to our enemies." 7

Pulling it off meant sailing their small skiff in the open ocean, beaching it north of Key Biscayne, and walking the last several miles to avoid detection. After six days with scant provisions, it was August 21 when the four crept along the pine and palmetto woods that surrounded the open lighthouse grounds.

The lighthouse "liberators" lacked enough ammunition to prevail in a shootout, so they decided on a ruse centered on Augustus Lang. He knew the keeper, Simeon Frow, and was aware that the tender from Key West was due to deliver supplies soon. The raiders remained concealed until midnight when they were sure both keepers were up in the tower. Then Lang emerged from the surrounding palm forest, shouting up to the tower that he had news from Key West. Both men gave a yelp of happy expectation as they recognized their friend's German accent and quickly scampered down to hear more.

"As soon as the door was opened, we secured them as prisoners," Paine reported. "The [raiding] party being small, and having only a small boat to return in, we concluded not to take them as prisoners." [8]

The keepers professed to be "strongly in favor of the South," noted Paine, but he would have none of it after the Papy episode. He "turned them away," and to make sure they had nothing to return to, "we brought away the Lamps and Burners, and broke the lens glass." [9]

For good measure, the raiders brought back to the darkened Jupiter Lighthouse "a sailboat, two muskets complete, two Colt revolvers, and three lamps and burners belonging to the Light." Augustus Lang was left in charge to guard everything at Jupiter Inlet while the other raiders returned to Paine's hometown of St. Lucie.

There they convened a meeting of local citizens at Paine's house to discuss the defense of the area against the growing menace of Federal gunboats. William B. Davis (who, oddly, would one day emerge as head keeper at Jupiter) was elected chairman and James A. Armour (who would succeed him) as secretary. The decision was to draft a letter to the governor requesting an artillery company to defend the Indian River Inlet, with James Paine to be made its captain. The group adjourned after passing a motion commending Paine, Lang, Ivey and Whitton "for their prompt action putting out the lights of Jupiter and Cape Florida." [10]

The request for a garrison seems to have been ignored. Still, Paine felt compelled to write outgoing Governor Perry explaining his recent heroics. "Our only desire," he added, "was to serve our Country, having performed a journey of about 140 miles, 90 of it on foot, being exposed to burning sun and drenching rains, and with a very scant allowance of food." [11]

Paine finally heard from Governor Perry in October. All confiscated material, he wrote the vigilante, "should be taken to St. Augustine and delivered to the officer in command of that post." But that didn't jell with the view of Paine's ally Paul Arnau, the former customs collector at St. Augustine. So on October 10 Paine wrote next to Christopher G. Memminger, the CSA treasury secretary. Paine said that because Arnau had opined that "any attempt to move the lens and machinery from Jupiter would result in material damage to them, I have thought it proper to submit the matter to you, as the proper officer, for your opinion and decision." [12]

There's no record of any reply from Memminger. Even more mysterious is the Jupiter lighthouse guardianship of Augustus Lang. Perhaps he expected the Confederacy to make him head keeper and furnish a regular paycheck. All that's known is that records show him going to Fernandina and enlisting in the Confederate Army as a private on January 27, 1862. He is then reported as having deserted on August 18, 1863. It may explain why Lang, a wanted man if he ventured anywhere near Confederate population centers, and equally sought by Union gunboat crews hovering about Jupiter Inlet, wound up spending the remainder of the war hiding out in the most isolated place he could think of.

Augustus Lang, at age 32, would become the first recorded white settler along pristine, 22-mile-long Lake Worth. There, on the east side of the lake near today's Bethesda-by-the-Sea Episcopal Church, he would build a palmetto shack and do what he liked most: cultivating exotic trees and plants that would one day provide sprouts for the first farmers in Palm Beach County.

Up in Washington, the news about the raid at Jupiter Inlet was not taken lightly. On August 28 Seventh District inspector Pickering notified the Light House Board that the Jupiter and Cape Florida lights were "extinguished by rebels." On September 9 Treasury Secretary Salmon Chase acknowledged receiving news of the "extinguishment of the lights at these points by a band of lawless persons…." On the same day he published a "Notice to Mariners" of the episode.

More importantly, the Navy decided that it was time to get serious about blockading the Indian River and Jupiter Inlet. [13]

ABOVE: The Cape Florida Lighthouse and keepers' quarters after George Meade oversaw restoration and extension of the tower in 1855. It was discontinued in 1878 and took on an eerie look as foliage grew up around it. *(State of Florida Archives)*

LEFT: Augustus Oswald Lang, gardener, Civil War lighthouse assistant, "kidnapper" of the light at Jupiter and the fugitive who became the first white settler along Lake Worth. *(Historical Society of Palm Beach County)*

Chapter 10

Gunboats

Key West was never a solid Yankee town, and if Southern sympathizers there had rallied to their cause immediately after secession, the Confederate Navy might have had a supply base that could have changed the course of the war. As early as November 1860, Captain Montgomery Meigs, another standout Topographical Engineer corpsman, was calling for reinforcements at Fort Taylor in Key West and Fort Jefferson in the Tortugas. The sizeable pro-South population of Key West was already talking secession, and unless fresh troops came immediately, Meigs warned, "a few ardent, desperate men" might take note of how thinly occupied the Federal forts were and try to "emulate the fame of Ethan Allen." [1]

By the time Florida seceded in January, Captain John M. Brannan, commander of the Key West Barracks, had already moved his men into Fort Taylor even though he still had no instructions to defend or hand it over. But soon the order came to defend at all costs and 66 soldiers arrived to reinforce Fort Jefferson. By February 6 Brannan wrote the War Department, "It is very doubtful now if any attempt will be made" on Fort Taylor. [2]

The Navy of the South Atlantic was now in position to become a major player in the Anaconda Plan.

Key West was responsible for feeding, arming and coaling the crews of the South Atlantic Naval Blockade. At its helm was Rear Admiral Theodorus Bailey. His instructions to the "officers commanding vessels of the Eastern Gulf Blockading Squadron" (including Jupiter Inlet), were:

1st. You will capture all vessels and cargoes owned by the rebels. Also, all merchant vessels, with their cargoes, under whatever flag they may be sailing, that have violated the blockade or attempted to violate it…however near or distant the vessel may be from such port or place. You will also capture all vessels employed in carrying contraband of war to the enemy.

2nd. To enable you to decide whether any vessel is liable to capture, you have the right to stop, visit and search her.

3rd. On boarding the vessel, the officer should, in a civil manner, demand of the captain the documents and papers belonging to the vessel or relating to the cargo for the purpose of examination and inspection.... [3]

The fine print in Bailey's order could have been written by Long John Silver himself. It gave the boarding party the right to inspect anything on ship and to bring both the guilty and suspicious back to Key West for adjudication. The reason even the suspicious weren't spared the tow ride to Key West was that if the court ordered a "prize ship" and its cargo auctioned off, the capturing captain and his crew were awarded a hefty share in the cash proceeds. With this one historical footnote we have the key to why recruiting men for the blockading squadron was a snap compared to the usual dragooning of foot soldiers. It also explains the super-charged excitement on both sides of the blockade: cats and mice alike stood to win bounties from the super-inflated value of the cargo, depending on who won the high-stakes sea chase.

Finally, the cash incentives also explain the relatively low number of all-out sea battles and loss of life in the South Atlantic. Sending all that expensive cargo down to Davy Jones was everyone's last choice. Besides, rescuing the shipwrecked and then having to feed them under the gentlemanly code of the sea expended energy and precious provisions.

Since blockaders reported their positions twice a month, we have an accurate picture of where and when they hung out. By early 1862 the East Gulf Blockading Squadron had built its fleet to about twenty gunboats and two tenders (not counting a half-dozen ships back in Key West for caulking and coaling). They covered an area from Cape Canaveral around to St. Marks on the Florida panhandle.

Because some ships had been hastily purchased and armed as war broke out, gunboats came in all shapes and sizes. Typical of a ship that was born to be a gunboat was the *U.S.S. Sagamore*. Built in Boston and launched in September 1861, the 691-ton *Sagamore* was a combination schooner-steamer, 158 feet long, 28 feet in the beam and with a 12-foot draft. It carried a crew of about 85 and 4 imposing cannons. Equally important, because the large displacement meant it couldn't enter all but a few of Florida's inlets, the *Sagamore* carried two thirty-foot cutters, held on hoists like lifeboats. It was the cutter crews who did most of the dangerous and dirty work of flushing out blockade runners and capturing their crews at gunpoint. [4]

At first the gunboats off Florida largely patrolled outside of inlets looking for trouble to come their way. But the more the state began to give up its pretense of a coastal defense, the bolder the gunboats became. The first organized raid on a coastal town came north of Tampa at Cedar Key in January 1862. Because the island town was the western terminus of the Florida Railroad, the blockader *Hatteras* dispatched a landing party, which destroyed the railroad wharf and depot along with seven freight cars. Also wrecked – all within an hour – were a telegraph office, a turpentine warehouse depot, seven sailboats and the already-abandoned Confederate fort. The *Hatteras'* commander crowed that "we were extremely successful with the expenditure of very little gunpowder and no one killed."

Twenty-three Confederate soldiers had been detailed to protect Cedar Key. When 14 of them tried to pole a makeshift raft into the mangroves, the water was too deep for their poles and they were soon overtaken by Union cutters. But they may have had the last laugh. When the captured rebels were ordered aboard the *Hatteras,* the ship's physician refused to take them as prisoners because some of the men had measles. The entire *Hatteras* crew had to be quarantined for a month. [5]

Florida's east coast got its first raid-in-force on March 22, 1862. Federal gunboats learned of a large arms shipment heading for Mosquito (now Ponce) Inlet. The Confederates had just evacuated St. Augustine, so the inlet leading to New Smyrna was their next best option. Someone tipped off the Confederates, who were spoiling for a fight anyway after giving up St. Augustine without a shot. When a Federal gunboat put 52 men ashore, they were quickly ambushed.

Only ten came back, and for that the Union navy took a fearsome revenge. On July 26 four gunboats entered the inlet at high tide and fired 500 shells into the little town of New Smyrna. Then a landing party went ashore and burned every house still standing as their helpless owners cowered behind trees in the underbrush. [6]

As gunboat crews became more acquainted with the lay of the land, they began sending cutters farther up shallow estuaries to scout for saltworks. During the first months of the war, those who boiled brine on inland shores had been largely ignored, but now the gunboat captains began to hear stories of prodigious production facilities. What the Federals found astounded them, as evidenced in the following example.

In the fall of 1862, the three-masted gunboat *Albatross* poked its prow just inside St. Andrews Bay (off Panama City) and anchored for the night. As dark came on its commander, John Hart, saw the sky lit up a bright orange over the bay's distant creeks and bayous. Beginning the next day, cutter crews from the *Albatross* followed the billows of smoke and wound up spending an entire week burning and whacking sledge hammers at salt pans, furnaces, pumps, tubs – even Lighthouse Service harbor buoys that had been cut in two to make brine boiling kettles. At the town of St. Andrew the men torched salt warehouses and wharves. Then they destroyed any animal or vehicle that looked capable of hauling bushels of salt. All this, Hart said, was "constantly watched" by a company of Confederate cavalrymen who "took good care to keep out of danger." [7]

Just ten days later the *Albatross* sent sixty marines up another arm of St. Andrews Bay. Fog hung over the bay in early morning, but soon, said Commander Hart, "we thought we heard voices on shore. As we came nearer we not only heard voices, but dogs barking and horses neighing."

Next the men could make out wagons lining the shore. Hart ordered a shell to be fired over the hubbub, "and in a minute there never was heard so much shouting and confusion." A few people tried to harness mules and wagons, but most ran off into the woods.

The marines waded through 200 yards of shallow water, posted guards around a perimeter behind the beach where they could see people watching from the woods. The rest of the day was spent using axes, sledge hammers and shovels "to render everything completely unfit for future use," said Hart. "We had to knock down all the brickwork, destroy the salt already made, knock in the heads and set fire to barrels, boxes and everything that would hold salt. We had to burn the sheds and houses in which it was stowed and burn the wagons we found loaded with it." Then they killed all the mules and cattle they could find.

After seven exhausting hours, they still weren't done. The marines "proceeded down the bay," destroying no less than 198 private establishments which lined each side of the bay for seven miles. Most averaged only two boilers and ten kettles each, but when Commander Hart sat down at the end of his very busy day, he reckoned that the destroyed distribution center had employed 2,500 men and that the whole operation around St. Andrews Bay was producing over 1,800 bushels of salt a day. At a conservative $10 per bushel (salt would hit $20 a year hence), it meant that the combined entrepreneurs were taking in $18,000 a day or $6.75 million a year. [8]

It also explains the other side of the equation. Saltmaking was as profitable then as producing cocaine is today. And so, month after month during the course of the war, gunboats would return and find the salt operations rebuilt and teeming with activity.

In far-away Washington, southeast Florida was on the fringe of The Big Picture except for the inconvenience Union ship captains encountered when navigating past darkened lighthouses. For example, on July 9, 1862, the Navy Department ordered one of the gunboats to investigate Indian River Inlet. Word was that rebels had built a road at the top of the river so that blockade runners could unload onto wagons headed for New Smyrna and points north. On July 26 the Department received a brief message that "reconnaissance finds no activity in the area."

Hindsight shows that the navy was missing the boat – lots of them. With Jacksonville and St. Augustine both blocked from the sea, inlets to the south had become a necessity, even when it meant hauling precious provisions from Jupiter Inlet up the Indian River. With the major Confederate saltworks under constant attack, blockade runners now carried salt from the Bahamas as commercial ships had before the war. But salt was like turpentine from Florida pines – something one added to a cargo of cotton. Cotton was the gold standard. It could be traded for anything and some of it returned to the Confederacy in the form of badly needed uniforms.

There is no doubt that "abandoned" Jupiter Lighthouse played a big role in the growing traffic up and down the Indian River. Rebels climbed the tower to search the sea for Federal ships before running a boat out of the inlet for a rendezvous with a Nassau-bound blockade runner. The oilhouse and tower base were convenient places for storing bales of cotton and other outbound goods. Finally, the men of this back-alley distribution network could use the empty keeper's quarters for shelter and its cistern for fresh water. It's also likely that Augustus Lang was there to supervise the grounds in the first months after he helped douse the light. And when he left to join the Confederate army, it would seem that James Paine looked in on the operation from time to time.

By fall 1862 the Union navy realized its mistake and tried to rectify it with a compromise. On one hand, the gunboat assigned to the job, the 691-ton *U.S.S. Sagamore*, was one of the largest and most powerful in the Blockading Squadron. On the other hand, the *Sagamore*, not the most nimble ship in the fleet, was ordered to patrol *both* Jupiter and Indian River inlets. The best it could do was float well out to sea and try to keep an eye out for what might be headed toward Nassau from either inlet. Occasionally it would put a cutter crew inside an inlet to see who or what might be hiding in the mangroves. When that happened, of course, it was open season at the other inlet.

―――――――――――――

The *Sagamore* served longer at Jupiter and Indian River inlets than any other Union gunboat, and fortunately, ship's logs in the National Archives tell where she was at any one time and what the weather was like. From the same archives are reports filed by Union captains describing the captures of blockade runners (often using dramatic license to underscore their claim to the prize money).

Finally, from the archives of Yale University Library come the daily journals of Walter K. Scofield, who served as assistant ship's surgeon. Scofield was a 23-year-old Yale Medical School student when he signed on to the navy in July 1861, intending to be a career navy physician. Letters to his parents in Stamford, Connecticut, date from his first assignment on a recruiting ship in Boston Harbor, where he undoubtedly probed and poked hundreds of raw recruits who had signed up for the chance to put Johnny Reb in his place.

The letters sparkle with the newness of a lad's first day at school. As Scofield explains a photograph he enclosed with the letter: "I purchased a sword for $20, a belt for $4, a tassel for $2.50 and a cap for $10." Anticipating a mother's concern about his quarters, he writes: "I ordered the other day 3 sheets, 3 pillow cases, 3 napkins and paid $2.46 therefore. They are of good material."

For Scofield, it would not be swords and swashbuckling, but years of combating malaria, measles and malnutrition with inadequate medicines. Why did an upper-middle-class Stamford youth sign his life away? His parents must have asked, because he answers the question head-on:

My salary is $1,050 per annum, or $2.8750 per day. If I should be sent on sea service, it would be $1,350.00 per annum. This is a desirable position and one much sought after, and happily outside the pale of political influence. It is not as fatiguing as a country practice of the same value would be, by any means. It also gives me the opportunity of becoming acquainted with the government officers, who are generally well educated and accomplished men. [9]

Thinking of Mother again…..

As for washing, there are plenty of women who are ready and willing to do all the washing they can get at 60 cents per dozen articles. I wear paper collars, so there is no need for washing them. Whenever we have washing to be done, we give it in charge of the corporal of Marines who sees to it and returns it in good order. [10]

From the stream-of-conscious jottings that Scofield made in his 4-by-6 inch pocket journal, one can follow him from his boarding the *Sagamore* at Key West in March 1862 to his last shipboard entry on March 14, 1864. Here are some snippets of life aboard a Union gunboat during the rainy, sticky, stormy Florida summer of 1862 as the *Sagamore* plied the state's waters from the Panhandle to Key West, then all the way around to Jupiter and the Indian River.

As July began, the *Sagamore's* crew already had a grueling, grinding eight months at sea. Confederate ambushers at St. Andrews in the Panhandle had peppered its cutters with bullets (wounding three crewmen) the previous spring. In June the gunboat had shelled Tampa in an unsuccessful bid to make the tiny town surrender. By July Yellow Fever was creeping into Key West and into some of the blockading fleet's supply ships. However, the *Sagamore's* crew seems to have suffered more from bug bites, spotty provisioning and acute bouts of homesickness. Colic and its "debilitation" would soon force its captain to the hospital in Key West and his mate, George A. Bigelow, would take charge.

We enter Dr. Scofield's world on Independence Day, 1862. The big gunboat lies at anchor with two others at Egmont Key, a makeshift navy re-supply "base" near Tampa that had become a magnet for escaped slaves and outcast Unionists hoping for handouts of food or a ride to Key West. It seems that Scofield's every spare moment is spent studying some aspect of medicine as he anticipates a navy-paid return to medical school after the war.

July 4. Sagamore *draped in flags with bunting and numbers. Washington's Farewell Address read by Mr. Huntington, also the ship's prayer. Mr. Bigelow unwell after last night's misuse of his stomach. Went on the* Ethan Allen [another gunboat] *at 1:30 p.m. Found dinner waiting. Great spread for the 4th unnecessary.* [Am reading] Gray's Anatomy, *Latin and Greek testament. Stormy afternoon.* [Received on board] N.Y. Herald *of June 15 and Savannah papers of June 5th.*

July 7. [Coal ship] Guard *alongside our ship all day. Dr. Gilbert* [the Guard's physician] *disappointed, leaving private practice in Central New York to go in the Navy for glory, and then being sent on a ship containing an old grocery and "coal yard." Mosquitoes very thick. Great pests. Must sleep in the daytime.*

July 11. Departure of Ethan Allen. *Three cheers by our men & theirs. Waited outside for a wind. Sailing in sailboat. About half the men off swimming near shore. Several officers, myself included. Fifty men at Tampa when we bombarded it* [a few days beforehand]. *Now there are 200. Writing letter, drawing.* [Seaman] *Badger a stout, strong man, yet very despondent. "The last work I shall ever do. Would give all I have to be home and die with wife and child beside me."*

July 16. Five gophers [tortoises] *brought on board by the Negroes* [escaped slaves living on shore] *for gopher soup and as gift to one or both supply steamers. Sent for by the Negroes* [in hopes the ships' doctors will] *go ashore and "see dem women – some o' dem sick." Cleaning sail boat on shore. Chase of sloop yesterday was unsuccessful. Went ashore at 4 p.m. to visit* [refugee] *patients. Want of camphor. View from top of lighthouse* [at Egmont Key] *extensive. Men on shore setting out green potato tops near lighthouse, expecting them to sprout and grow. Negro and white refugees dread attack by the rebels. Return of boat that started for Point Harrison saying that rebels were concealed & watching us on Mullet Key.*

July 28. Mosquitoes last night were excessively troublesome, obliging most of us to go without sleep during the night. Supposed to have been brought [on board] *by the bathers last evening. All three of the fishing smacks left early this morning. All hands turned out of bunks by mosquitoes & slept on deck. Captain Drake attack of colic. No appetite for weeks. Debilitated.*

August 13 [after a week in Key West]. *Arrived 12 miles off Lighthouse at St. Marks & anchored. Waited 2 hours but saw no* Young Rover [another gunboat assigned to the area]. *Pulled anchor at 10 a.m. and off for Apalachicola. Arrived at 5 p.m. Steamed in to pilot's cover. There we found the U.S. bark* Amanda *& the bark* Young Rover *with captains on board. Sent medicines to* [the Amanda's surgeon].

August 14. Officers of the two [other] *vessels on board the* Sagamore. *Gale blowing very hard. The* Amanda *got adrift and came down to us & was only stopped a few feet from crushing in our bow. Boat ashore this morning fishing. About four bushels* of shiners caught. Made way at 11 a.m. Captains, purser and master's mate went out over the bar with us. En route to New River Inlet. Ships J.L. Davis and Fort Henry arrived there at 2 p.m. Signaled for a boat. Captain McCauley of the Fort Henry and Assistant Surgeon Stevens, Purser Price of the J. L. Davis came out to us. Sent in the box of medicines to Dr. Jackson. Capt. McCauley an ardent admirer of photography. Kept up til midnight listening to the arguments between him and Captain Bigelow. "Now," [McCauley] said, "you are just commencing your life as a commander in the Navy. Put your right hand upon the Bible and your left hand stretched forward to do your duty. At 60 or 70 when you wind up on the retired list, you will feel great satisfaction, but you will return with no more idea of the true aim of life than you do of the coming events tomorrow."

August 16. Thurlow sick and groaning. When asked where the pain was, replied "I have no pain. I am starving to death. There is nothing fit to eat forward. The beans would knock a man down if they could hit him." 2nd cutter shore drawing seine. Few fish. Crabs abundant. Thunder and lightning and squalls most every afternoon. [Gunboats] Kingfisher and [Samuel] Rotan still here. Young alligator caught, irritating him.

August 20 [anchored off St. Andrews]. Leonidas Rhody gun shot wound. Piece of tompkin [gunshot] weighing a drachm or two & made of brass entered the arm severing an artery. Removed by forceps and hemorrhage restrained by coagulation. * * * Boat ashore fishing and crabbing. Mrs. King came on board after one of her slaves but did not get him. Professes to be [for the] Union now but threatened to boil Yankees in her salt kettle a few days ago.

September 9. Large shark caught with a hook. Cut into two and hung over the stern. The piece was seized by another large shark, which made many ineffectual attempts to devour the piece. It could not bite through the tough tail part of the shark, nor was it obliged to turn upon its back to bite. Fishing for snapper on Hurricane Island. Great success of Mr. Babson and Mr. Sidell.

September 11. Started at 7 a.m. for St. Andrews. Arrived at 9:30 a.m. Sent a flag of truce ashore to say that the authorities mean to destroy all your salt-works but will not enter your houses or molest any other property. Work of demolishing kettles commenced at 10 a.m. Launch with the howitzer, second cutter, first cutter and gig all shore. Rebounding of their sledge hammers in the attempts to destroy the kettles of cast *iron turned upside down. Rain and thundershower at 1 p.m. Nearly all the officers and half the men ashore. Salt nicely crystallized in cubical crystals. Destroyed 30 salt kettles during the day.*

September 12. Work of destroying wrought iron boilers continued. Much hard labor performed during the morning. Came off at 2 p.m. Many pans had been removed during the night. Spoils brought off [included] *hammers, axes, spades, old iron and young pig. Boatload of oysters from Catfish Point brought on board.*

Went ashore fishing at N. end of Hurricane Island. Eight large fish, 3 lbs. each, caught in five minutes before it began to thunder.

September 17. Went out to the Tahoma [a sister gunboat]. *Worked a long time in piloting her in. Mr. Fales could not find the harbor and got the steamer aground. Searched two hours for the channel without an outside buoy. Anchored inside at 5 p.m. Mr. Hurley, Acting Master* [of the Tahoma] *died on board a few minutes before we spoke* [signaled] *the steamer at 2 p.m. Buried at 6 p.m. Our officers requested on board in dress uniform and swords. Coffin put in Tahoma cutter and* [taken ashore] *where the Episcopal burial service was held. Boards driven into the sand as headmarks. Mr. Hurley was said to have died of Yellow Fever. Unnecessary exposure of our men on board the infected vessel.*

September 19. [The supply ship] Connecticut *steams by the* Sagamore *and* Fort Henry *but will not stop to offload provisions or receive letters. The "Conn." will not stop at Key West, where Yellow Fever prevails with much malignancy. Steamer* Fort Henry *in an un-seaworthy condition.* [Am reading] Fevers of the United States *and* The Book of Surgical Operations.

October 2. Boatload of 20 bushels of oysters. Men out oystering on St. Vincent's Island. Destroyed salt works yesterday. Obtained newspaper of Sept. 20 from Columbus, Georgia. Battle at Harpers Ferry. Whiskey served to launch and cutter's men.

October 16. Flag of truce from town [of Apalachicola]. *Want surgeons to dress stump of a man who had his arm blown off at Apalachicola. Drs. Stevens and Draper went up under flag of truce. Started at sundown for Key West* [after the steamer Somerset arrived with orders to report there].

On October 19, the *Sagamore* steamed into Key West harbor, mainly to take on its usual 94-ton capacity of coal. The next day Assistant Surgeon Scofield collected his back pay, sent $50 to his father in Stamford, and went about collecting a dozen letters from home and the most breathlessly current newspaper he would read during his entire tenure with the Blockading Squadron. It was the *New York Times* of October 13, hurtled down to Havana on a clipper ship and routed to Key West on the same day.

On October 22, 1862 the *Sagamore* and its 85-man crew were bound around the other side of Florida on a roving mission. Reports had reached the fleet admiral in Key West that as Union gunboats became better at sealing off busy shipping corridors like Charleston, Wilmington and Jacksonville, the more the blockade runners ventured southward toward sparsely-populated inlets. Word was that two growing favorites were Jupiter, with virtually no population to bother them, and Indian River, with a mere hundred or so souls eking out a living in the shadow of the abandoned Fort Capron.

The *Sagamore* was dispatched on a brief scouting trip. On October 25 the ship anchored off Jupiter Inlet because its 12-foot draft was 3 times more than the stubborn sandbar would tolerate. The next day, as sharks swirled all about the bobbing *Sagamore*, cutter number two was lowered, with instructions to go scouting up to Jupiter Narrows to see what might be lurking amidst its dense mangrove islands.

No vessels were found, but on the way back the cutter stopped at the supposedly abandoned Jupiter Lighthouse. The shuttered keeper's house had a lived-in look and a walk around the grounds produced 50 pumpkins, 1 live chicken, 4 bushels of salt, 2 muskets, 1 chair and 2 barrels of sperm oil – all taken aboard.

The *Sagamore* next steamed up to Indian River Inlet for a look-see and quickly nabbed a prize ship before it could even anchor. Boarded six miles outside the Inlet, the British schooner *Trier* produced 100 bags of salt, a case of dry goods, 2 boxes of candles, 4 boxes of tea and 4 boxes of soap. [11]

When a cutter crew was sent inside the inlet, they noted that inhabitants along the riverfront had hastily deserted their houses – hardly a sign of Union fealty or even neutrality. A hog and 2 chickens were spotted in one of the backyards and they were soon passengers on the cutter, along with 2 bushels of oranges. [12]

Clearly, rebel activity swirled at both ends of the Indian River. Back in Key West, Admiral Theodorus Bailey aimed to get to the bottom of it. But that would mean a sharp change of *persona* for his most available vessel. Although it was one of the fleet's biggest, best equipped gunboats, the *Sagamore* — meaning the whole package of captain, men, guns, etc. — had become known as a ship that followed orders reasonably enough, but no more. It had no élan, no fire for the chase, and not a whole lot of internal discipline. Orders would be followed as long as there was time for crabbing, fishing, hunting on shore and that the officers didn't search a sailor's gear too diligently for hidden stores of whiskey.

All that would change. On November 1, just as the ship returned to Key West, Admiral Bailey announced that a new captain would be in charge, someone who would aggressively pursue blockade runners and send a message that the partying in Nassau would soon be stopped. [13]

The new skipper was Earl English. Then 38, the Naval Academy graduate (specialty: gunnery) had served in campaigns off Mexico, Newfoundland, Ireland, India, China, and Japan. He was already a commander and seemed intent on using two sailors to demonstrate the fact. During its first week out of Key West, the *Sagamore's* log notes that "by orders of Captain English conferred double irons on William Carrls, mate, for disorderly conduct. Also, Leonard Sim, mate, is to be disrated and confined in double irons during night time and to do extra duty during the day until further orders." [14]

On Sunday, November 23 the *Sagamore* was back at Indian River Inlet. Despite heavy, rolling seas, the officers had managed to lead a worship service on deck when someone saw a sloop poke its bow out of the inlet. As soon as they saw a cutter being lowered, two men aboard the sailboat jumped off and swam to shore, leaving Captain English with his first prize ship, the sloop *Ellen*. The next day the captain sent the veteran acting master, Mr. Fales, and a cutter crew down Indian River and spent some anxious hours when it didn't return that night. But the next day at 9 a.m. Fales and crew rowed into view bringing a captured schooner, the *Agnes*, along with some "ammunition and trifles," as Scofield put it. Although neither sailboat contained a significant cargo, English thought they'd fetch a worthwhile sum in a Key West auction, so he ordered them towed. [15]

Towing was always tricky, and it would be especially so that day because the weather was changing abruptly from balmy to windy and cold. The captain decided to have each sailboat towed by a cutter down the inside passage to Jupiter Inlet. It meant calmer waters but an exhausting row for the ten men who manned each cutter.

The *Sagamore* steamed down to Jupiter Inlet to wait, and Captain English decided to spend some of the time exploring the lighthouse grounds for himself. His whaleboat returned with a large grindstone from the kitchen, having decided that he wasn't going to have it used to grind some blockade runner's flour or carted off to a rebel farmhouse. [16]

After two days at the oars, the cutter with the schooner *Agnes* arrived to meet the waiting *Sagamore* outside Jupiter Inlet. "Much hardship and difficulty," Scofield noted. The cutter crew "slept two nights in cabins of the [towed boat] filled with fleas." The men "have had colds [resembling] influenza. Sloop [*Ellen*] stuck on Couch's Bar but is now being towed down to the lighthouse." [17]

The *Ellen* and her cutter didn't appear until noon the next day. Wrote Scofield: "The whole party who went inland were very much fatigued." Meanwhile, the surgeon estimated that about half the men on the waiting *Sagamore* were affected by "severe headaches and distress generally" which he attributed to "the effect of the sudden change in the weather."

When the *Sagamore* and its two prizes reached Cape Florida, Captain English led a party ashore and returned with a half bushel of limes, the sailor's cure-all. Perhaps it was a gesture of atonement for underestimating the toil it took to row and tow a heavy sailboat for 35 miles. [18]

Cape Florida was used as an anchorage and mid-point depot just like Egmont Key on the west coast. Ships were towed there and left at anchor. Whenever convenient, transport steamers from Key West would come up and tow the captive ships through calm inner waters such as Biscayne Bay and Blackwater Sound.

Once having temporarily stowed its prizes at Cape Florida, the *Sagamore* was soon back patrolling between Jupiter and Indian River inlets — this time in sunny weather and calm seas. On December 1 a schooner was headed right for Indian River Inlet when its helmsman suddenly recognized the gunboat and took an abrupt tack. The chase began and finally required firing two shells over her bow before she dropped sail.

"Captain, identify yourself," a mate yelled out.

"*By George* of Nassau."

"Where bound?"

"Key West," came the nonchalant reply. But the captain's voice was all Bahama Conch, which made him a rebel trader. This time the boarding party found something worth claiming: 20 sacks of salt, 10 bags of coffee at 150 lbs. each, and 47 gross of matches — an all-too-typical trade package for a few bales of Confederate cotton.

With the very idea of towing enough to make most of the men cringe, Captain English decided to assign four men to sail the lightweight *By George* to Key West. But the winds were now calm and when the men tacked the schooner into the Gulf Stream, its three-knot current actually made them sail backwards. So out came the tow line again and off went the *Sagamore* to make a temporary deposit at Cape Florida. [19]

Cape Florida and the pretty grounds around the ruined lighthouse usually meant a pleasant day or so layover. This time it was bathing in the bay, catching kingfish, collecting coconuts and using ice and salt from one of the prize ships to preserve what was left of a cow that one of the cutter sailors had shot along the Indian River. Scofield even notes that it had belonged to "Mr. [William] Russell, the secesh [secessionist] judge." [20]

The next several days were again spent patrolling the Jupiter-to-Indian River Inlet beat and challenging passing ships to produce their papers. One excursion inside Indian River Inlet netted two small vessels, one of which was burned and the other sunk (the tow-by-row experience perhaps still too fresh in the men's minds). Amidst constant fishing for kingfish and bonita, the best "catch" of the entire expedition proved to be the schooner *Alita* with 13 bales of cotton (which if auctioned for $500 a bale, might fetch more than the ship itself). [21]

RIGHT: Sketch of the Union gunboat *Tahoma*, one of the South Atlantic Blocking Squadron based in Key West, and a frequent companion of the *Sagamore* on shore raids. *(State of Florida Archives)*

RIGHT: Walter K. Scofield, a young assistant navy surgeon, wrote his parents that "I purchased a sword for $20, a belt for $4, a tassel for $2.50 and a cap for $10" to have this photo taken. His diaries when aboard the gunboat Sagamore illuminate the days of the Union blockade off Jupiter and Indian River inlets. *(Yale University Library)*

BELOW: An anonymous soldier's sketch of the lighthouse at Egmont Key in 1862. It served Union ships as a mid-point base between Key West and the Florida Panhandle. *(State of Florida Archives)*

Chapter 11

Crane

On December 18, 1862, the *Sagamore* glided into Key West harbor for a welcome Christmas layover. To Scofield it meant picking up a dozen letters from home and catching up on current events with a cornucopia of old newspapers from many ships. For most of the *Sagamore* men the arrival coincided with a Christmas season "ball" aboard the *Magnolia*," which, says the prim and proper Scofield, "terminated in a disgraceful row."

Admiral Theodorus Bailey probably summed up the *Sagamore's* performance something like: "Not bad for a first effort, but not good enough to make a difference." One glaring problem was in having only one gunboat patrolling both Jupiter and Indian River inlets. It was obvious that rebels were using Jupiter Lighthouse as a lookout to see when the *Sagamore* was lurking about and to adjust their own shipping cycles to when it was forty miles north. Bailey couldn't spare a gunboat for each inlet, but he did tighten the noose a notch by deciding that two ships would cover *three* inlets — Jupiter, Indian River and Cape Canaveral.

Bailey's choice for the task was the *Gem of the Sea*, which steamed out to Jupiter Inlet the same day the *Sagamore* returned to Key West. Although smaller than its new partner and drawing 18 inches more water, the 116-foot *Gem* carried more than enough firepower to cow any blockade runner, which was built small and light enough to clear a Florida inlet's shallow bar. [1]

But the admiral still needed to address a second problem. Because nearly all of the men in the East Atlantic Blockading Squadron were northern-bred, every turn made by a cutter crew in a place like the Indian River was new territory, rife with dead-end rivulets, sudden shoals and uncharted places that could harbor an ambush. Moreover, people on shore could recognize the distinctive navy gray Union vessels so quickly that they could melt into the woods long before a boat reached shore.

Sometime before Christmas 1862, Bailey notified his captains that he wanted a list of especially "meritorious officers and men" recommended to him so as to make the blockade more effective and "cripple the rebels." [2]

The declaration almost seemed written specifically to accommodate a proposal that *Sagamore* captain Earl English had brought the admiral upon arriving in Key West. With him were seven tough, tight-lipped men in woodsman's garb who sauntered around town like a pack of wolves looking for a fight.

They were. On January 2, 1863, as the *Sagamore* steamed off toward Jupiter Inlet, Captain English carried the following orders from Admiral Bailey:

Sir: You will receive upon the Sagamore, *as supernumerary volunteers, for pay and rations, seven refugees* [Union sympathizers] *from Indian River. Proceed to the mouth of that river and allow them to leave you in the night in a boat, which they will take with them, on an enterprise proposed by them for the capture of a rebel streamer.*

Remain in the vicinity or at Jupiter Inlet sufficient time to satisfy you that they have succeeded or failed, say a week or ten days, and then return and report to me. Should the party not have returned before your leaving, you will give directions to the commander of the bark Gem of the Sea *to look out for them, and in case they return, to take them on board. Be vigilant in making captures of enemy's vessels and illegal traders breaking the blockade.* [3]

The next day Captain English gave an order to the "volunteer" group's leader, illuminating a few details:

You will proceed with the party under your command, capture and run the steamer down to the mouth of St. John's River, and then deliver her and report yourself and party to the officer commanding the blockade at that place.

Should you not find it practicable to run her down the river, you will burn her, bringing with you the valves and eccentric strap, and return to this place with your party, capturing any vessels you may see on your way down Indian River. [4]

The expedition leader was Henry Abijah Roberts Crane, and this would become just the first of several clandestine activities of a unit that could be described as a nineteenth-century amalgam of navy SEALs and army commandos.

What was this "steamer" that was so important to a rear admiral? Quite possibly it was no specific ship at all – just an official license to go hunting along the Indian River for bounty. Giving the admiral the benefit of the doubt, it was probably a large vessel that was hidden somewhere far upstream. Once several small boats had run over the Indian River Inlet bar and deposited their cargos in some hidden depot, the big supply ship would cruise downriver long enough to pick up the cargo and move it up to Titusville and/or New Smyrna. Finally, the cargo would be off-loaded and hauled overland by mule and ox cart to a wharf on the lower St. John's River – perhaps in Sanford (then called Mellonville). From there the trip to Jacksonville was safe and easy.

Who was Henry Crane? He was raised in New Jersey, went to Washington as a young man where he clerked in some unexciting office positions, then moved to Florida to enlist in the Second Seminole War. Crane settled in St. Augustine afterwards, married Sophia Allen and had six daughters and one son (who would split the family by enlisting in the Confederate army). The 1840s saw Crane in Mellonville (Sanford) where he farmed, ran a print shop and (probably because of his ability to print official documents) served as clerk of the Orange County Court. Four years later he was in Tampa as a full-time printer of the *Tampa Herald*. But when the Third Seminole Indian War broke out, he enlisted again, became a first lieutenant and gained local fame by making daring raids on Indian camps in marshy areas.

When the Civil War erupted, Crane was just past fifty and known everywhere as "Colonel" Crane. With Tampa tightly in the hands of the Confederacy, Crane and six fellow Seminole War veterans decided to venture across the state to see if they might have a hand in catching blockade runners for profit in the Indian River. Having lived in Sanford, then the southern terminus of St. John's River commerce, Crane probably knew a lot about how blockade runners made their runs to Jacksonville. But he sought help in the form of an old friend and Indian River resident named James Armour.

Most likely, the eight men simply walked out on the beach at Indian River Inlet in early December 1862 and signaled the *Sagamore* offshore they'd like to talk. What no doubt caught the captain's attention at once was their offer to use their own boats so as to escape detection in the Indian River. [5]

Crane was given the rank of master's mate on the *Sagamore* (although he was seldom on board). His fellow volunteer, James Thompson, was made fireman first-class. The rest enlisted as "landsmen."

Of the latter, James Armour is the only member whose name is known today, and it is high time he was properly introduced. Armour, who would in five years become the lighthouse keeper at Jupiter and the little town's father figure for over 42 years, was born in September 1825 in Amsterdam, New York.

For one who would loom so importantly to everyone who lived from Lake Worth to Titusville, little is known about him. That Armour was often described as soft-spoken and taciturn would seem to be borne out by the absence of any surviving letters or diaries. The best that can be offered up are a military payroll stub, some scraps of Lighthouse Service records and a 1910 newspaper obituary full of threadbare anecdotes. Maybe Armour wanted it that way, because his life story seems to be full of conflicting loyalties and financial gain derived from mysterious sources.

As the obituary tells it, Armour discovered early that he disliked city life.

Under a boyish impulse, he shipped on an American clipper ship, but tiring of the sea, he began a business career in New York. Again the wanderlust called him and he followed it inland and south. In the early 1850s he came to the Indian River and located at Sand Point, now Titusville. [6]

One genealogy shows him serving briefly as sheriff of sparsely-populated Brevard County. U. S. Army records show James Arango Armour collecting $50 a month from June to September 1858 as a navigation pilot. He probably had other paychecks as well because he was still employed at Fort Capron in July 1859. He had to have been hired in part because he could negotiate the tricky mangrove islands in the Jupiter Narrows. If so, he would have known all about the coming construction of Jupiter Lighthouse, the biggest event for miles around. And since the 1860 census lists James Arango Armour as a "carpenter," he must surely have stopped by the construction project and offered his services to Edward Yorke.

Continues the obit:

Pioneering on the Indian River…was not the life for a weakling, for beneath the veil of calm serenity that nature had spread over the section was a rugged existence in which only the fittest survived. Life during those years preceding the outbreak of the Civil War was strenuous, but the virgin, hospitable land, was, withal, filled with peace and plenty, and to his liking.

The War Between the States brought a change to the little group of pioneers on the Indian River, who held strong opinions and strove to express them vigorously. Believing in the Union stand, Captain Armour joined the Union naval forces as a volunteer coast pilot. [7]

Fine as far as it goes. The obituary helps in explaining the survival-of-the-fittest mentality that governed coastal pioneers, but then the fog rolls in. The 1910 newspaper eulogy seems to forget that in 1861, when James Paine and his neighbors formed a committee to petition the Confederacy for troops to garrison the Indian River, James Armour was its secretary.

Here's another military record. On June 12, 1862, James Arango Armour showed up at Camp Ward, Florida, to enlist in Company G, Eighth Florida Infantry Regiment of the Confederate States of America. Since Florida was desperate to meet its recruiting quotas at the time, it's possible that Armour walked into the post office one day looking for his mail when a couple of recruiters hauled him off to boot camp. In any case, the records show him deserting on July 25th, a mere six weeks later. [8]

Whatever the circumstances, deserting no doubt saved Armour from an early death. If one could name the Confederacy's ten most murderous battles, scholars would agree that the names of Manassas, Antietam, Fredericksburg, Chancellorsville, Gettysburg and Petersburg would be among them. The Eighth Infantry Regiment fought in all of them and the number of men in Armour's boot camp who survived all of those slaughters was next to nil.

But a burning question remains. In the small, close-knit, rabidly secessionist Indian River community centered around his home in Sand Point (Titusville), how could someone so imbedded in its infrastructure suddenly cast his lot with the gunboat marauders that had already enraged people by killing their cows and kidnapping their chickens?

Even though the absence of information must leave the question unanswered, there are only two motives to choose from. One is that northern-bred Armour, after months of discomfort in trying to blend in with the secessionists all around him, finally summoned his courage and declared for the side of righteousness. The second option is that life on the river was indeed "strenuous," as the obit says. Cash was scarce and the smell of it powerful enough as to overcome any loyalties and other sentiments that couldn't be taken to the bank.

Perhaps James Armour helped himself to a little of both.

As the *Sagamore* was winding down its Christmas layover and making ready to sail, the *Gem of the Sea* was already busy at Jupiter Inlet. As soon as the bark's first cutter came ashore at the lighthouse on the sunny, balmy morning, of December 30, 1862, it was obvious from the warm ashes in a campfire, from the trodden grass and newly-discarded tins of food that the rebels had probably bivouacked there from the instant the *Sagamore* had steamed off to Key West. One of the men climbed the tower stairs and, as if on cue, an old sloop appeared below, meandering northward on its way to Jupiter Narrows. In seconds the ten crewmen were in their cutter rowing to the coxswain's cadence. The sailboat had scant wind and its four-man crew could only watch as the hard-stroking cutter closed in on it.

The quarry was the *Ann*, a barely-seaworthy three-ton tub from Nassau, manned by an Englishman and three native Bahamians. Two cutter crews worked to anchor the *Ann* just inside Jupiter Inlet, then inventoried its cargo: 76 bags of Bahama salt, 3 bags of coffee, 4 gross of matches, a barrel of potatoes and assorted crew provisions.

The next morning the *Gem's* master, Lieutenant Irwin B. Baxter, did what would become standard procedure for captured vessels deemed too leaky, creaky or wormy to be worth towing to Key West. First, he ordered her decks stripped of all rigging, sails, anchors and tools. Then, after taking off the few armloads of food and sundries, his men used the captured matches to torch the entire ship and its cargo of salt. Salt they already had aplenty. [9]

———————————

On Sunday, January 4, as the sun rose out of the sea on a clear, crisp morning, the *Sagamore* glided towards the entrance to the Indian River and hailed the *Gem of the Sea*. The rendezvous had just two purposes. First, the two captains agreed that the *Sagamore* would bring the four crewmen of the burned *Ann* to Key West for safekeeping. Then Captain English told the younger Baxter about Henry Crane and his special mission. Early that evening a cutter would take the volunteers inside the inlet where an old cracker sloop was stashed among the mangroves. With provisions securely packed, they headed quietly upriver, the moon lighting their wake, until the men in the cutter could see them no more.

As the admiral's orders had stated, "wait seven or ten days" and see if anything happened. During the interim, the two gunships had their own agendas. The *Gem* would send a cutter down the river to Jupiter to see what was lurking along the inside passage. Along with the 10 rowers went 18 lbs. pork, 25 lbs. bread, 1.5 lbs. coffee and a large metal kettle.

The *Sagamore* would also head to Jupiter Inlet in hopes the *Gem's* cutter could capture enough nautical game to justify the long tow to Key West. But it didn't have to wait that long. No sooner had the gunboat arrived outside Jupiter Inlet when it found the mice at play again. Almost as quickly as the two cutters entered the inlet the next morning, they practically ran into the *Avenger* from Nassau, loaded with gin, salt, coffee and dry goods. [10]

This time the hunters tried setting a trap. The *Sagamore* would disappear out beyond the horizon, leaving the captured *Avenger* anchored just inside the inlet with an armed crew hidden aboard. Sure enough, two days later a small English sloop glided into the inlet and pulled alongside the *Avenger*, no doubt to exchange provisions and intelligence. The captain was roaring drunk, and after swaying back and forth on his deck and making sure that what was he was seeing was the barrels of ten rifles pointed at his heart, he bellowed out a string of epithets at the commanding officer. Then the bellow gave way to a whine. The bleary-eyed captive wailed that he was pressed into this line of work against his will. He had been a farmer in Jupiter and had his fields flooded out the previous summer. Then he calmed down and decided that a few months in the Key West stockade was a better idea than challenging ten guns.

The new prize was the *Julia*, with a cargo entirely of salt, and soon it was again next to the *Avenger*, this time at the end of twin tow lines to Cape Florida.

In pre-Coast Guard days, warships often performed rescue missions, as did the *Sagamore* on its way back to Key West. As it approached Carysfort Reef off Key Largo, the crew saw a merchant ship, *Lucinda* from New York, struggling in the reef's clutches. Since the ship wasn't beached ashore, Captain English ordered lines attached and began pouring on the coal to tug her out. "After several minutes steaming at full speed did she move," wrote Walter Scofield. "Her captain was very thankful and said he would report us in New York." [11]

Another effort was not so fortunate. As the *Sagamore* passed Carysfort, a crewman spotted a second ship inside the reef, wallowing on the beach, with wreckers already taking its tackle apart. The ship was the *Sparkling Sea*. It was carrying the men of the 25th New York Battery and they had been at sea since December 7. They had also begun the journey with 120 horses, and now there were only 80 alive. Captain English took all of the men aboard, save three men assigned to try keeping the panicked horses alive until a barge could be sent for them from Key West. [12]

On its return trip ten days later, the *Sagamore* passed what was left of the *Sparkling Sea,* "dismasted and with the seas breaking over her," as Scofield noted. Approaching Indian Key the gunboat itself became the latest ship to run aground in the heavy winter seas. In eight feet of water, the Sagamore "went on easy without feeling it," recorded Walter Scofield.

[We] *backed the engine for sometime without effect, got our kedge anchor and used foresail and mainsail and engine. But without moving her. Anchor that would hold the* Sagamore *in a gale of wind drawn home by the captain. Worked from 6 to 10 p.m. Left kedge and small boat, kedge to windward with taut cable until 1 a.m. when the tide will be at the full.*

The struggle continued all the next day. Finally, notes, Scofield: "Got steamer off the sticky, muddy bank at 11 p.m. Hilarious at our success." [13]

———————————

After days of rolling and heaving in seas so rough that they could not disembark at Jupiter, the *Sagamore* could only toss and turn, anchored in 25 fathoms off the inlet. At sundown a Union supply ship approached and briefly considered pulling alongside, but "excessive rolling in the trough of the sea prevented it," noted Scofield. The night wasn't all wasted, however. "Had hold of trolling line when an amberjack weighing 40 pounds was caught," noted the young medic. [14]

On January 21 the *Sagamore* appeared off Indian River Inlet. It had been over two weeks since Henry Crane and his men went upriver. Where were they? Commander English decided to find out. Lowering a cutter into the choppy sea was delicate enough, but riding the breakers into the inlet was worse. "Nearly swamped coming out in the breakers," noted Scofield, who seems to have been in the boat. "One more wave would have disposed of its contents to the sharks."

Yet, by January 25, without further explanation, "Col. Crane" and his men appear in the diary, pronouncing the singing at the Sunday shipboard service "good – better than the Methodist singing at Key West." He also refers to Crane's having brought a "Mrs. Hall and children down to the tent, or encampment on shore at the entrance of the inlet."

That a young medic wouldn't be privy to details of discussions between his elders, Crane and English, is understandable. We learn more from a letter Crane wrote to Captain English on February 7. The "encampment" by the inlet was a clue that the party didn't get as far as planned. The letter begins by apologizing for the "noncompliance with your instruction to me dated January 3, 1863." Crane then explains:

The evening we left your ship and got underway, Mr. Thompson, one of our party, was taken quite ill. We continued up the river, however, until Indian River Narrows, when, coming suddenly upon a boat and finding ourselves discovered, determined to capture her. She proved to contain the crew of the schooner Pride *from Nassau, after salt discharged by that vessel and near at hand. After destroying 47 sacks (188 bushels), we returned to the Inlet with the boat and prisoners and turned them over to Captain Baxter, commanding bark* Gem of the Sea. *The medical officer of that ship reported Mr. Thompson as seriously ill and unfit for duty, which determined me to report my command to Captain Baxter for service.* [15]

Crane's letter goes on to say how he and his men worked with the *Gem's* cutters while Thompson recuperated: capturing a boat with two "rebel spies" on January 7; taking the unmanned schooner *Flying Cloud* on January 9; destroying 45 sacks of salt near Couch's Bar, Jupiter, on the 16th and finding four bales of cotton on the 18th. The list goes on to February 3 when "I detached a party of five men in the morning to Jupiter Narrows, who succeeded in finding 4 bales of cotton and bringing with them two.

"Thus," he says, getting to just why he cited all his captures in painstaking detail, "it will be seen [that] we have not been very idle. * * * Mr. Thompson has returned to our party and we are now ready for our original destination." [16]

Clearly, Henry Crane hadn't gotten near the big ship he was supposedly sent to catch, and clearly he wanted another chance.

Curiously, Crane's litany of progress fails to mention what must have been a big feather in any Yankee cap. At a time when Scofield was writing that he feared landing ashore because "the whole of this part of Florida is held by rebels," lighthouse vigilante James Paine was seeing things quite differently. Somebody from a gunboat, doubtless Crane's men and *Sagamore* seamen, had raided his homestead in St. Lucie and left him devastated enough to write Thomas Martin, Chief of the Confederate Light House Board. A letter dated January 15 states:

I beg to inform you that since the 26th of Oct. last, the Yankees have had entire control of Indian River, from Jupiter Inlet to Banana River, some 50 miles north of the Indian River Bar. They have blockaded both entrances to the river with war vessels and operate on the river with launches and barges, destroying and stealing wherever they go.

They make such frequent visits to the Lighthouse that I therefore left the Light after removing the oil and placing it in the mangroves, where I think they will be unable to find it.

After leaving Jupiter I went to my place on the Indian River, but was driven from there by them. They stole and destroyed nearly everything belonging to me. I was then compelled to accept the hospitality of a neighbor for my wife and children, and even there they found me out, and made three attempts to capture me by coming to the house with an armed force of 30 or 40 men. They have stolen one of my boats along with the one belonging to the Light House and swear they intend to have me for robbing the Light House of the property. In consequence with their threats, I was compelled to build a camp in the woods, and have slept away from my family for about two months.

Under all circumstances, I thought it best to come to this place [presumably the clandestine camp] where I arrived on the 15th Ultimo and thought it fit to make known to you my situation. I shall go down to Jupiter as soon as I think it safe to do so, to look after [lighthouse] property there. The property I had with me at Indian River I have carefully stored away in a palmetto hut in the woods where I think it will be safe.

Trusting that what I have done may be approved by the Dept., I am [etc.].

While Crane and the cutters were away in the river, the *Sagamore* was anchored off Jupiter Inlet, intercepting sloops from Nassau (one captain, a Bahamian named Sweeting, admitting that this was his second capture), and broadening its menu fare with fishing and oystering excursions inside the inlet. At 4 p.m. on February 8, the gunboat was off in high, stormy seas again for Key West with two towed sloops, various prisoners, Crane's supernumeraries and the aforementioned Hall family of refugees (for whom the crew had collected a $50 donation). [17]

Henry Crane hadn't achieved his objective — a big prize steamship — but he and his volunteers had proven their courage and work ethic. And so, they got another chance from the admiral.

Off the *Sagamore* went again in mid-February. Approaching Jupiter Lighthouse as the gunboat rode the Gulf Stream on a cold, crystal clear night, Walter Scofield and a few sailors stood at the deck rails pointing westward and buzzing among themselves. Could it be that someone had re-lit the beacon? It seemed to be shining with a steady light almost like a huge sparkling gemstone. At last an old navigator pointed out that the planet Jupiter had arisen in a position just behind the eight-foot-tall lens. In a celestial tribute to Jean-Augustin Fresnel, the intricate assemblage of prisms had taken in the glow from a distant planet and projected it into the Bahamas Channel almost like a working navigational light.

An omen, perhaps? By February 19 the gunboat was again at Indian River Inlet and Crane's raiders were already returning from an expedition upriver. Noted Scofield: "Col. Crane and his party had found and destroyed 158 bags of salt and found four bags of cotton, a tierce [42 gallons] of sperm oil and the [Jupiter] lighthouse apparatus." [18]

That the "apparatus" was recovered along the Indian River and not Jupiter Inlet strongly indicates that Crane struck where James Paine had hidden it. And who would better know the lay of the land around Paine's homestead than his former neighbor, James Armour? Indeed, over the years, oral tradition has always credited Armour as the man who uncovered it.

That same night all three *Sagamore* cutters started to go after the cotton (worth about $500 a bale) but the surf was breaking too hard on the bar. The next day, as they brought off five 250-pound bales of high-quality Sea Island cotton, Scofield elaborated on what he had meant by lighthouse "apparatus." Along with the cotton, he wrote, came "the two lighthouse lamp jumps, four or five lamps with concentric tubes, two copper nails and one hundred gallons of sperm oil." [19]

No sooner had Crane and crew come back than they were off again upriver, moving at night to escape detection. By the morning of February 22 they had gone 15 or so miles upstream into the Indian River Narrows, just north of today's Vero Beach. On the river's eastern shore they discovered several "clearances" where bales of cotton were stacked. Soon they came upon what Crane called a "perfect ship yard, with a trail leading to the beach." At the end of it, he later told Captain English, "we had a full view of the blockading bark [*Gem of the Sea*] and your steamer. One could easily see boats [cutters] leaving either vessel."

By 2 p.m. the next day the raiders had pressed up the inland lagoon to a point five miles north of the Sebastian River. Suddenly a large schooner appeared, bearing hard and filled with men on deck "acting in a careless manner." Crane decided his crew of six were going to track down and attack the ship, but on their own terms. After melting into the mangroves as the schooner passed by, they slipped their whaler out of its hiding place and followed southward, keeping just out of sight. When the steamer reached the shallow Indian River Narrows, its crewmen began to lower sail and climb into the water to haul her over the oyster bars.

As Henry Crane related,

The moon was high and shone very clear. Keeping out of view as much as possible was important, as the darkness would favor our disparity of numbers. At or near midnight the masts of the schooner were visible, and [we] *could easily hear the crew hauling her over the oyster bars. At this juncture I placed a man in our stern, with instructions to push us for her with all his force. In a few minutes we came alongside, mounted her deck, and demanded a surrender, which was instantly complied with.* [20]

Crane counted twelve men on board the captive ship. His vigilantes quickly seized all the arms and whatever paperwork they could find. The ship was the *Charm* of Nassau, empty of cargo, but obviously on its way to pick up the bales of cotton from the makeshift wharves in the Narrows. In fact, no sooner had Crane's men boarded the *Charm* when they spotted another vessel in the distance. Figuring that it had probably had a load earmarked for the Nassau-bound *Charm*, Crane ordered the sails raised on his newly-captured ship and "determined to run her down at all hazards." When the Union raiders overtook the ship and boarded it, they found no one aboard — nothing but luscious bales of cotton from bow to stern.

The seven "supernumeraries" were already near exhaustion — they'd been up for two days without sleep — but now they decided to take both prizes 18 miles down to Indian River Inlet, all the while keeping their guns trained on their dozen captives. When patriotic fervor ran out, the prospect of auction money surely supplied the extra energy to go the last mile. At a time when the average clerk or farmer earned $300 to $400 a year, two ships worth perhaps $5,000 between them and several bales of cotton worth $500 each in a normal market amounted to a heap of prize money even when split with a large gunboat crew.

When Crane and party reached the inlet on the morning of February 27 they had been without sleep for 72 hours. They desperately needed help from the *Sagamore*, but it was nowhere in sight (it had gone off to Cape Canaveral). The only choice was for two men to walk several miles back up the beach until at long last they saw the *Gem of the Sea* rolling at anchor and waved a white shirt at it frantically. The seas were so violent that it wasn't until the morning of March 1 that the *Gem's* cutter could get into the inlet and bring back the prisoners. The best Crane and his totally-spent-but-happy volunteers could do was secure their prizes in the inlet, sprawl out on their decks and fall fast asleep. [21]

The booty represented by the two prizes must have been impressive because it was enough to embroil the *Sagamore's* Earl English and the *Gem's* Irwin Baxter in a tiff that only Admiral Bailey (and eventually the court) could settle. Baxter's hackles were raised at learning that English had written the admiral in Key West reporting that Crane's group had captured two boats and "delivered them over to the U.S. bark *Gem of the Sea* for safe keeping." The clear intent was to claim the bounty for the two prize ships for the *Sagamore's* crew.

Two days later a piqued Baxter wrote his own letter to the admiral. Sir, he said in essence, it was our ship who took off the prisoners and fed them for six days. We also gave Crane's party provisions and pulled their prize ships off the bar at the inlet when they drifted aground. We treated the Crane party as part of our crew, and the *Sagamore* never showed up until three days later. The *Sagamore's* claim is an insult to the officers and crew of our ship. [22]

More about the outcome of the dispute later. The whole episode quickly took a backseat to a new development that would require both gunboats to cooperate because their lives depended on it. The *Sagamore*, it turns out, hadn't been idling about. It had steamed to Mosquito Inlet and somehow learned of a large cotton carrier that had been supplying the mice from Nassau. The vessel was the 150-ton *Florence Nightingale*, the largest ship the *Sagamore* would encounter during the war, and quite possibly the prize Henry Crane initially had in mind capturing. Captain English had actually nosed into Mosquito Inlet far enough to actually "see the schooner inside" loading up at a wharf. English ordered a couple of shells lobbed in its direction, but with no effect. When he saw what looked like a canon positioned near the end of the inlet, he decided on another strategy. [23]

Back at Indian River Inlet on March 1, all agreed that the *Nightingale* was too large to be stormed by Crane and a crew that was still bone tired from its long struggle on the river. Besides, the *Sagamore* crew wanted in on the action.

The night of March 2, reports Walter Scofield, "thirty men volunteered and sent a petition to Captain English stating that 'we the undersigned respectfully request that we may be permitted to go and cut out the schooner in Mosquito Inlet.'"

The task was entrusted to a young, promising Master's Mate named Jeffrey A. Slamm. As dawn broke the next day, two cutters and a smaller launch manned by 39 men stole silently into Mosquito Inlet. As the sun began to penetrate the gray sky, Slamm could make out a large vessel of about 150 tons, laden with cotton "only waiting," he surmised, "for the [high] tide to cross the bar." A short distance away, he added, "there appeared to be a considerable amount of cotton in a warehouse." [24]

No one seemed to be aboard the *Nightingale*. But as the launches approached, suddenly a few men with torches came from nowhere and in seconds the ship was on fire. Slamm ordered his men to fire on the embankment by the wharf, mostly to cover his sailors as they boarded the schooner with orders to douse the fire and run it out the inlet. But the rifle cover had no effect. Some 25 or 30 men had been concealed in the bushes behind an embankment near the ship and they opened fire.

Wrote Slamm later: "Finding it impossible to extinguish the fire, the vessel hard and fast on the bottom, the tide still falling, and the object of the expedition being accomplished, I deemed it folly to expose my men any longer, so [I] ordered a return to the ship." [25]

But at a great cost. One sailor was shot to death, three were severely wounded and three others slightly so. Suddenly young Walter Scofield became the most important man on the *Sagamore* and his eye more discerning than Acting Master Slamm, as he lists his casualties in order of severity:

1. Hugh McGuire was killed instantly. He was climbing onto the schooner and was shot in the chest. He held on for a moment then fell backward into the water.

2. Roswell C. Lewis, gunshot wound. The ball entered the chest a little to the left of the heart between the 4th & 5th ribs, passed through the left lung and came out on the back just below the shoulder blade. Dangerous wound.

3. Neil McDonald, gunshot wound of hand. The ball entered the knuckle of the first finger, traversed the hand, breaking one bone and passed out at the wrist. Serious injury to hand.

And so forth. The next day the doctor reported: "Wounded men cheerful. Sent in a sick report with nine [names] on it, more than at any other time. Dr. Walton of the bark *Gem of the Sea* on board. Examined the wounded men. Two hands better than one." [26]

The *Nightingale* had gone down. Mission accomplished, but not to men who also dreamed of bounty. A 250-pound bale of cotton became a thousand pound bale when drenched in seawater. Impossible to bring up without a crane. And who had one except maybe in Charleston?

Turns out that the captured *Charm* and "sister" sloop proved to be better cotton producers. When all was loaded aboard the *Sagamore*, the total haul was 29 bales.

With wounded men aboard, there was pressure to speed on to Key West. But a brief stop at Jupiter Inlet netted a third sloop to be towed with four more bales of cotton. By March 10 the *Sagamore* was home again, ready for a new assignment.

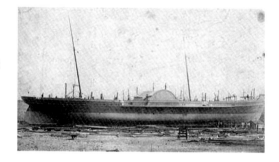

RIGHT: An unnamed Confederate steamer, probably about the same size as the large cotton transport that Henry Crane and men from the *Sagamore* burned to the waterline just inside Mosquito Inlet. *(State of Florida Archives)*

BELOW: Sketch of the newly-minted Union gunboat fleet as it sailed from Boston Harbor toward Key West in 1861. *(Harpers Weekly magazine archives)*

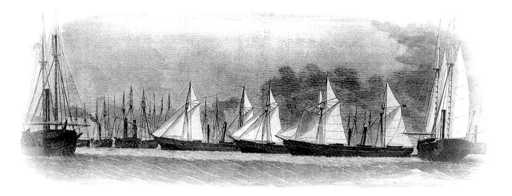

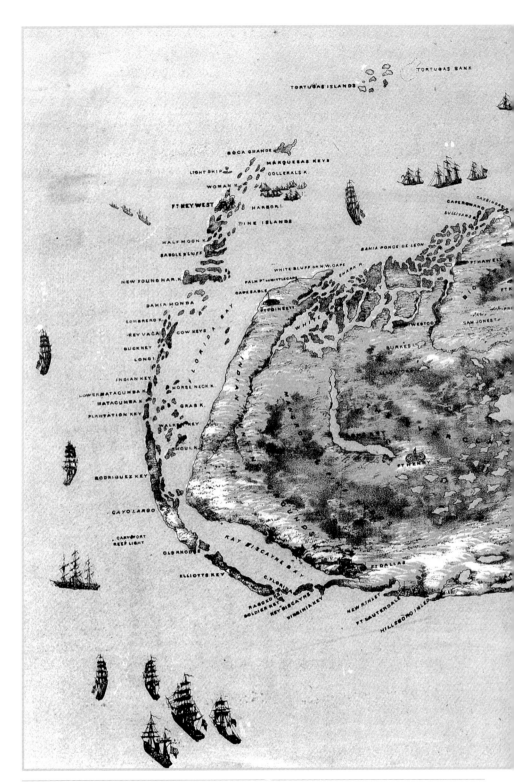

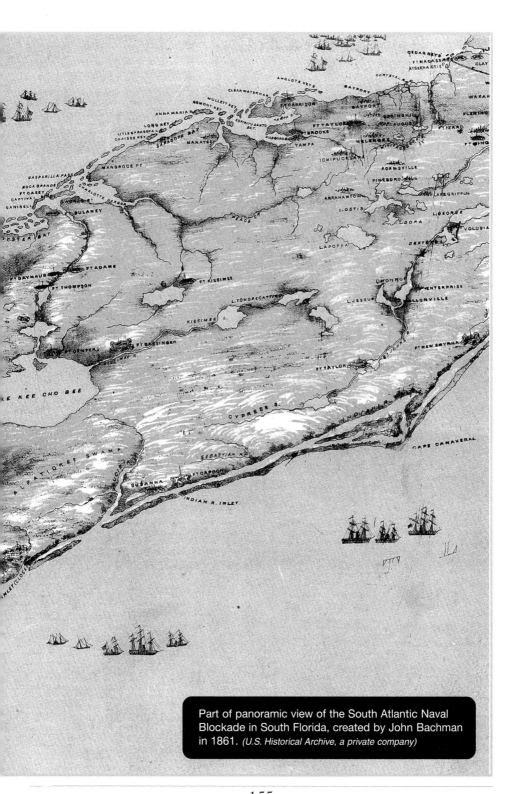

Part of panoramic view of the South Atlantic Naval Blockade in South Florida, created by John Bachman in 1861. *(U.S. Historical Archive, a private company)*

Chapter 12

Breakup

On April 9, 1863, Acting Captain Baxter of the *Gem of the Sea* observed to the admiral that "I am confident that no vessels have run in or out of either Jupiter or Indian River inlets since the 6th of March, as our boats are in the river whenever the bar will permit them to cross." He added that "the bar at Jupiter is nearly dry at low water."

Indeed, the *Sagamore* had already steamed off to Tampa Bay, making only an occasional stopover at Jupiter during the remainder of the war.

Volunteer Acting Master Henry Crane was off on another adventure as well. After the Mosquito Inlet campaign, *Sagamore* Commander English had sung the praises of Crane and his "supernumeraries" to Admiral Bailey, and the latter had extolled them to Navy Secretary Gideon Welles. After reporting an account of the *Florence Nightingale's* destruction, Bailey cited Crane, "whose history and services merit the attention of the Department."

Their...operations, in concert with the boats of the Sagamore *and* Gem of the Sea, *have been of efficient service in clearing out the rebels from Indian River and in breaking up their connection with the lawless traders of Nassau; and it is scarcely too much to say that without the local knowledge and personal acquaintance possessed by these men it would have been nearly impossible to effect this very desirable object. This last achievement of theirs, wholly unassisted as they were against nearly double their own numbers, and showing such determined bravery and endurance, is of a brilliancy to merit special recognition from the Government.*[1]

It did. Within a month, Henry Crane had been made a captain in the Union army and was back in his familiar territory around Tampa Bay. On its outskirts he would lead a commando-type raid to break up the cattle operations that had been sustaining the Confederate troops in Alabama and Mississippi with a staple of beef.

It's doubtful that James Armour went with him. Tradition along the Indian River has Armour being rewarded for his valorous role by being made "keeper of prize ships" in Key West. There's no record of it as yet, and it's unlikely that

Armour would have rated such a plum job as supervisor of all the hundred or so captured ships that were moored in Key West harbor at any one time. More plausible is that when Crane agreed to undertake his next daring mission for the Union, he prevailed on the admiral to make sure that one of his most trustworthy men stuck around Key West to make sure that captives like the *Charm*, left tethered to a buoy in the harbor, weren't ransacked or hijacked by vandals or — the more likely — their former owners. If so, Armour's unofficial job description might have read more like: "custodian in charge of making sure Crane & crew get their fair share of the auction money."

By summer, even James Paine had left the Indian River. On June 17 he wrote another letter to Thomas Martin, the Confederate lighthouse chief.

> *I have to report that the enemy has succeeded in getting possession of the oil and other property belonging to the Light House at Jupiter. I received the information from a captain of a blockade runner* [no doubt the Charm]*, who was taken off Indian River bar, and presume it can be relied on as true.*
>
> *He was captured by the Gun Boat* Sagamore*, and saw the lamps landed from her at Key West. He learned the purpose of searching them out, and had spent several days before they found them. I endeavored to place them beyond reach, and hoped that they were safe and regret that my efforts were not successful.*
>
> *The boxes containing the tools, wicks and cleaning material, concealed at Indian River, I hope are still safe. I should have gone down to look after them, but have had information that the river is still under Blockade, and no boat can pass up or down without great danger of being taken.* [2]

Owing "to the condition of things," said Paine, "I have concluded to go with my family to Charleston until the troubles are over." With him went "the clock belonging to Jupiter Light, as I have no safe place to leave it."

Finally, Paine asked to "retain the appointment of light keeper" (which he'd apparently been given) and directs the bankrupt Confederate treasury to send any "pay for past services" to his new address in Charleston.

While things were looking bleak for all of the vigilantes associated with the lighthouse raid in August 1861, the U. S. Lighthouse Service was already making plans to re-install the light at Jupiter. Its records show that on May 22, 1863, the inspector of the Third District in New York reported that the steamer

China from France had just docked at the Staten Island depot with "a new illuminating apparatus for Jupiter Inlet, Florida." [3]

By July 1863 the Jupiter-Indian River-Cape Canaveral patrol was being performed by the *Beauregard* and *Roebuck*. But at Mosquito Inlet, just north of that territory, the blockade had again become porous. The two gunboats needed help, and again the *Sagamore* steamed up from Key West. New Smyrna was hopping with smugglers yet again, and this time Admiral Bailey was determined to put on a show of force. Enough of this sneaking up in the night and capturing a cotton schooner. Enough of his men being fired on and killed. Three gunboats would steam as close as they could get to the inlet and open fire on the whole town of New Smyrna.

As the *Sagamore* anchored off Jupiter on its way to the rendezvous, Commander English did what he'd done just after taking command nine months before. He held a shipboard court martial – a sailor accused of stealing $18 – as if to serve notice that no break in discipline would be tolerated as his men entered a life-threatening conflict.

On July 24 two cutters snuck up the Indian River and captured a sloop with 11 barrels of turpentine (worth $1,760) "all ready for shipment."

So much for capturing prizes. The next day the *Oleander*, a 306-ton Union side-wheeler, hove into sight on its way south and agreed to take part in the assault. By nightfall the *Para*, a mortar schooner, had also come by and enlisted.

The next afternoon, which was also high tide, the five-ship fleet – the largest the terrified citizens of New Smyrna had ever beheld – boldly slipped over the bar at the inlet. The *Beauregard* immediately went aground, but the others kept steaming until they were directly opposite the town. The only eyewitness is surgeon Walter Scofield, with hardly a military man's perspective:

Steamer [he doesn't say which one] *went up 800 yards farther to the large white hotel house and began to shell rapidly. Soon after the boats pushed up the river according to Mr. Babson's orders from Captain English.* Oleander *shelling all day.*

Mosquitoes numerous and toward night became with the sand fleas exceedingly troublesome. Firing into the houses, woods, swamps and everywhere. Wasteful use of ammunition. Shells fired during the evening. Flash smoke and whirring noise & explosion. Pacing deck tormented by mosquitoes till 11:30 p.m. Handkerchief over face.

Ought to have a wire mask and leather gloves so as to leave no flesh exposed. Laid down in cabin by candle light and wrapped overcoat over head, but no go. Wrapped navy blanket around head but did not succeed in keeping off the pests. Went on deck and did not sleep in a chair or in any other way. 4

Scofield thought he was glad to see the break of day and "to be relieved of our torments." But they would be replaced by another type. Thirty or forty shots rattled into the ships from a "long house" on shore. The Union fleet unleashed a fusillade at it. "Expended 280 shells wastefully," the young medic wrote.

A party of twenty sailors went ashore, covered by intense fire. "Set fire to houses," Scofield wrote. The ships trained their guns on a group of rebels apparently trying to carry the contents of a household across a creek. "[Shot away] parts of the piano, chairs, mirrors, tables, hens, pigs, and papers," Scofield reported. But, miraculously, "no man injured or in need of a doctor," which was especially fortunate because Scofield was the only one on all five ships.

In another hour the gunboats had gotten out of the river and back over the shallow bar. As if to sum up all the ebb and flow of life on a gunboat, Scofield ended his New Smyrna notes with this:

No sleep and was very glad to get out of the wretched place. Felt refreshed to sniff the ocean air fresh and pure. No wonder that men have fevers in such a comfortless place as this. Enough to make anyone sick. Greatest punishment for a blockade runner is to… put him ashore in the state of Florida [with its] *swamps, mosquitoes and sand fleas!* 5

As the game of cat and mouse continued at the blockaded ports, the number of prize ship adjudications in Key West began to grow. So did the interest of any gunboat crew that happened to be in town for a break. Cases were scheduled to coincide with the arrival of the capturing ship so that its captain and officers could testify. At such times the crewmen would loiter about the low grey building that housed the U. S. Court for the Southern District of Florida with an ear cocked for the bang of the judge's gavel and a ruling that would put some more dollars into their pockets. Proceeds from auctions would be forwarded to a special U.S. Treasury account in Washington, then routed piecemeal to each of the sailors whose names and shares had been supplied by the captain. Although it might be months before they received their federal bank drafts, the judge's decision was enough to send the men whooping off to the saloons across the street to celebrate.

Of course, not all of the prize money went to officers and crews. "Administration" always took its cut first, as one of the smallest awards illustrates. On August 8, 1863, on its way back from a raid on New Smyrna, the *Sagamore* was already towing two prizes when it captured the small sloop *Ann* heading for Jupiter Inlet. Back in Key West, after the district attorney had scrubbed up the case and presented it for adjudication, the owner appeared to swear his loyalty to the Union and vow that he was simply blown off course on his way from Green Turtle Cay to Key West. But the judge chose to believe Captain English that the ship was captured in calm waters. He declared the *Ann* a prize ship and ordered the sloop and its contents to be auctioned off at the courthouse in November. A week later he certified that the sloop had fetched $240 and the meager cargo $82.61.

Instead of splitting an already-slim $322.61, the men of the *Sagamore* got just $175.40. Right off the top came the Key West establishment's cut:

Marshall's fees, including wharfage, storage, advertising, auctioneer's commission	$67.80
District attorney's fee........................….....	21.61
Prize commissioner's fees and expenses........	31.90
Clerk's fees......................................	25.90
Total	$147.20 [6]

The higher the stakes, the more time the case took and the greater the "establishment's" share. But the rewards for officers (and sometimes even crew) could be downright invigorating, as the case of the *Charm* illustrates.

Let's revisit the scene on the Indian River on February 23, 1863. It was only after an exhausting all-night row and tow back to the inlet that Henry Crane's seven volunteers found help from the *Gem of the Sea* and touched off the controversy as to whether the *Gem* or *Sagamore* was entitled to claim the schooner and its 29 bales of cotton.

All of the men aboard the *Charm* except for the captain had sworn they were merely trying to escape the Confederacy's new Conscript Act, which allowed recruiters to press into service any able-bodied man found to be living in the South. On May 8 the judge had ordered the schooner and its 29 bales of cotton sold at auction. At the same time, he agreed to hear separately a plea from one Henry J. Waltjen, who claimed ownership of four bales of cotton.

Waltjen testified that he was a citizen of Bremen, Germany, and had never been naturalized or sworn allegiance to the Confederate States of America. When the Conscript Act was passed he had purchased four bales of cotton, which he was to pick up on a dock at the mouth of the St. Lucie River. He was aboard the *Charm* and just about to load up his four bales (presumably to be converted to cash upon his arrival in Nassau) when the *Sagamore's* volunteers seized the schooner. [7]

The fact that it took nearly a year from Waltjen's capture to settle his appeal indicates that his case didn't fit the usual mold. After all, a citizen of non-combatant Germany, trying to escape a common enemy with his own private property had been seized at night, not by uniformed sailors in a navy vessel, but by a scruffy group of men using an unmarked civilian craft. This was nothing short of piracy!

It may be that the court delayed the trial so long while attempting to dig up enough on Henry Waltjen to brand him a repeated blockade violator. In any case, Admiral Bailey's edict trumped all arguments: no person or vessel of any kind was allowed to run the blockade. Waltjen lost his case.

On February 26, a year and two days after the *Charm's* capture at Indian River Inlet, Judge Homer G. Planta announced that a public auction had netted $673 for the vessel, $6,629.95 for 21 bales of cotton, $1,236 for 4 bales of Sea Island cotton and $1,216 for 4 bales stamped "S.L." (Waltjen's St. Lucie River cotton).

From the total of $9,756.25, "Administration" helped itself to $1,107.54. Then the judge settled the little dispute between the crews of the *Sagamore* and *Gem of the Sea*. Earl English, his crew, and Crane's volunteers divvied up $7,649.36. The *Gem* crew split $1,089.35. [8]

At a time when the dollar was worth about 50 times of its present value and when an ordinary seaman earned $300 a year, prize money could finance a serious binge or realize that dream of a cottage with the white picket fence, depending on the recipient's view of what's important in life. Since the *Sagamore* captured twenty vessels off Jupiter Inlet and Indian River alone (in addition to its prizes on the west coast), it's safe to say that Earl English easily doubled his navy pay in prize money.

By the winter of 1864 blockade runners still arrived in Nassau Harbor every day, but the cargoes were smaller, the ships grubbier and their captains grim and grimy. The dances still went on nightly at the Royal Victoria Hotel, but they had begun to take on the blue airs and black humor of a Last Tango. Lee had paid a dear price (the loss of Stonewall Jackson) in the bitter Battle of Chancellorsville. The tide had turned at Gettysburg. And as Grant now prepared to march 120,000 men against Lee's 62,000 at Richmond, everyone knew that Nassau would soon melt into the sweaty, sticky provincial place it had been before the prince had kissed Sleeping Beauty.

Florida knew it, too. Henry Crane's special forces had already seized 2,000 head of cattle that were being run north to feed Confederate armies in Mississippi, and now the closest rebs were getting to beef was gnawing on strips of leather for survival. In Tallahassee the *Florida Sentinel* suspended publication due to lack of paper. Governor John Milton, preparing to evacuate the city, received a telegram warning that a band of 100 Confederate deserters were bent on capturing and delivering him to a Union gunboat.

On the seas, 34 Union ships now made up the East Gulf Blockading Squadron compared to just 21 a year earlier. The *Sagamore* and *Gem of the Seas* were off to more challenging duties, chasing swift blockade runners from Cuba and conducting raids on the ever persistent saltmakers of St. Andrews Bay. Now policing the Jupiter and Indian River inlets (and sometimes Cape Canaveral) was the 455-ton, 138-foot *Roebuck*, with help from other ships that could be deployed on short notice.

The *Roebuck's* logs are a microcosm of what was unfolding around Florida's coastline. Whereas a captured blockade runner just a year before might be expected to be at least twenty tons and carry twenty bales of cotton, the quarry in 1864 became smaller, older and leakier with each succeeding week. A few snapshots:

January 8. John Sherrill, the *Roebuck's* acting master, is patrolling off Indian River Inlet when told that two boats from the Bahamas have run into Jupiter Inlet. He dispatches two cutter crews to head down the Indian River and intercept them. On January 12 they return towing the 8-ton *Maria Louise* of Green Turtle Cay and the 6-ton *Susan* of Nassau.

The *Maria Louise* carries 2 men, 3 passengers and 20 bales of cotton.

Making sure he shares in as much booty as possible, Sherrill frisks the passengers and makes sure the court knows he has confiscated $725 in gold and silver, 3 gold watches and $240 in Confederate notes. The *Susan* has slimmer pickings: 43 bags of salt, $265 in Confederate notes and some "sundry boxes." [9]

January 19. Sherrill reports the capture of the Nassau schooner *Eliza*, "one mile inside Jupiter Inlet." Just over 5 tons, the *Eliza* carries 14 bales of cotton. Not wishing to trust towing "such a frail craft at this inclement season," he promises to forward it to Key West "the first opportunity." [10]

February 27. Back at Indian River Inlet, Sherrill overtakes the schooner *Rebel* out of Nassau. Total haul: "salt, liquors, a box of sundries and one bale of cotton." Adds the captain: "The vessel, being in bad condition and leaky, will be destroyed [and] the cargo sent to Key West." [11]

June 30. *Roebuck* captures a tub fittingly named *Last Resort*. After taking aboard the crew of three and six bales of cotton, Sherrill declares the bark "unfit to send to Key West" and has it scuttled. [12]

July 11. *Roebuck's* cutters nab the *Terrapin* from Nassau inside Jupiter Inlet with 4 bales of cotton and 3 barrels of turpentine. Also aboard are 130 rounds of rifle cartridges. "Over one third were of caked powder and useless." [13]

But it wasn't all routine. Like its predecessors guarding Jupiter and Indian River inlets, the *Roebuck* sometimes had to "rescue" cargo that its quarry tried to dump overboard and contend with leaving captured crews ashore while it tended to other business at sea. And sometimes it had to deal with more than one captured crew at a time. Here is an example:

On January 14, 1864, the *Roebuck* reported that it had "chased the British ship *Young Racer*, caused her to be destroyed, and received on board 21 crew and passengers." They had to be left ashore because the *Roebuck* had other quarry to chase. A few days later the sloop *Mary* tried to hurdle the bar at Jupiter Inlet in a heavy surf and ran aground. As the *Roebuck* drew near, the *Mary's* desperate crew tried to lighten the sloop by pushing bales of cotton overboard. The result was a hectic scene with some of the *Roebuck* crew diving into the crashing surf to gaff the heavy wet cotton bales (their bounties always uppermost in mind) while others rounded up the crew — all as the captives from the *Young Rover* watched from shore.

Master Sherrill had clearly bitten off more than he could chew. By the unwritten mariner's code of honor, he could not let the captured crews starve on shore. Yet, sightings of still more sloops approaching Jupiter meant that he couldn't take his prisoners back to Key West just then. The *Roebuck's* log indicates just how much of a bite the captives' appetites took out of its precious stores:

January 24. "Sent 11 barrels bread to the refugees on shore."

January 26. "Sent on shore to refugees 1 barrel bread and 100 lbs rice."

[Undated] "Sent to the refugees as follows: 200 lbs. bread, 30 lbs. pork, 20 lbs. beef, 30 lbs. rice, 3 lbs. coffee, 2 gallons molasses. Caught 100 gallons rain water" [for refugees]. [14]

In hindsight, July 1864 marked the last month that Jupiter Inlet would be a factor in the War Between the States. From that point on there are no records of blockade runners captured at Jupiter Inlet, nor any gunboats stationed there. The *Roebuck* was occupied solely at Indian River Inlet.

Blockade Runners Captured from Jupiter Inlet to Indian River Inlet

1862

January 17. Tender *Union*, 24 miles N.W. of Jupiter Inlet light hales and boards Havana schooner *Emma*. Towed to Key West.

October 28. Gunboat *Sagamore* captures British schooner *Trier*, bound from Green Turtle Cay, Bahamas to Indian River Inlet with 100 bags of salt and several boxes of sundries.

December 2. *Sagamore* captures blockade-running English schooner *By George* off Indian River Inlet, along with cargo of coffee and sugar.

December 5. *Sagamore* captures and sinks two unidentified schooners off Jupiter Inlet.

December 10. *Sagamore*, now at Indian River Inlet, captures Nassau schooner *Alicia* with cargo of cotton.

December 12. Union bark *Gem of the Sea* captures and scuttles sloop *Ann* six miles inside Jupiter Inlet. Cargo netted: 76 bags of salt plus crew supplies.

1863

January 5. *Sagamore* sends armed crews up Indian River. The next day they capture English sloop *Avenger* from Nassau loaded with coffee, salt, gin and "baled goods."

January 7. *Sagamore* sends a cutter into Indian River, captures two men "believed to be Rebel spies."

January 8. *Sagamore* seizes British sloop *Julia,* carrying salt, ten miles north of Jupiter Inlet.

January 9. Henry Crane's crew from *Sagamore* captures and burns unmanned schooner, *Flying Cloud,* in St. Lucie River.

January 12. *Gem of the Sea* takes small, unidentified schooner in tow for Key West.

January 16. Volunteer Henry Crane and others from *Sagamore* destroy 45 sacks of salt at Couch's Bar near Jupiter Inlet.

January 25. *Sagamore* captures and destroys British blockade runner *East Yarmouth* off Jupiter Inlet.

January 28. *Sagamore* had just captured the schooner *Agnes* when sloop *Ellen* darts out of Jupiter Inlet. Sea chase ends with capture of cargo of cotton and turpentine.

January 28. Nassau sloop *Elizabeth* runs aground crossing Jupiter bar in full sight of *Sagamore.* Captain escapes. *Sagamore* orders the ship burned.

January 28. *Gem of the Sea* captures "small boat" of Jupiter Inlet.

February 3. Volunteer Crane sends five men up Jupiter Narrows. They confiscate several bales of cotton hidden along shore.

February 4. Cutters from *Sagamore* capture schooner *Pride* in Indian River Narrows. Crew taken prisoner, along with 188 bushels of salt.

February 5. Crane and cutter crew from *Sagamore* find 58 sacks of salt and several tools at Jupiter Inlet Lighthouse.

February 22. Cutters from *Sagamore* seize schooner *Charm,* 11 men and 29 bales of cotton in the Indian River.

February 24. *Gem of the Seas* captures sloop *Petee,* which was attempting to run a cargo of salt out of Indian River Inlet.

March 8. *Sagamore* captures sloop *Enterprise*.

April 8. *Gem of the Seas* captures 26-ton, British blockade runner *Maggie Fulton* off Indian River Inlet. Ship and cargo of salt and general merchandise towed to Key West.

April 18. *Sagamore* sinks British sloop *Elizabeth* off Jupiter Inlet.

April 18. *Gem of the Seas* sinks British schooner *Inez* and her cargo of salt off Indian River Inlet.

April 23. Navy bark *Tioga* seizes the sloop *Justina* in the Indian River with a cargo of salt.

April 26. *Sagamore* captures sloop *New York*.

June 23. Bark *Pursuit* captures sloop *Kate* at 12 miles north of Indian River Inlet.

August 8. *Sagamore* captures sloops *Clara Louisa, Southern Rights,* and *Shot* – all a few miles off Indian River Inlet. Later that day the *Sagamore* captures schooner *Ann* off Gilbert's Bar.

August 22. *U.S.S. Beauregard* boards schooner *Phoebe* off Jupiter Inlet, then allows it to anchor. When the suspect ship tries to send a crew ashore at night to unload suspect goods, the ship is captured and towed to Key West.

December 13. Bark *Roebuck* seizes unnamed schooner off Indian River Inlet.

December 17. *Roebuck* takes English schooner *Ringdove* bringing salt, coffer, tea and whiskey from Bahamas.

1864

January 8. The *Roebuck* sends two armed cutters inside Indian River Inlet with orders to rendezvous at Jupiter Inlet with any captured blockade runners. The cutters arrive on January 12 towing the *Maria Louise*, an 8-ton Savannah-registered sloop with 3,000 pounds of cotton. Also in tow: the 6-ton *Susan* of Nassau with 43 boxes of salt and several sundry boxes. *Roebuck* skipper Sherrill decides to equip the *Susan* with a howitzer and send it back into Jupiter Inlet as a river patrol boat.

January 11. The gunboat *Honeysuckle* captures English schooner *Fly* a mile off Jupiter Lighthouse after firing a shot across her bow.

January 14. Cutters from *Roebuck* chase British blockade runner *Young Racer* and force her aground north of Jupiter Inlet. Cargo of cotton destroyed by *Young Racer's* own crew.

January 14. British schooner *Minnie* tries unsuccessfully to outmaneuver patrol boat *Norfolk* at mouth of Mosquito Inlet. The *Minnie* makes a dash for Indian River Inlet, the *Beauregard* captures its cargo of salt, liquor and earthenware.

January 16. *Roebuck* captures Confederate sloop *Caroline*, carrying salt, gin, soda and dry goods, as it attempts to run into Jupiter Inlet.

January 19. *Roebuck* catches British schooner *Eliza* escaping Jupiter Inlet laden with 14 bales of cotton.

January 19. *Roebuck* heads to Indian River Inlet and captures British sloop *Mary* with 31 bales of cotton. The ship and crew are beached on Hutchinson Island until they can be towed to Key West.

February 4. *Beauregard* sends cutters into Jupiter Narrows to seize schooners *Lydia* and *Hope* with cargoes of cotton and turpentine.

February 26. *Roebuck* seizes British sloop *Two Brothers* carrying salt, liquor, coffee and cotton from Bahamas into Indian River Inlet.

February 27. *Roebuck* forces surrender of British schooner *Nina*, then on same day captures and burns Nassau schooner *Rebel*.

March 1. *Roebuck* seizes British schooner *Lauretta* and her cargo of salt at mouth of Indian River.

March 11. *Beauregard* and *U.S.S. Nantucket* intercept unidentified schooner hauling salt, liquor, coffee and dry goods into Indian River Inlet.

March 30. *Roebuck* longboat captures sloop *Last Resort*.

April 7. *Beauregard* captures sloop *Spunky* and cotton cargo at Indian River Inlet.

June 10. Union supply vessel *Union* fires two shots at Nassau sloop *Caroline* near Jupiter Inlet. *Caroline* comes alongside and is towed to Key West.

June 30. Cutters from *Roebuck* capture sloop *Last Resort* with six bales of cotton and two passengers at Jupiter Inlet.

July 10. *Roebuck* hauls beside and captures British schooner *Terrapin* at Jupiter Inlet as it tries to run blockade with cargo of cotton and turpentine.

December 4. Gunboat *Pursuit* captures cotton boat *Peep O'Day* in the Indian River.

1865

March 16. The British sloop *Mary*, already captured once, auctioned, and somehow back with her owner in Nassau, tries again to run Indian River Inlet and is captured by the *Pursuit*.

Chapter 13

Escape

On April 1, 1865, Florida Governor John Milton, named for his ancestor, the great English poet, shot himself to death at his home in Marianna. On April 9 Lee surrendered to Grant at Appomattox, Virginia. On April 14 Abraham Lincoln was murdered at Ford's Theater, and the voices of those who had urged compassion for the leaders of the defeated South were quickly drowned out by a blood-thirsty cry for revenge. On May 10 a dragnet of Federal patrols captured President Jefferson Davis in his wife's clothing as the last remnants of the fleeing Confederate cabinet scurried into the night from their makeshift camp in the woods outside Irwinville, Georgia. A few days later, indictments of treason were returned against most of Davis' cabinet and top generals.

Southeast Florida, hardly the center of the Civil War, happened to be the place that would best symbolize the last dying gasp of the Confederacy.

On June 1, 1865, six men pushed and pulled an old lifeboat the last few feet to Carlile's Landing, at the northern end of the Indian River. It had already been an exhausting clop by horseback from southern Georgia, always with flies to provide ear music and mosquitoes feasting on any uncovered skin. Most recently, having reached the southern tip of Lake George, the weary travelers had dug up and cleaned out the old lifeboat, stolen by locals from a Federal gunboat several months before and hidden in the sand. They rowed the old boat as far south as Lake Harney, whose headwaters (flowing south to north) presented a hundred possible dead-ends to the strangers. At that point they had hired a team of oxen, and with the men pushing the boat along and cursing the reluctant team, they managed to haul the boat over twelve miles of bumpy, sandy scrubland to the edge of the Indian River.

One of the men described the creaky craft at Carlile's Landing as "a small man-of-war's gig, only 17 feet in length, open, and with little freeboard." For power it offered four oars and a small mast which could accommodate a sail, provided that one of the men held the end of it in both hands. After some quick caulking and patching, the men began to load the only provisions they had acquired for a long journey: gunpowder, bacon, sweet potatoes, a twenty-gallon jug of water and some rum. Friends along the way had given them salt and cornmeal, but heavy rains had dissolved the salt and left the meal too mushy to take aboard. [1]

When all six crowded into the boat and shoved off, its gunwales nearly touched the water. And yet, the Indian River looked cheerfully inviting compared to the windless, blistering, buggy Florida interior they had just come through. The men could already see fish jumping all about and the cool breeze that wafted across the rippling waters lifted their hearts at the prospect that only a tolerable number of mosquitoes would join the trip. [2]

Who were these men? Sergeant Joseph J. O'Toole and Corporal Richard R. Russell were simply paroled Confederate soldiers who had agreed to hire out their services for the trip. The others were Colonel John Taylor Wood, General John Breckinridge, Colonel James Wilson (Breckenridge's top aide) and Tom Ferguson (the general's man-Friday and life-long slave).

Of these, Breckinridge and Wood ranked at the top of the Most Wanted list of Confederate fugitives. Washington had ordered the Eastern Gulf Blockading Squadron to hunt them down as zealously as pursuing a prize ship, and word spread that a gunboat had dropped off soldiers at Fort Pierce and the abandoned Jupiter Lighthouse to make sure they didn't escape down the Indian River.

Forty-five-year-old John Breckinridge probably had more to fear than any Confederate leader save Jefferson Davis. The Kentucky native had served as vice president under James Buchanan, had headed the Southern Democrat ticket in 1860 and had continued to serve in the U.S. Senate until well after the First Battle of Bull Run. After being at the epicenter of conflict on Capitol Hill for his ardent southern views, Breckinridge left town just one step short of arrest and became a general in the Confederate army. He would later become Davis' secretary of war.

The name John Taylor Wood meant as much to newspaper reporters as did that of Breckinridge. A nephew of Jefferson Davis, the handsome Wood traded his U. S. Naval Academy commission in 1861 for a Confederacy lieutenancy and quickly began a well-publicized career as a bold leader in naval gun battles and a blockade runner *par excellence*. It was Wood who was blazing away at the aft gun of the *Virginia* when it out-dueled the ironclad *Monitor* at the mouth of the James River. It was Wood who daringly led a series of raids against Federal gunboats, always keeping a whole fleet guessing as to where he might strike next. Finally, in August 1864, when the rest of the South had little else to cheer about, Wood steamed the *C.S.S. Tallahassee* out of Cape Fear near Wilmington and spent the next month capturing over 35 Union vessels. Since some of them were harmless fishing boats as far away as Maine, the name "John Taylor Wood" had an especially odious ring throughout the northeast.

With all his maritime experience (and creative ingenuity, as it would turn out), Wood was generally looked to as leader of the band of six as it headed down the Indian River. Still only 35, his dashing, good looks were now well hidden beneath a thick beard and layer of grime, sweat and mosquito welts. All of his personal baggage had long since been abandoned, leaving him with the tattered clothes on his back, a "hickory shirt" and one pair of extra socks.

For four days the group meandered down the Indian River in the torpid heat. As Wood recalled, the only signs of humanity were a few cabins, burned out by raids of gunboat cutters.

> *We passed a few cabins, around which we were able to obtain a few cocoanuts and watermelons, a most welcome addition to our slim commissariat. Unfortunately, oranges were not in season. Whenever the breeze left us, the heat was most suffocating; there was no escape from it. If we landed and sought any shade, the mosquitoes would drive us at once to the glare of the sun.*

> *When sleeping on shore, the best protection was to bury ourselves in the sand, with cap drawn down over the head (my buckskin gauntlets proved invaluable); if in the boat, to wrap the sail or tarpaulin around us. Besides this plague, sand flies, gnats, swamp flies, ants and other insects abounded. The little black ant is especially bold and warlike.* [3]

When the fugitives came to within ten miles of Indian River Inlet, they began to worry about the prospect of a military guard on duty there. Wood's answer was not to tarry and to trust what he'd learned from his many months of midnight runs around Federal blockade ships. That night everyone's apprehension rose as they glided down river. Sure enough, they soon saw the red glows of campfires on the western shore. But by staying in the middle and dipping their oars delicately, they slipped by without a sound and continued ten miles downstream. [4]

The next thirty or so miles found the saltwater lagoon broad and easy to run, but then it abruptly gave way to what Wood called the "Juniper Narrows." There, he wrote,

The channel is crooked, narrow, and often almost closed by the dense growth of mangroves, juniper, saw-grass, etc., making a jungle that only a water snake could penetrate. Several times we lost our reckoning and had to retreat and take a fresh start; an entire day was lost in these everglades, which extend across the entire peninsula. Finally, by good luck, we stumbled on a short "haul over" to the sea, and determined at once to take advantage of it, and to run our boat across and launch her in the Atlantic. [5]

Since Wood describes the haulover as "a short half-mile wide," it would be somewhere on Jupiter Island between two and three miles north of Jupiter Inlet. A half mile portage was nothing compared to the 28-mile haulover of the week before, and Wood triumphantly proclaimed that "at last we were clear of the swamps and marshes of Indian River and reveling in the Atlantic — free, at least for a time — from mosquitoes, which had punctured and bled us for the last three weeks."

On Sunday, June 4, the little lifeboat, straining in the open sea to stay far from any military unit that might be camping at the lighthouse, "passed Jupiter Inlet, with nothing in sight."

Their goal was to reach Green Turtle Cay, just eighty miles across the Bahamas Channel, but first all six agreed that they had to heed the rumble in their stomachs. The provisions had dwindled to two days' worth of sweet potatoes.

Down the coast they sailed in lazy summer waters, with still no sign of human activity. Near today's Palm Beach they went ashore to hunt for turtle eggs. Russell and O'Toole were veteran beachcomers, and they began walking the shore, methodically poking sharpened sticks into the sand as they went. Indians and black bears had already been digging before them, so it took a few hours to find a nest that hadn't been destroyed. When they finally did, "I do not think prospectors were ever more gladdened by the sight of 'the yellow' than we were at our find," wrote Wood.

The men spent two days resting on the beach and mixing turtle eggs ("the flavor is not unpleasant") with snails and shellfish. Suddenly a ship loomed into view heading south and quite near the beach to avoid the swift Gulf Stream current. Wood at once spotted it as a Union navy cruiser. Instantly the fugitives pulled their lifeboat "well up into the sands," pushed it over on its side and made for the palmetto brush. "To our great relief, the cruiser passed us," said Wood. When it had gone some two miles, the men ventured out to their overturned lifeboat. "Just then the sharp lookout saw us," recalled Wood, "and to our astonishment, the steamer came swinging about." [6]

Here is where John Taylor Wood allowed himself to be ruled by the survival instincts he had honed in running blockades and boarding enemy ships. Breckinridge and the others had begun to run for the bush, hoping a shore party would leave their boat alone. But in an instant Wood realized that the sailors would be sure to destroy the boat, dashing its crew's hopes of escaping a treason trial. "Besides, the mosquitoes would suck us dry as mummies," he thought.

Wood quickly scooped up two buckets of turtle eggs, ordered Russell and O'Toole to push the lifeboat into the sea, and climbed aboard. The two ex-soldiers were the only ones in the party with parole papers that guaranteed safe passage. As they rowed out, the steamer put out a launch and met them halfway. As Wood tells it:

I had one oar and O'Toole the other. To the usual hail I paid no attention except to stop rowing. A ten-oared cutter with a smart looking crew dashed alongside. The sheen was not quite off the lace and buttons of the youngster in charge. With revolver in hand he asked us who we were and where we were going.

"Cap'n," said I, "please put away that-ar pistol. I don't like the looks of it, and I'll tell you all about us. We've been Rebs, and there ain't no use sayin' we weren't. But it's all up now, and we got home too late to put in a crop, so we just made up our minds to come down shore and see if we couldn't find something. It's all right, Cap'n. We got our papers. Want to see 'em? Got 'em fixed up at Jacksonville."

O'Toole and Russell handed him their paroles, which he said were all right. He asked for mine. I turned my pockets out, looked in my hat, and said, "I muster dropped mine in camp, but 'tis just the same as theirn."

He asked who was ashore. I told him: "There's more of we'uns b'iling some turtle eggs for dinner. Cap'n, I'd like to swap you some turtle eggs for tobacco or bread." His crew soon produced from the slack of their frocks pieces of plug, which they passed on board in exchange for our eggs. I told the youngster if he'd come to camp we'd give him as many as he could eat.

Our hospitality was declined. Among other questions, he asked if there were any batteries on shore — a battery on a beach where there was not a white man within a hundred miles! [7]

The sweetest sound the six fugitives ever heard were the "youngster's" orders to his men: "Up oars. Let go forward. Let fall. Give Way." As they shoved off, the grizzled coxswain said to the young officer, "that looks like a man-of-war's gig, sir." But he was paid no heed.

———————————————

Green Turtle Cay was still the objective, but the required four or five days' supply of food and water was still beyond their reach. And even with proper provisions, any waves over two feet would wash over the gunwales and threaten to swamp the little boat.

Down the coast they sailed. Somewhere off today's Boynton Beach they saw a party of Seminoles poking in the sand for turtle eggs. "They received us kindly and we were very anxious to obtain some provisions from them," said Wood, but all they could offer was some koontie.

This is an esculent [edible] *resembling arrowroot, which they dig, pulverize and use as flour. It makes a palatable but tough cake, cooked in the ashes, which we enjoyed after our long abstinence from bread.*

The old chief took advantage of our eagerness for supplies, and determined to replenish his powder horn. Nothing else would do — not even an old coat, or fishhooks or a cavalry saber would tempt him. Powder only he would have for their long, heavy, small-bore rifles with flintlocks, such as Davy Crockett used. We reluctantly divided with him our very scant supply in exchange for some of their flour. We parted friends after smoking the pipe of peace. [8]

Again, they wallowed down the coast, rowing lazily against the gentle zephyr from the Caribbean. But soon Wood would once more summon his verve and experience in boarding enemy ships. On June 7, off today's Fort Lauderdale, the six fugitives spied a small sailing craft sitting almost motionless in the calm waters. Straining at their four oars to overtake it, they soon came upon three men in a somewhat larger boat actually made for ocean sailing.

Wood noted their tattered Union navy uniforms and decided they were deserters. He figured the three probably had enough ammunition to make it an even fight if they shot first, but Wood could see he had the advantage. "They were thoroughly frightened, for our appearance was not calculated to impress them favorably."

One of them, who seemed to be the leader, whined that the war was over and asked by what authority these grubby pirates had come. With a wave of the hand, Wood announced that "the war was not over as far as we were concerned." All three Yankees, he said, were "deserters and pirates, the punishment of which was death." But rather than turning them over to the first cruiser to loom on the horizon, the benevolent buccaneers would simply "take their paroles and exchange boats." [9]

Acting like they already owned it, Wood and Breckinridge climbed aboard and shoved their revolvers in the leader's face. All three quickly gave up their guns and knives as Wood began taking stock of the ship's stores. All he found were some "salt horse," hardtack and a beaker of water, which he exchanged for some koontie and turtle eggs before sending the refugees off in the old lifeboat. The one real prize was the ship itself, which Wood found to have "more beam, plenty of freeboard and well-found in sails and rigging."

All that was needed now for a real run to Green Turtle Cay was four or five days' worth of provisions. The only place that might have inhabitants and/or a trading post was the old, abandoned Fort Dallas at the mouth of the Miami River. "We knew not whether we would find friend or foe," worried Wood. But after stopping again on a beach and finding nothing but some onions, washed up from a passing ship, "nothing remained but to make a venture of stopping at the fort." [10]

One day later the sailboat edged cautiously towards the mouth of the Miami River, the shoreline lush with "many flowering plants and creepers" reflecting their colors in clear waters. There in a clearing with coconut trees in the foreground were the still-white buildings of Fort Dallas.

What ruined the pretty picture was the group of thirty or so men waiting by a small wobbly wharf. They were "of all colors, from the pale Yankee to the ebony Congo," noted Wood. "All were armed, and a more motley and villainous-looking crew never trod the deck of one of Captain Kidd's ships."

We saw at once with whom we had to deal – deserters from the army and navy of both sides, with a mixture of Spaniards and Cubans, outlaws and renegades. A burly villain, towering head and shoulders above his companions, and whose shaggy black head scorned any covering, hailed us in broken English and asked who we were.

Wood's quick wit went to work again.

Wreckers, I replied. We had left our vessel outside and had come in for water and provisions. He asked where we had left our vessel and her name, evidently suspicious, which was not surprising, for our appearance was certainly against us. Our headgear was unique: the General [Breckinridge] wore a straw hat that flapped over his head like the ears of an elephant; Colonel Wilson an old cavalry cap that had lost its visor; another, a turban made of some No. 4 duck canvas. And all were in shirt sleeves, the colors of which were as varied as Joseph's coat.

Wood told the man his ship was "northward a few miles." Determined not to bring the boat within a hundred yards of the shore, he hollered out that one of his men (O'Toole) was ready to go ashore and buy supplies if they would send a canoe out for him.

No, only the captain would do, they shouted back. Too bad, said Wood, holding up a handful of gold pieces. He would have to go elsewhere for provisions. As the six got out their long oars and began to row away, they could see the men on shore huddling. Then quickly "some 15 or 20 men jumped into 4 or 5 canoes and started for us."

No parlaying this time. Even Tom, the general's servant, loaded a revolver. When the first of the canoes came within range, Russell fired a lone shot. Reported Wood: "He broke two paddles on one side and hit one man — not a bad beginning."

The other canoes began to open fire, but they were now rolling in waves and their shots went high and wide. Russell fired again and the bow man in the nearest canoe slumped over, nearly spilling his two companions as well. Convinced that the strangers were serious, the canoes clustered for another meeting. Soon one of them approached with a white flag.

A white man, standing in the stern with two Negroes paddling, said, "What did you fire on us for? We are friends."
"Friends do not give chase to friends."
"We wanted to find out who you are."
"I told you who we are. If you are friends, sell us some provisions."
"Come on shore and you can get what you want."

More haggling ensued. Eventually, O'Toole, with five ten-dollar gold pieces, was sent ashore in a canoe – but only after Wood made it clear that if he were not back in two hours he would hail the first gunboat that came along and "have this nest of freebooters broken up." [11]

Two hours passed. Then another half hour. The five agonized. They worried about O'Toole, "a bright young Irishman whose good qualities had endeared him to us all." They had ordered him to be "dumb as an oyster." Had he been robbed and tortured? Meanwhile, a plume of black smoke had gone up ashore. Was it a signal to some bigger pirate ship, lurking about in some nearby cove, to come and see if the little sail boat contained any more gold coins? They pulled anchor and made ready to leave when just then the sight of an approaching canoe made them heave to.

It was O'Toole… a bag of hard bread, two hams, some rusty salt pork, sweet potatoes, fruit, and, most important of all, two beakers of water and a keg of New England rum. While O'Toole gave us his experience, a ham was cut, and a slice between two of hardtack, washed down with a jorum [large bowl] *and water, with a dessert of oranges and bananas, was a feast to us more enjoyable than any ever eaten at Delmonico's or the Café Riche.* [12]

Yes, O'Toole reported, the brigands *did* have a schooner coming, which is why they tried to delay O'Toole. Moreover, they had been told to be on the lookout for escaping Confederate bigwigs and had suspected the party was just that. It was time to move on.

After a mosquito-infested night in the mangrove islands of Biscayne Bay, the fugitives had decided that their only hope now was to continue down the Florida Keys and make a break for Havana. But early in what could have been a smooth journey, a forty-ton schooner hove into sight, and all concluded that it must have been the ship attached to the motley occupants of Fort Dallas. Whatever its port, it was doggedly determined to run down the escapees. And so, for an exhausting day, the larger ship remained as close to the coast as it dared while the smaller one darted over brittle reefs and paddled between narrow mangrove channels.

At one point during low tide Wood could see nothing ahead but a flat expanse of shoal. The schooner was now "coming up hand over hand." Wood ordered all the ballast thrown over. Still the keel grated over coral and "that peculiar tremor most unpleasant to a seaman under any circumstances, told us our danger." The schooner was no more than a mile away and gaining. *Clunk*, the little ship's keel hit another reef and stopped. Without hesitation, hams, hardtack and all the heavy provisions went overboard. Then went the anchor, chain and rope.

It wasn't enough. In desperation, all six men plunged into the water, three on each side of the boat, and heaved it upward with their shoulders as they struggled for a foothold atop the breaking coral. Inch by inch they moved the boat forward. Between the coral branches they would sink to their necks in the slime and water, their limbs bleeding from coral cuts.

After a hundred yards they were on the shore side of the reef. Just then they looked up to see the schooner hauling by the wind, opening fire with the mighty blasts of nine and twelve-pounders. But their fears were allayed at realizing the range was too long. The shots were falling far short.

"Wet, foul, bleeding, with hardly enough strength to climb into the boat, we were at least safe for a time," said Wood. Their spirits soared when Tom, ever mindful of his master's needs, pulled out a jug of rum that he had kept "while you all was pitchin' everythin' away."

They would need their little burst of energy. As the fugitives had walked their boat over the ring of reefs, the schooner had found an opening it could sail through. Now it was just a half mile away and putting out a cutter. Now its small canon fired, with the men shooting their own small arms. The boat gun's second shot grazed the mast and carried away the luff of the mainsail. The six targets crouched below the gunwales as several Minnie balls thudded into the sides without penetrating. At one point when the heaving gunwales revealed a break in the reef, they quickly raised what was left of the sail and raced through it. "The schooner was now satisfied that she could not overhaul us, and stood off to the northward," the weary Wood would write.

As the men glided toward Elliot Key, they took stock. The remaining provisions consisted of 10 pounds of hard bread, most of a 20-gallon beaker of water, and 2 gallons of rum. The ship had no ballast and no ground tackle. All they could do was pull up on the sand at Elliot Key, wrap themselves in the sails from head to feet, and wait for dusk to bring clouds of mosquitoes

By next morning all agreed that they would not endure another night like the one that just passed. They would bet everything on reaching Havana, and before they left they would strip Elliot Key of everything edible.

They began by spotting a half-dozen cocoa-palms, each forty or fifty feet high. Tom went to the boat, brought off a piece of canvas, cut a yard-long strip and made two holes for his big toes. Then he was up the trunk of the first palm, throwing down green nuts. Soon they had enough for a half pint of milk, and General Breckinridge was stirring up a morning rum and milk punch.

Next was ballast. They fetched the jib sail from the boat, laid it on the shore, piled sand atop it and bound it into a heavy sack that all wrestled aboard..

What about meat? The General went off with his revolver and came back in an hour with two pelicans and a "white crane." In the stomach of one pelican were "a dozen or more mullet from six to nine inches in length, which had evidently just been swallowed," said Wood. "We cleaned them, and wrapping them in palmetto leaves, roasted them in the ashes. And they proved delicious."

Tom, who had cooked just about everything in battlefield camps, next skinned the three birds, broiled them over a camp fire and laid the first one before the general on a leaf. "I fear it's as tough as an old Muscovy drake," he said.

Breckinridge cut off a mouthful while the rest anxiously awaited the verdict. He chewed some, then without a word rose and hastened into the bushes. Returning in a few minutes, he told Tom to take the birds away.

Night was falling. Whatever more sustenance the men had expected to gain on Elliot Key would have to remain undiscovered. Their bodies were already the color of mahogany. Their feet were swollen and blistered. Their lives would depend on decent weather and the ability to outwit the Union navy and outrun the demons of starvation.

After putting Breckinridge in charge of doling out water and rum at regular intervals, the last remnants of Confederate rule in Florida sailed into the sunset on June 8, 1865.

After yet another near-death experience (see page 245), the six starving fugitives would arrive in the harbor of a Cuban town a day's carriage ride from Havana. All had just surrendered their last gold coins for a hotel room and could only think of sleeping for a week. But Cuba was ardently rebel-friendly. Word spread that some Confederate dignitaries had arrived after a heroic escape. As the men put their heads to their pillows, a crowd gathered outside shouting for them to appear. Once they did, they were swept up in a celebration, feted with food, drink and public acclaim — perhaps the answer to their most fervent prayers when they faced starvation at sea.

ABOVE, LEFT: John C. Breckinridge in his spit-and-polish days as Confederate Secretary of War. (State of Florida Archives). RIGHT: Dashing John Taylor Wood as top aide to Jefferson Davis, then captain of a gunboat that bedeviled the Union navy. *(Battles and Leaders of the Civil War)*

When Taylor, Breckinridge and crew slept covered with sand, they were copying what soldiers on both sides had learned to do along the Florida coast. This Civil War drawing is entitled "Mosquito Control."
(State of Florida Archives)

182

Artist's rendering of the six rebel escapees commandeering a larger sloop manned by three Union deserters in May 1865. *(State of Florida Archives)*

ABOVE: With shots from a bounty-hunting privateer whizzing over their heads, the desperate fugitives tossed everything overboard and pushed their sloop over the sharp coral reefs just south of Miami. *(Century Magazine)*

BELOW: The escapees found subsistence in turtle eggs, just like this beach digger at the turn of the century. *(State of Florida Archives)*

Timelines: 1861-1889

1861 – January. Florida secedes from Union.

1861 – April. Civil War begins with firing on Fort Sumter, South Carolina. President Lincoln orders blockade of all southern ports.

1861 – August 15. Confederate band captures Jupiter Lighthouse, renders the light inoperable, then goes on to destroy the light at Cape Florida.

1862 – June 10. Navy Secretary Welles alerts Key West that Confederates are bringing goods northward over land from the tip of the Indian River.

1862 – summer. *Sagamore* and other federal gunboats conduct raids on salt works Florida's Panhandle.

1862 – October 15. Gunboat *Sagamore* seizes the English *Trier* near Indian River Inlet, the first of its 24 captures of blockade runners off southeast Florida.

1863 – January. Union navy intensifies blockade of Jupiter and Indian River inlets. Volunteers enlist to patrol Indian River.

1863 – February. Missing parts of Jupiter Lighthouse found by gunboat crews on James Paine's property around St. Lucie.

1863 – March 3-4. The *Sagamore* slips into Mosquito Inlet, firing and sinking the cotton-laden *Nightingale* and sustaining its first combat death.

1863 – July. Four Union warships shell and ransack New Smyrna.

1864 – Lighthouse Establishment adopts lard oil as standard illuminant, replacing colza, rapeseed and sperm oil.

1865 – April. Lee surrenders to Grant at Appomattox. Lincoln assassinated five days later. Jefferson Davis and cabinet become fugitives.

1866 – July. Jupiter Lighthouse again illuminated. William Davis becomes head keeper.

1869 – U.S. Lighthouse Service adopts a distinctive flag: triangular, with a red border and blue lighthouse on a blue field.

1869, December 16 – James A. Armour named head keeper at Jupiter, a job he will keep for forty years.

1872 – August. Henry Titus accuses Armour of gross neglect of duty.

1872 – October 20. Merchant ship *Victor* wrecks in reefs off Jupiter, disgorging its valuable cargo.

1873 – March 26. Light House Board drops rules that charges against James Armour be dropped.

1877 – Kerosene used in lighthouses for first time; becomes the principal illuminant within a dozen years.

1879 – January 12. Jupiter and Cape Canaveral lighthouses survive Florida's only recorded earthquake.

1883 – February. Construction begins on new head keeper's house at Jupiter Inlet. Assistant keepers' house renovated.

1884 – Light House Board mandates uniforms for lighthouse keepers. Regulations increased.

1885 – Federal government builds a chain of life saving stations along Florida coast.

1885 – December. New 41-mile railroad connects Sanford to Titusville, allowing rail-steamboat service from Jacksonville to Jupiter.

1889 – July. Indian River Steamboat Company opens Titusville-Juno service, with short-line railroad linking Jupiter to Lake Worth. Two steamers serve as floating hotels near Jupiter Inlet.

PART III
A Settlement

1870 chart shows Florida's pivotal role in ocean shipping from New Orleans and throughout the Caribbean. Note the busy trade at Cedar Key, which was linked by rail to Fernandina, Jacksonville and points north. South Florida was still a wilderness. *(State of Florida Archives)*

Chapter 14

Restoration

The nation's system of navigational aids was just one of a thousand shattered pieces of government that had to be picked up and patched together by Andrew Johnson and his post-war administration. The Topographical Engineers had been pulled apart by the army's need for men who could build bridges and roads under battle conditions. Now, Colonel John James Abert was dead and Hartman Bache had retired to Philadelphia. The Corps itself gave way to the much larger Army Corps of Engineers, but at the time the successor agency's main priority was to support westward expansion.

The Light House Board was busy reclaiming and repairing the stations it had lost to its Confederate counterpart. In Florida the few active beacons in the old Seventh Lighthouse District had been run from the Key West navy base. The District supervisor knew one thing for sure: in the land that had cast not one vote for Lincoln, he couldn't re-open and staff his lighthouses unless he was willing to appoint men who, just a year or so previously, may well have been snuffing out beacons or running cotton past Union blockaders.

This explains why the first postwar keepers at Jupiter Inlet were men who had been, shall we say, generous to both sides with their allegiance. The new head keeper was 65-year-old William B. Davis, known in the upper Indian River community as a long-time homesteader, expert river pilot and sometimes supply runner from Fort Capron to Fort Jupiter. He had been described earlier by one neighbor as a "strong and muscular man, full of life and daring, bluff of speech and manner, frank and hearty always, and ever ready to do his best for the good of settlers." [1]

It was Davis who had once carried the mail from Fort Capron to Fort Dallas during the Seminole War era and who had led the volunteers who tried to re-open Jupiter Inlet in 1844. It was also Davis who had praised the "patriots" who had extinguished the Jupiter light and who was later elected chairman of the local committee that petitioned the governor of Florida to send Confederate troops to defend the Indian River.

When Davis was named head keeper at Jupiter on July 10, 1866, his first assistant was none other than James Armour, his former neighbor on the Indian

River. It was Armour who had been elected secretary of the committee and who had enlisted in the Confederate Army in June 1862. It was the same man who deserted six weeks after enlisting and who served the *U.S.S. Sagamore* so vigorously in pursuit of blockade booty. Local tradition has it (thus far undocumented) that when Armour applied for the assistant keeper's post, he had in a hand letters from *Sagamore* Captain Earl English and Key West admiral Theodorus Bailey praising his Yankee zeal.

As before the war, a Jupiter Lighthouse keeper's biggest burden was isolation. It made every fever or animal bite a potential threat to life. It made for a monotonous diet and limited one's company to a handful of fellow humans whose voices probably grew tiresome after months in the same solitary station. And with no women around (families would come later), three robust males surely longed for a woman's touch, be it even in the form of an apple pie.

To give some indication of the area's loneliness and lack of communications, one need only cite the summer of 1866. Michael Sears and his son George had ridden the Gulf Stream from Key Biscayne to the Indian River in their small sailboat and were hugging the coast on the way back. It had rained heavily the day before. As the two boaters were about ten miles south of Jupiter Inlet they noticed something they hadn't seen on the way up – a stream of fresh water flowing out to sea. Curious (especially because there were so few inlets in southeast Florida) they waited for the tide to change and maneuvered their shallow-draft skiff through the narrow opening. Soon they were in the midst of Lake Worth, with no end in sight from north to south. After heading a few miles southward they pulled up to the only cabin they saw on the waterfront and introduced themselves to its lone occupant. The man was Augustus Lang, lighthouse raider and self-exiled Robinson Crusoe. "How is the war going?" he asked after deciding that the arrivals weren't Federal agents.

Lang reportedly was astonished when told the Civil War had been over for a year. Within a few weeks he was gone, not appearing in public records again until November 1867 when he bought some land along the upper St. Lucie River. [2]

Isolation, however, was also the main reason Jupiter Lighthouse got early attention when it came to repairs. Maritime merchants and their insurance companies knew only that they wanted to get on with making money, and that depended greatly on safe shipping. In September 1865, nine months before Davis arrived as head keeper, Seventh Lighthouse District records show the president of Atlantic Mutual Insurance Company writing the Light House

Board to urge early restoration of the lights at Jupiter and Cape Canaveral. In January 1866 a congressional committee complied with an insurance industry petition to appropriate the necessary funds. In March, in his annual message to Congress, President Andrew Johnson took time to note that "an experienced agent has been sent to [Jupiter Inlet and Cape Florida] with instructions to use every exertion to re-light those points…." [3]

The files then become fragmentary, but show steady progress:

On April 17, 1866, the Third District lighthouse inspector reported that a new first order Fresnel apparatus (lens) marked "Jupiter Inlet Lighthouse" was being sent from the Staten Island depot to Key West along with a year's supply of oil.

On May 21, both were reported shipped to Jupiter on the tender *Narragansett*.

On July 12 Seventh District Engineer M. C. Dunnier wrote the Light House Board that the lens was lit on July 10 (exactly six years after its first shining) and that a Notice to Mariners had been properly published. [4]

In 1866 if you had climbed the 105 steps of the lighthouse and stood on the cast iron gallery resting on the railing, your eyes would sweep over a vast wilderness of water and trees. To the east you could make out the end of the narrow inlet through the pine trees as it met the sea three-quarters of a mile from the tower.

Looking south you could barely make out the arm of the Loxahatchee that limped into Lake Worth Creek, which in turn dissolved into a hundred dead-end rivulets before ever reaching the northern end of the pristine lake. Indians had made a haulover for their canoes over the years, and the slicked-down sawgrass left a trail of sorts for weeks after they departed. But as soon as the sawgrass grew tall again, finding the haulover was a gamble. Mostly, Lake Worth, ten miles off, was only something you could see the tip of from the lighthouse gallery on a very clear day.

To the west the broad Loxahatchee gradually narrowed to the width of a half-dozen canoes as it wound towards the swamps that fed it, some 14 miles away. You would see absolutely no sign of mankind except for the tip of the crumbling cabins that remained from abandoned Fort Jupiter two miles upriver.

To the north the old trail from Fort Capron was already covered by a thick growth of jack pine, cypress and saw palmetto. The inland waterway called

Jupiter Narrows looked nothing like today. It consisted of a maze of shallow mangrove islands so dense and mysterious as to defy all but wizened local boat captains like James Armour.

Life as a lighthouse keeper was a grinding routine. Typically, one of the men would climb the tower just before 11 p.m. He'd remain there until a half hour after daybreak, then shuffle down the 105 steps, make a big breakfast, then roust the two sleepers.

Each night's work in the tower began by providing enough fuel to last until dawn. Originally, most lighthouses used sperm oil, but as the whale population declined, lard oil proved to be almost as efficient at half the price. It came in 100-gallon "butts" – the mariner's term for barrels – and each night the keeper on duty would lug a 30 lb. iron container up the winding staircase. He'd then pour some in a container beneath the five concentric wicks that gave the Fresnel lens its light.

Charles Pierce, who was just eight when his father, Hannibal, became assistant keeper for a short spell, recalled over fifty years later,

An hour before sundown the keeper and his two assistants would go up in the tower, take enough lard oil to last the big lamp throughout the night. Each evening the outside of the lantern and the glass prisms of the great lens were cleaned with Spanish white and spirits of wine and carefully wiped and polished. Then the clock mechanism that turned the lens was wound, started and timed to a second so that the flash, varied by fixed lights, would be in the exact time allotted to the Jupiter Lighthouse. The work was usually finished some fifteen or twenty minutes before sundown…and while waiting for darkness, the men would go out onto the balcony for a breath of fresh air and to view the scenery spread out before them for many miles in all directions. [5]

Once or twice during the night, the lone keeper on duty would have to crank up the rope that was attached to a 250-pound metal cylinder that made the lens carriage go around the stationary lamp, or illuminant. Working on the same principle as a grandfather clock, the weight of the descending iron tube rotated the carriage on its ball-bearings and let the lens create its special signature to ships at sea. When the heavy metal weight had descended about forty feet below the gallery floor, the keeper on duty would crank it up again as the rope wound around the large drum by his side.

In between "crawling the drum" and minding the wick, the keeper would make entries in his watch book, read, or perhaps get a head start on a daytime chore, such as scraping rust from the iron railings so they could get one of their periodic paintings.

After breakfast, the two "fresh" keepers had their own set routine: polishing lamps and prisms, shining brass fixtures, tuning the turning mechanism, replacing broken glass panes and carrying butts from the oil house to the tower base. Then there was the business of living: tending the small garden, hunting for fresh meat, fishing, and tidying the keepers' quarters. Probably because builder Edward Yorke had used most of his wood getting through the ice in the Delaware River, he built most of the 20-by-36 foot keepers' house of two-foot-thick coquina rock. Its only household convenience was an underground, indoor cistern, built in hopes the building could be defended should Indians attack.

In exchange for these round-the-clock chores with no days off, Captain (the title bestowed on head keepers) Davis received $820 a year. Armour and second assistant keeper Dempsey Cain, who had held the same post at Sand Key Light, each got $460. Both salaries were a decent bump over pre-war levels. Davis now held a coveted position that few salaried workers in Florida could match. And with his staples paid for by the government, he could probably put most of his paycheck into a savings bank if one existed. Moreover, for the true outdoorsman, the Jupiter station was a *carte blanche* to partake of the world's best hunting and fishing. Some places may have had better hunting and some better fishing, but none had a more glorious combination!

What caused the most problems wasn't so much the routine, but the *unexpected*: things wearing out, breaking down with no means of repair and no replacement parts. On December 26, 1866, just six months into Davis' tenure, the superintendent of lights in Key West reported receiving a letter from the Jupiter keeper "complaining of the condition of the lighthouse and its illuminating apparatus." Only summaries of correspondence have survived from the first years after the Civil War, but they indicate the kinds of trouble that plagued the keepers at Jupiter:

January 17, 1867. The Seventh District Inspector in Key West reports "lantern glass damaged by wild fowl" (so many flocks of migrating birds flew smack into the beacon at night that it's said that one could often walk around the base of the tower in the early morning filling a washtub with dead ducks for the evening meal).

March 27. A lampist (Fresnel lens expert) arrives from Key West to fix the broken illuminating apparatus "but lacks the necessary tools for repair."

March 31. The inspector in Key West reports receiving a shipment of plate glass for Jupiter (which the keepers have been requesting for some six months). [6]

From the Seventh District's annual report in 1868: "The walls of this tower are damp during the rainy season, causing the plastering to fall off. The proper remedies will be applied. The gutter around the porch floor [of the keepers' house] is needed." [7]

Aggravating the whole maintenance problem was the difficulty in keeping the Jupiter station supplied with parts, fuel and household staples. Although the tenders of the Seventh District had the task of re-supplying its lighthouses in the open sea, the off-loading of heavy crates onto a lifeboat in rolling seas wasn't a crew's idea of fun. Worse was when the seas were so bad or the shipment so bulky that they had to anchor off Indian River Inlet and bob at sea for several days while the supplies were rowed 35 miles to Jupiter. Thus, tender captains tended to put off the odious chore as long as they could. More than one inspector asked Washington to assign him another lighthouse further up Florida's west coast if only "other arrangements" could be made to supply troublesome Jupiter. [8]

Jupiter's surest means of getting attention and supplies was the threat of running out of fuel for the beacon. On December 2, 1867, the superintendent of lights in Key West lamented that whereas Jupiter had just reported itself short on oil, his only tender was over on the state's west coast. Two months later, on February 2, 1868, District Inspector B. M. Dove got a letter from Jupiter stating that "there will be no light at the house unless oil is supplied by the 10th." On the same day the captain of the tender *Pharos* reported that due to the turbulent surf, he had "no success" in trying to land supplies on the beach at Jupiter. Three days later Inspector Dove reported "oil and lightning conductors supplied [to Jupiter] by the U.S. steamer *Don*" [were they transferred from the *Pharos?*]. [9]

By 1868 the elderly Captain Davis had a problem with what today might be called "personnel retention." When second assistant Dempsey Cain left on May 14, 1868, his replacement was Allen Padgett, a one-time Davis neighbor from around Fort Pierce who seems to have spent much more time roping wild cows in the piney flats than on developing any lighthouse credentials. Padgett lasted five months before open spaces again called. He would be heard from again in six years when he and two other nomad cow catchers murdered Augustus Lang because his house happened to be on a patch they fancied for a corral (for more see page 244). [10]

Next up was John Umfreville, a 48-year-old English native. He served five months before dying on the job on May 8, 1869. Umfreville, who is presumed to be buried somewhere on the lighthouse grounds, was the first of three keepers who would give up the ghost while on duty, causing one to wonder if the repeated climbs to the tower in all kinds of weather may have triggered disaster for men with undetected heart conditions. [11]

Before the year was out another second assistant keeper had come and gone, and so had Captain Davis himself — no doubt to enjoy what time he had left at his homestead on the Indian River. Watching — and enduring — during all this time of revolving personnel was James Arango Armour, and on December 16, 1869, he got a letter from headquarters promoting him to the head keeper's job.

ABOVE: In early lighthouse days planks of wood sufficed for bringing supplies from dockside. Water's edge had several chickee huts for doing laundry, cleaning fish and accommodating Seminoles who visited to trade deerskins and venison. *(State of Florida Archives)*

ABOVE RIGHT: Small steamers like this one, usually chartered by owner-guides, brought hunters and fishermen through the Jupiter Narrows and onto the mysterious Loxahatchee. The lighthouse was a lone outpost in a land that visitors from "up north" deemed as wild as "darkest Africa." *(Historical Society of Palm Beach County)*

RIGHT: Isolated Jupiter Light, one of the nation's most difficult to supply, usually got its staples and spare parts twice a year when a passing Lighthouse Service tender rowed crates ashore and left them on the high-tide line. *(Loxahatchee River Historical Society)*

Chapter 15

Armour

A captain's title and a hefty raise to $820 a year was just the boost needed for a man who had recently decided to settle down and raise a family. On December 4, 1867, the 42-year-old Armour had married 18-year-old Almeda Catherine Carlile, youngest daughter of David and Eliza Carlile. In 1852 the Carliles had hitched up a mule team in Mississippi and driven all the way to homestead eighty-acres along the Indian River in what would become the settlement of LaGrange. Sand Point, soon to become the busy little town of Titusville, was just two miles south. [1]

The land the Carliles picked had a strategic value besides farming. If one wanted to travel or ship goods north from the tip of the Indian River, one had to take an ox cart over ten rough miles of sand and pineland until it reached the St. Johns River, which ran all the way north to Jacksonville. The ox-cart trail, as Confederates John Breckinridge and John Taylor Wood found during their escape, ended right around Carlile's dock.

Whether Armour's bride stayed very much at Jupiter Lighthouse in her first year or so of marriage is unclear but unlikely. For one thing, she would be the only white woman in a hundred-mile radius. She'd be living in a cramped keeper's quarters with three men, no doubt cooking and picking up after them, too. Moreover, two months after her marriage, Almeda would become pregnant with Kate (Katherine Dickerson), the first of her seven children. Living a hundred miles from even a midwife — and a three-day river trip at that — doesn't seem like the sort of thing her anxious parents would condone for their youngest daughter.

Besides, running the lighthouse was far from smooth. In February 1870, the second full month of Armour's reign, the British brig *Merino* ran aground at Jupiter Inlet. Later that same month, the schooners *Minerva, Mattie Richmond* and *Rafborn* also ran onto the beach at Jupiter on different days. Insurance and lighthouse officials must have been flabbergasted as to how four vessels could wreck independently of one another in the same month in the same general spot.

Then, October 20 of the same year, the 200-foot, 670-ton steamer *Varuna* sunk in high seas a few miles northeast of Jupiter Inlet, losing 52 lives and sparing only five crew members. A report by the U. S. Steamboat Inspector estimated its lost cargo at $300,000. [2]

In the midst of such events, the passing parade of assistant keepers continued under Armour. Nehemiah Crowell came aboard in August 1869 and left the same month a year later. O. P. Barnes took his place and was gone by April 1871. Daniel O'Hara joined the same day as Barnes and lasted until October 1871.

Increasingly, Armour turned to friends and relatives along the Indian River. On September 8, 1871, Charles Carlin, his friend from Titusville, signed on as an assistant keeper and would stay until 1885 when he was named (through Armour's contacts?) to head the new U.S. Life Saving Station on the beach at Jupiter. Carlin was a Carlile family friend, described by one of them as "an ex-sailor of Old Ireland" who lived in a ten-by-twelve-foot log cabin beside the Titusville dock "with his little sloop anchored out front." He and his wife Mary would soon become innkeepers and leading citizens of Jupiter.

Armour's reservoir of relatives was even more plentiful (Almeda had six grown siblings, all living in Brevard County). A month after Charles Carlin boarded up his cabin in Sand Point and moved to the lighthouse, he was joined by Andrew Carlile, Almeda's 24-year-old brother. Within the next eight years, what was becoming the "family seat" at the lighthouse would be passed on to another of Almeda's brothers, Robert, and to Carlile nephews Joshua Smith and David K. Harrison – all when in their early twenties. [3]

Could all this commotion, job turnover and unusually large number of wrecks around Jupiter have anything to do with Armour himself?

In late August, 1872, the Light House Board in Washington received a letter dated August 10. It was written from Titusville. Today, the outer edges are charred from the Commerce Department fire in 1920 that destroyed so many lighthouse records. But the writer clearly thought James Arango Armour a scoundrel.

This will inform you, not as an [words burned away], *but as an agent for underwriters, that the Light House Keeper at Jupiter Inlet does in no manner as his duty requires. He is a man totally unworthy of so important a situation. The Light is frequently out long before daylight whilst this man Armour is away at Sand Point* [Titusville] *most of the time as long as six weeks at a time. He has just left here when his first assistant Charles Carlin comes up. If this is in accordance with the* [unintelligible] *these worthies spend their principal time on the beach wrecking. That is, the assistants, whilst only one* [charred]. *This man Armour also barters off the oil and it is now high time it should all be stopped.*

This man Armour the Keeper was tried at Key West for piracy and convicted for two years by the U.S. government and got out and is a man of the very worst character and should be [removed] *at once.* 4

The writer was none other than Henry T. Titus, owner of Titus House hotel, wholesale liquor dealer, part-time "special agent" for the Board of Underwriters, and the local postmaster who managed to get the town named after himself. Then about 50, the "Colonel" (a title he apparently also appropiated), surely must have known Armour, Carlin and the Carliles personally in a town whose entire orbit couldn't have contained more than 300 souls. If so, it didn't soften his enmity. The letter concludes by promising to produce affidavits from various local luminaries to vouch for his charges.

On September 23, 1872, Titus wrote the Board again and enclosed the "sworn upon his oath" testimony of Daniel O'Hara, who had resigned in October 1871 after 14 months as an assistant keeper under Armour. He testified that he and the other assistant keeper, O. P. Barnes, were

...on several occasions sent to the beach to pick up wrecked goods from wrecked vessels whilst the said James Armour took care of the Light, he only giving such a flow of oil so that it would burn out in the night. So that I have as well as O. P. Barnes [been absent?] *from the light on* [charred] *times for two to three days, no one being at the light but the said James Armour. It was understood that the goods were to be divided between us, and further* [charred] *that James Armour often left the light house for six weeks at a time whilst the light is left in charge of two assistants and that the two assistants also go away frequently and are gone from their post for weeks. He* [O'Hara] *also states that he was employed with O.P. Barnes about one year at said Light House.*

[The undersigned] *states that this James Armour, tried and convicted for felony and piracy and* [unintelligible] *during the war and sentenced to imprisonment but got out after having served some time, and that his first assistant is one Charles Carlin, a foreigner and not a citizen of the United States.*

The letter was notarized by the local justice of the peace and the character of O'Hara was attested to by Titus, the J.P. and one I. D. Parkins of Titusville.

Let us leave aside the character and motives of Henry Titus for the moment. A vital question at this point is when James Armour was made aware of the charges and what the Light House Board did about them.

The summary of another destroyed-by-fire letter shows that on August 22 Rear Admiral C. S. Boggs, the Board's naval secretary, wrote the Seventh District inspector to have the local lighthouse superintendent investigate the charges. Or, if he lacked "implicit confidence" in the superintendent, he should take on the task personally.

On October 9 Boggs again wrote the inspector, enclosing the second Titus letter and O'Hara affidavit. Apparently no inquiry had been made yet, because Boggs urges him to "please report upon this matter and inform this Office whether removal of this Keeper would or would not be for the benefit of Commerce and the good of the Light House Service."

Since the mails to Key West took two to three weeks, it's highly unlikely that the inspector there would have received it by October 20 and visited Armour at Jupiter Inlet by then.

Why is October 20 so important? Because on that day an event would occur that everyone within a hundred miles of Jupiter would long remember – one that also afforded an opportunity to measure the character of James Armour.

October 20, 1871, was exactly one year after the *Varuna* and its $300,000 cargo sunk in a storm off Jupiter, drowning 52. On October 20, 1872, around ten in the evening, another Mallory merchant ship, the steamer *Victor* was on its way from New York to New Orleans with a cargo of general merchandise valued at $150,000. As if on cue, a late fall tropical storm flared up as the big ship lurched toward Jupiter Inlet. In the midst of the storm the *Victor's* propeller shaft bent and jammed itself against the prop. Now the boat had no ability to navigate and began to bounce and twist as it was driven into the chain of reefs just off Jupiter's coastline.

Up in the lighthouse tower watching the tragedy unfold was Hannibal Pierce. He had no lighthouse training, but he was thankful to James Armour for making him assistant keeper just a month before. Pierce, his wife Margaretta and young son Charlie had recently come from Chicago to try their luck in Florida. The little family had just set up housekeeping south of Fort Pierce when a fire raged through their crude palmetto shack and turned all of their clothing and furniture to ashes. Armour had apparently heard about it and offered Pierce a job at the lighthouse until he could "get on his feet." 5

A month later, the Pierces still had only the clothes they were wearing when the fire destroyed their home. Earlier that day Margaretta had even wistfully wished that a passing ship might providentially dump a case of dry goods overboard when passing Jupiter. Now, as her husband saw the broad merchantman begin its slow twist of death in the clutches of a reef, he took stock of the four-foot breakers crashing on the beach. Although he wasn't due to be relieved by Charles Carlin for an hour, Pierce scrambled down from the tower and told the head keeper what he'd seen.

Armour was already in bed (the other two had night duty) and his sleepy reaction was that his greenhorn assistant was most likely mistaken. He added that it was probably the inspector's boat, since he was due anytime now.

Pierce climbed the tower again but quickly returned. "That's no inspector's boat," he said. It was a large steamship. It was now broadside on the beach and waves were breaking over her from the northeast, pushing the *Victor* southward along the surf.

By now it was midnight and time for Carlin's watch. Armour and Pierce jumped in the captain's dinghy. Since this account comes from young Charlie's journal and since he stayed behind, we know only that the two keepers presumably spent the night rescuing passengers. Charles Carlin came down from the tower at sunup and headed for the inlet in his little *Sea Gull*. Charlie Pierce tells us that "three women and the children" were left alone at the lighthouse.

Around 9 a.m., Charlie wrote, he glanced south where Lake Worth Creek flows into the Loxahatchee and counted seven canoes, loaded with people, and coming straight for the lighthouse landing. He ran to the front porch and pointed as Almeda Armour stood up from her chair. "Oh goodness, they are Indians!" she exclaimed.

From the other corner of his eye, Charlie spotted Carlin's *Sea Gull* in the inlet and approaching the dock. With the wind in his favor, Carlin and several cold, wet passengers in his little skiff made it to the dock just ahead of the Seminoles and their crowd. Turns out that the Indians, their wives and children had just set out on a trading mission from Lake Worth to Titusville. As for Charles Carlin, his *Sea Gull* had returned with a woman and her daughter, a merchant from New Orleans and the ship's stewardess.

The captain and most of the crew had remained aboard hoping to be picked up by one of the many Mallory steamers that passed by regularly. They had initially tried using blankets to stuff the hole made by the broken shaft. But by mid-morning the captain feared the hole would burst and the ship break up. Afraid to trust his lifeboats in the churning surf, he had tossed a cable to the crewmen on shore. They had found a timber and jammed it into the sand in hopes of creating a sort of clothesline that people could grasp while pulling themselves onto the beach.

Back at the lighthouse, the bedraggled passengers were followed up the steps to the keepers' porch by a gaggle of Indians. The latter stayed for about an hour, then suddenly bolted for their canoes, determined to make camp on the other side of the inlet and see what goodies from the *Victor* might come their way if it lost its battle with the reef.

The wind continued to blow hard from the east, and on the third night the ship began to break up as feared. All three lighthouse keepers ran down to the beach after breakfast, recalls Charlie, because "they knew the steamer would not last long in that sea, and they wished to be on hand when the wreckage started coming onshore." 6

Father returned at half past eleven, but Captain Armour and Carlin remained, busy picking up the goods that came piling in on the beach. While father was at dinner, I went to look down the river to see if there was anything to report. The tide was coming in on a full flood and water was full of wreckage of all kinds that had washed in through the inlet.

On the east side of the dock a dry goods box and a big Saratoga trunk had grounded, and barrels and boxes of every description were floating by me. I flew back to the house and between gasps told father what I had seen. Forgetting his hunger, he jumped up from the table and ran to the landing. Seeing that the box and trunk were not likely to float away, he turned his attention to the things going upriver on the top of the tide.

He pushed out in Captain Armour's little catboat, Kate, *after some of the stuff that was floating toward the Indian camp. At the moment of pushing away from the dock an immense box and trunk came floating past. He got a line fastened to it and hauled it onshore. This carton, when opened later, was found to contain fifty men's suits.*

After landing the big box, he saw two Indians trying to get a large container into their canoe. He sculled up alongside and told them it belonged to him; they gave it up without protest or hesitation as there were too many other things floating in the river to waste any time disputing the ownership of any one particular box. In telling of the incident later, father said he knew as soon as he came near that it was a sewing machine and that the Indians wouldn't have known what to do with it. As he had suspected, it was a Wheeler and Wilson machine, and mother used it for many years. [7]

The booty brought back to the lighthouse was overwhelming. Examples: several hundred bottles of perfumes, 10 hundred-pound kegs of fine creamery butter, bolts of high-quality muslin and a whole trunk of patent leather valises. Not the least prized were three pedigreed collies that were liberated by Captain Armour. He named them Storm, Victor and Wreck, and they served as lighthouse mascots for many years. [8]

The Indians wound up with an ample supply of fancy colored shirts and bright ribbons. But what they sought most were the many cases of Plantation Bitters that washed up the river. "There was more whiskey than bitters in the stuff, and it allowed the Indians many a big drunk," said Charlie.

A week after the storm the Atlantic was like a quiet lake, and another Mallory steamer picked up the captain and crew. The Seminoles continued up the Indian River on their way to Titusville, where, says Charlie, "people there had their first news of the shipwreck at Jupiter." At the lighthouse, nine of the butter kegs were buried under the shade of a big tree for future use and life returned to its routine.

As for the *Victor*, no wrecking crews ever showed up from Key West. Charlie Pierce reported that later examination by the keepers showed that "there was still a lot of cargo in the hold, held there by a mass of wire rigging and the iron parts of the ship." Probing with a crowbar, the lighthouse keepers broke one crate free of its binding and found themselves with a fifty-gallon barrel of "French cognac of the first quality." [9]

After the keepers had their way with her, the ship wasted away in the surf by Jupiter Inlet until years later when only two rusty boilers remained.

Curiously, young Charlie reports that "one afternoon near the first of December, Colonel Henry T. Titus of Sand Point [some folks hadn't gotten used to the new name, Titusville] came sailing in and tied up at the lighthouse dock." With him were two locals headed for Lake Worth to gather crabwood, which, says Charlie, "was used to make fancy walking canes." It seems that Titus and Captain Armour talked only about crabwood and Lake Worth. He sailed off with the men and stopped by on his way back, ten days later. [10]

Henry Titus probably did have a genuine interest in obtaining crabwood. Leo Titus, a descendent writing in a family history, notes that "He had a machine to make shingles and all types of fancy canes, cups, saucers and napkin rings out of native wood." But Titus was foremost an importer of liquor and wine who also advertised himself as "General Marine Underwriter's Agent American and Foreign." Thus, it would be easy to conclude that "special agent" Henry Titus was on a spy mission for his insurance client. Titus was already incensed that the bumbling bureaucrats in Washington hadn't satisfied his earlier charges against Armour. In January 1873 (the exact date is burned away) Titus sent another letter to the chief clerk of the Light House Board. In a text that suffers as much from Titus' poor handwriting as from fire, he begs to report more on the "outrageous acts of the Jupiter Light House keepers on this coast." If something isn't done about it soon, he adds, "I shall take another course."

For I cannot conceive for a moment that the Government of the United States employs men to steal goods from stranded [wrecks] *on the coast. And as lights keepers* [portions missing] *and luxury goods taken from the steamer* Victor. *Mr. Armour, the chief Light Keeper, was here* [in Titusville] *and frequently stays here for a month. At a time he returns. Then the Assistant Light Keeper Carlin is now here and has been* [absent] *from the light over 20 days in no accordance with the Law and Rules of the Light House Board.*

Titus goes on to say he has reported "all of these facts" to one J. D. Jones, head of the "Board of Underwriters in New York" and vaguely threatens that Jones is prepared to take some sort of legal action in accordance with laws that bar employees of the United States government from "pilfering property belonging to the underwriters." [11]

Well, now, let us re-assemble the charges. According to Henry Titus, the U.S. Lighthouse Service had erred in the first place by hiring a convicted felon. Having gotten the job, James Armour was often AWOL from his post – while collecting his paycheck – for extended periods, leaving the lighthouse short-handed. He allowed the Jupiter light to burn out at night so he could conserve his government-issued oil supply and barter it (perhaps to steamer captains) in Titusville. In so doing, he committed the lighthouse keeper's most egregious sin – endangering ships that passed near the dangerous reefs off Jupiter Inlet. Indeed, he ordered his men to roam the lonely shoreline for washed-up merchandise, took it to Titusville to sell or barter, and divvied up the sales from other people's property with his men.

Serious accusations, and all attested to by his former assistant and accomplice!

Now let us delve a little deeper into the character of Henry T. Titus. He first emerges into public view as a soldier of fortune who was such an ardent anti-abolitionist that he rushed to the Kansas frontier in 1854 to confront the crusading John Brown. After joining military campaigns from Nicaragua to the Wild West, he then turned up in California with soldier of fortune John Fremont. Titus next surfaced in Jacksonville, Florida, serving as mayor, collector of customs and member of the state legislature. He even ran unsuccessfully for governor. Along the way, Titus married Mary Hopkins, daughter of a wealthy planter in Darien, Georgia.

How did Henry Titus come to Titusville? When war broke out, the South had no more rabid supporter. But Titus wasn't just a "supporter." He was a *doer* who had to be in the thick of things. Most nineteenth-century frontier men could handle small boats, and when the enterprising Titus saw how be could combine his Southern patriotism with making money as a blockade runner, he knew he had found his calling. Other sailors of fortune had established themselves on popular runs to places like Jacksonville and New Smyrna, but Sand Point, at the tip of the Indian River, offered a splendid "franchise" location for a newcomer. For good measure, Titus established a hack service that hauled goods from the river to the wharf on Lake Harney, which flowed into the St. Johns River and up to desperately needy Jacksonville.

No one knows how many successful runs Titus made between Nassau and the Indian River. All we know is when he got caught.

The captain of the *Charm*, whose adjudication was described on page 161, was none other than Henry Titus. When Henry Crane and his crew surprised him at Indian River Inlet on February 23, 1863, James Armour would have been among the men who seized his boat and sent it to Key West. Armour may even have gotten his "keeper of prize ships" job in Key West mainly to make sure that swashbucklers like Henry Titus didn't try to sneak into the island harbor and take back the *Charm*.

Titus insisted that the *Charm* was unarmed and owned by a non-combatant (the actual owner may have been Titus himself) who had no allegiance to either side. Seizing it was nothing short of piracy — especially because the assailants were not in navy uniform and came from an unmarked civilian riverboat. That he should despise Armour as part of the capturing crew is understandable. That they were on speaking terms when they discussed crabwood at the lighthouse nine years later is puzzling indeed. Since Charlie Pierce, who reported the conversation, was a mere boy of eight at the time, it may be that a lot of undetected acrimony was exchanged.

Now for James Armour's perspective. The criminal cases of the U. S. District Court for Southern Florida (Key West) have also been lost and no trace can be found so far of Armour's being convicted for "piracy" or anything else. Yet, it seems unlikely that anyone would make such a statement to the Light House Board if he couldn't count on records to back it up.

It's possible that some time in the early days of the war, Armour may have done something (trying a blockade run or appropriating military property?) that got him hauled off to Key West and tossed in the hoosegow. Perhaps in late 1862, when Henry Crane came to Key West and persuaded the admiral to let him form a volunteer vigilante corps, he asked that Armour be sprung from jail to join him because his knowledge of navigating Jupiter Narrows was so valuable.

But another scenario is more likely. Crane had known Armour since their days together in Tampa and it seems more plausible that Armour was already with him before he first walked out on the beach to signal the *Sagamore* that he'd like to come aboard and discuss an idea.

If so, that would make Henry Titus the sort of man who would tell a bald faced lie and bribe a former Armour assistant to achieve his aims.

Let us continue the guesswork in answering the other charges against James Armour. Operating on the theory that no one performs extraordinary deeds that are not justified in his/her own mind, the Jupiter lighthouse keeper might have responded to Henry Titus as follows.

"Did I 'steal' other people's property by scavenging for washed-up merchandise? You must realize that we are in a wilderness here. The nearest 'store' of any kind is a 10-by-10 foot palmetto hut 35 miles upriver in St. Lucie. Anything we appropriate would spoil or soon gain a coat of mildew if we didn't put it to good use immediately. Besides, we are so poorly provisioned by the Lighthouse Service that it's understood by all that we must supplement our supplies by garnering as much as we can from the sea.

"Henry Titus? Henry *Titus*? Please! How do you suppose he is compensated as a 'special agent' for insurance companies? He gets a percentage of the value of any goods recovered from the wreck. I just happened to be there first. Besides, he certainly seemed to enjoy that French cognac I offered him when he stopped by the lighthouse.

"Did I cause ships to wreck because I let the light go out in order to save fuel? No. I had to let the light go out at times because those laggards who run the Lighthouse Service tenders didn't deliver our supplies on time. Yes, I sold some oil in Titusville, but it was rancid lard. Lighthouse Service rules prohibit the use of rancid oil in the lamp, but don't prevent it being used for other purposes.

"Did I hire only cronies and relatives? I didn't at first, but I soon found that they made the most reliable employees. I never gave them special favors.

"Did I spend too much time away from the lighthouse? The District authorities know full well the cramped, deplorable condition of the keeper's house, which was only built for two families in the first place. Besides, I have a young wife who just had her first baby. Raising an infant a hundred miles from a doctor is risky, as Almeda's parents kept telling me. I wanted to be near my wife and baby, so I spent some time in Titusville. The lighthouse was left in capable hands."

(Armour's second daughter, Mary Elizabeth, was being raised at the lighthouse when, at age two, she suddenly began having convulsions. James and Almeda loaded their sailboat with sand. On top of the sand they built a wood fire so they could heat water and apply alternating hot and cold packs to Mary's forehead as they plied the hundred miles to Titusville to see a doctor. But Mary died before they reached it.) [12]

The bottom line may be that both Titus and Armour were right in their own eyes. Both had done what they could to survive in a turbulent period. As soldiers of fortune, both had "sailed close to the wind" on matters of law and ethics. But the difference may have been this: bombastic, blustering Henry Titus was known to sit on the steps of his Titus House with a shotgun across his lap because he had so many enemies (even though he gave generously to local civic causes). Quiet, courtly James Armour had many friends and admirers (even though he was beginning to acquire land on a scale suggesting far more income than a lighthouse keeper's salary).

The bottom line for the Light House Board was a terse communication on March 26, 1873. Seventh District Inspector Albert Kantz had visited Jupiter and tendered his report. "Removal of the keeper cannot be recommended," he wrote. [13]

A thousand miles away in Washington, the pros and cons were simply too muddy to see through. And besides, where were they going to find another head keeper for such a forlorn place?

Increasingly, almost imperceptibly at times, more activity began to swirl about Jupiter, with the lighthouse usually at its center. For one thing, Lake Worth began to be settled, starting with Hannibal Pierce. With wife Margaretta always busy at her "new" Wheeler and Wilson sewing machine, the three Pierces had re-clad themselves and even saved a little money. By the summer of 1873 Margaretta's brother Will Moore had joined them in Jupiter and all were itching for their own place. This time it would be as the second home on 23-mile-long Lake Worth. After outfitting one of the *Victor's* lifeboats with a sail, they were off that fall to try their luck. Within a year or two, another dozen or so families would stake homesteads on Lake Worth and begin to surmount a serious set of obstacles to raising crops for market. As the community grew along the lake, the intrepid farmers would stop by the lighthouse in their little skiffs to borrow a tool or ask James Armour's advice about the business of survival. [14]

Mostly, the lighthouse became a magnet for a growing number of hunters, surveyors, scientific expeditions and Indian traders. Word about the splendid pompano and tarpon fishing in the Loxahatchee and the "Garden of Eden" along Lake Worth was beginning to filter north among farmers and work its way into popular adventure magazines like *Harper's Weekly* and *New Century*. It was now common for hunting and fishing parties to camp on the river just outside the lighthouse reservation. Indians showed up at any and all hours, bringing venison, honey and buckskin to sell or swap for lighthouse stores. They had one price and it never changed: a dime a pound for venison and a dollar for a buckskin. [15]

Early on, the Armours learned to be gracious and unruffled at the sight of a boatload of visitors approaching the lighthouse dock at all hours. And sometimes one didn't even get *that* much notice. One day Almeda Armour turned around from her stove to see an Indian sitting at the kitchen table staring at her silently. On another occasion she opened the door to the keepers' house to find a tall Seminole with a knife clenched in his teeth. She suppressed the urge to scream (the men were all off the grounds anyway). As she gulped and stared the Indian ceremoniously handed her the knife. Turns out that the gesture was sign language for friendship. He merely wanted permission to camp for the night.

James Armour continued to face the usual frontier problems and improvise his own solutions. The lighthouse withstood a major hurricane in the fall of 1876, and in 1879 the tower shook during what may have been Florida's first recorded earthquake. On January 12, according to the U.S. Coast and Geodetic Survey, South Florida recorded shocks of thirty seconds each at 11:45 and 11:55 p.m. Up at Cape Canaveral light, the tower shook so severely that oil was sprayed all over the lens. Perhaps it answers why, when a year or so later Armour was climbing the ladder from the gallery to the walk-around above it when the iron rung broke in two, nearly plunging him backward and almost over the railing. Dr James Henshall, a hunter-sportsman who was staying with Armour at the time, wrote that "a less cool-headed man than Armour would probably have been dashed to the ground, but he is noted for intrepidity and level-headedness." [16]

Seventh District reports indicate the same old problems at Jupiter, enough to make the inspector renew his plea to headquarters to obtain "relief from his charge" at Jupiter. As usual, flocks of ducks had knocked out three glass panes in the lantern in 1874 and replacements didn't arrive until May 1876, just a few months before the big hurricane knocked out even more panes. The inspector's quarterly report for January 1874 cited the need for a separate kitchen building, then decided that all of the keepers' quarters were "entirely insufficient." [17]

The keepers' house, in fact, bred tension both among its occupants and between Armour and his supervisors in the Seventh District. The one-and-a-half story house was built originally with two four-room apartments. Fitting three families in meant carving up the two units in awkward ways (and perhaps explaining Henry Titus' claim that one keeper was invariably at Titusville). Records show the house was "repaired" in 1875 and "thoroughly overhauled" in 1880, but it was like putting a tuxedo on a pig. Armour insisted that the only answer was a separate new house for his growing family. [18]

In early 1883 Armour got his wish, but not without some begrudging snickers by Seventh District Engineer W. H. Heuer. In a letter to the Board commenting on Inspector Kantz' approval of the project, Huer wrote in part,

In my report to the Board of July 31ˢᵗ, 1880 (the station was thoroughly overhauled in that month) will be found a complete statement of repairs made at this place. At a place like Jupiter, where there are 3 keepers with very little work to do, one would suppose that they would try and make small repairs and keep their building in order, but it is difficult to get them to do anything other than manage the light. They are even too lazy to make monthly reports of the condition of their station. [19]

Heuer's letter enclosed copies of Armour's handwritten report for September 30, 1882. In it he had cited the need for new windows and frames in the tower, "top to bottom" repairs in the dwelling and the oil house. Said the keeper: "The oil room floor is rotten and will not hold the oil butts. I have put on some two inch planks for stands, which does very well." [20]

Lazy or not, Armour got his house. Materials were delivered by barge on February 3, 1883, and by April of the same year Inspector Kantz was reporting the whole project complete. On April 25 Engineer Heuer was able to tell the Board in Washington,

I sent by today's mail in a separate package two photographic views of the Light Station at Jupiter Inlet, FL. One [shows] *a view of the new dwelling just created and the other of the old dwelling, which has been thoroughly overhauled and made almost as good as new.*

The station is at an out-of-the-way place and difficult of access, and has been placed in such good order recently that it is hoped no more repairs or renovations will be required there for several years. The [photos] *were made by the assistant light keeper at the station.* [21]

Indeed, the visual history of the lighthouse, aside from George Meade's blueprints, really begins in 1883 with the photo of the crew at work on renovating the old keeper's house. For that we can thank Melville Evans Spencer, a millwright from Pennsylvania who had come to Titusville and worked for Henry Titus as a carpenter while he built himself a boat on his off-days. He sailed his *Bon Ton* down the Indian River in September 1878, signed on as assistant keeper with James Armour, and would stay on for five years before joining the stream of homesteaders to Lake Worth.

Curiously, Armour, the man who never missed a commercial opportunity, may have been the cause of Spencer's fame today. According to one lighthouse visitor, it was the captain who suggested that his assistant learn this intriguing new trade and that the two of them split the proceeds of a new business selling photos to hunters and fishermen who stopped by expecting hospitality. Soon Spencer was lining up anyone who would pose: Indians, shark fishermen, people holding up their catches, James Armour with a trophy wildcat and, of course, the lighthouse from a dozen angles. Although Spencer and his works helped shed more light on nineteenth century Jupiter than just about anyone else, it's interesting to note that in a 12-page memoir he dictated in 1936 at age 85, he never once mentioned his photography. [22]

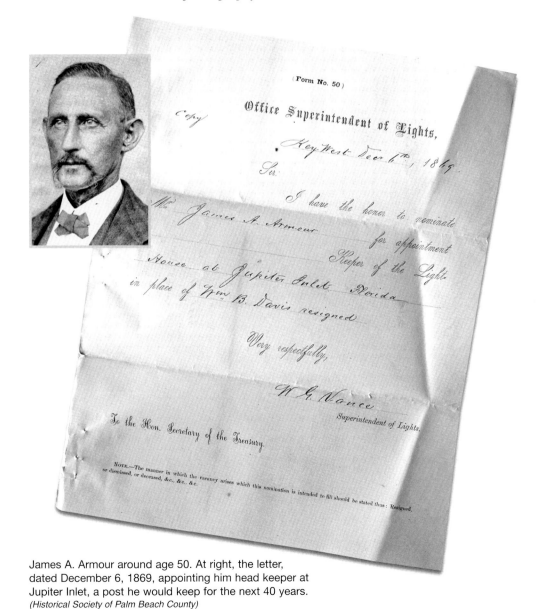

James A. Armour around age 50. At right, the letter, dated December 6, 1869, appointing him head keeper at Jupiter Inlet, a post he would keep for the next 40 years. *(Historical Society of Palm Beach County)*

The first of three letters Henry Titus, the major domo of Titusville, wrote to the Light House Board calling Armour a "scoundrel" and unworthy of his post. The charred fringes are from a government archives fire in 1920. *(National Archives and Records Administration)*

ABOVE: A riverside view of the wharf at Titusville (circa 1890), showing several warehouses and a steamboat loading up. *(State of Florida Archives)*

RIGHT: Henry T. Titus, a one-time soldier of fortune, moved to Sand Point to relieve his rheumatism, and soon had the town re-named for himself. His hotel and liquor importing business were the town's economic mainstays. *(Historical Society of North Brevard, Inc.)*

BELOW: When the blustery, combative Titus died, the local *Florida Star* gave the event all of 14 words in its column of miscellaneous gossip. However, the publisher had no problem charging the deceased with one more ad for his three businesses. *(North Brevard Public Library)*

—The moon quarters Aug. 16th at 11.31 a. m.
—The thermometer stands at 76 at 9:00 a. m.
—We are having delightful weather.
—We notice Messrs. White and Allen from down the river.
—Business is livelier than common at this time of the year.
—Our people are, as usual, grumbling about the taxes. How natural!
—Titusville has lost an energetic citizen in the death of Col. H. T. Titus.
—The proprietor of the STAR expects to build us a new office in his new block this Fall.
—The Fall Term of Court will be held in the commodious building of Capt. T. W. Lund.
—No Enterprise Mail via Smyrna yesterday. Our Northern mail facilities are bad—bad enough.
—Mr. W. H. Gleason, well known to parties on the river several years ago, was in town on Saturday.
—Mr. Fisher has had a new smoke stack built for his steam saw mill. Mr. J. W. Zeller's was the builder.
—Our latest advices from Washington report the President better and improving as rapidly as could be expected.
—Judging from appearances, our new Board of County Commissioners

AURANTIA MILLS.
PLAINED LUMBER
a speciality.
Matched Flooring, and Ceiling.
NOVELTY & COMMON
SIDING.
Orders filled promptly and at short notice; address Titusville Fla.
12   3m   F. B. SACKETT.

HENRY T. TITUS, Titusville, Fla.
General Marine Underwriter's Agent
American and Foreign,
——also——
Notary Public at Large for the State of Florida.

DEALER IN PURE LIQUORS.
Imported wines, ales etc. Old Port and Sherry wines kept expressly for Invalids, warranted pure
The Titus House is now open for the winter and Hacks will connect with the boats at Salt Lake.

THE   TRADING   SLOOP.

RIGHT: James Armour in early sixties.
(Historical Society of Palm Beach County)

FAR RIGHT: Construction crews
renovating the old keepers' house
(foreground) for two families and
building the new head keeper's quarters.
(Historical Society of Palm Beach County)

BELOW: The completed keepers'
quarters at Jupiter, 1884.
(Historical Society of Palm Beach County)

BELOW RIGHT: James Armour,
approaching 80 and retirement.
(Historical Society of Palm Beach County)

Chapter 16

Settlers

By 1876, a decade after the War Between the States ended and the year of the young nation's Centennial celebration, the Indian River was still a wilderness viewed by northerners with guarded fascination. No one accustomed to the comforts of civilization would venture south below Sanford, where Lake Monroe formed the link between South Florida and the St. Johns River transportation system. Any stranger who sailed into the Indian River was a daring adventurer whose only interest could be hunting, fishing, surveying or collecting specimens for a museum.

Game fish, shellfish and wildlife were in such abundance that visitors killed them in a reckless frenzy that mirrored the slaughter of buffalo on the Great Plains. Witness these excerpts from the letters of Francis Stebbins, the Michigan furniture manufacturer who had claimed to view Indian mounds surrounding Jupiter Lighthouse during one of the ten winters he spent on the Indian River:

February 6, 1879, (the first day after sailing off from Titusville). "Just before noon the warm sun brought out the huge lizards, and the cry of "there's a gator" from the pilot-house brought us to the front with our rifles — for I started to Florida with 'malice'…against alligators and a good Winchester in my hands. In less than an hour its deadly 44-calibre pellets sent three fine fellows to their rest and furnished fifteen hundred pounds of meat for the buzzards."

February 19, 1879. "Talk about fishing! You ought to have been with us! Yesterday, four of us caught three hundred pounds in two hours of surf fishing. Today I went out, and in less than an hour caught over one hundred pounds."

February 2, 1881. "About ten o'clock a huge porpoise broke water [in the Indian River] about six rods distant. As he rose I sent a Winchester ball "plumb" through his body, about a foot aft of his forward fin…. He tried to swim away from us but I got another ball into his head, and he turned up a dead porpoise.

February 3, 1882. "This afternoon two of us went ashore with our guns. One discharge of both barrels of my Parker brought down seven ducks."

March 10, 1882, (after arriving by night at what is now Pelican Island National Wildlife Refuge). "We could hear their cawing in the trees, and…banged away all our barrels where we thought they ought to be. We picked up a white ibis, two egrets and a fine man-of-war or "frigate bird," which measures seven feet from tip to tip of wings."

One carcass after another was simply left to rot. Why? Stebbins was no kid with more testosterone than judgment; he was in his sixties, a solid citizen of Adrian, Michigan, who had recently run for mayor. Why such destructive exuberance? He reflects on the question lamely in a couple of letters:

February 6, 1879, (after shooting alligators as he cruised along the shoreline). "I really feel a little sorry for these monsters; and the wanton shooting of them is possibly inexcusable in a strict code of life, but they are such a concentrated combination of repulsive ugliness, without a single redeeming trait, that one can easily give way to the organ of destructiveness when he sees one, and has a good rifle in his hands. Besides, what will become of the national bird of the cotton belt, the pet scavenger of the south – the buzzard – if he doesn't have something to 'scavenge' upon!"

February 21, 1882. "We have a great love for ducks, and we shoot ducks to keep them from the mouths of the alligators, and we shoot the alligators to keep them from killing the ducks. Thus, we kill two birds with one stone." [1]

In the 1880s the immediate area around the lighthouse began to sprout with people – not enough to call Jupiter an actual town with a mayor and all, but certainly a "settlement." The first attraction was Lake Worth, because if it hadn't been for pioneer farmers stopping at Jupiter on their way between Titusville and an area that would soon become known as Palm Beach, Jupiter would still be no more than a scenic lighthouse to delight passers-by.

The reason they didn't pass by, or so quickly, was that you couldn't get to the tip of Lake Worth by inland waters. Oh you could have an ocean steamer drop people and supplies on the beach opposite Lake Worth, or you could usually squeeze a skiff through the shallow, unpredictable inlet that the local men had cut through with picks and shovels. But if you were a farmer, you had no reliable way to sail your fresh tomatoes or pineapples up to Titusville before the sun and wind turned them to mush.

If you wanted regular mail, you still had to rely on a frontier system. The only regular service came from Titusville to St. Lucie (James Paine, now collecting a Yankee paycheck as postmaster) once a week by small sail boat. Anything addressed to a Jupiter or Lake Worth resident would stay at St. Lucie until somebody picked up the mail for himself and all his neighbors. If he were only going to Jupiter, he'd leave the bundle at the lighthouse. If and when someone said they were on their way to Lake Worth, Captain Armour would give him the whole pouch to distribute along the shoreline. Charles Pierce recalled that no one ever refused to deliver every piece of mail and "not a paper or letter was ever lost." [2]

So, Jupiter's transition from outpost to town began at the old Indian haulover, the thousand feet or so thicket of rivulets and sawgrass trails that continued to baffle anyone but Indians trying to reach Jupiter by inland water from the top of Lake Worth. The first, albeit weak, remedy for the haulover came in 1874 when two men were assigned to place stakes in the water and tie pieces of white cloth to their tops so that boaters could see the boat channel over the tall sawgrass. The problem was that they used fresh-cut limbs. In a few months the green shoots had blended in with a million others like them, and the cloth markers had rotted away.

It was time to get serious. In November 1878 the men of Lake Worth set out with their tools from home, bent on building a thousand-foot wooden tramway over the haulover. They had already ordered cast-iron wheels and axles from Jacksonville. They had also scoured the beach for wood and found enough 4 x 4s from wrecked ships and spilled cargoes to use for tracks. Then they found enough other washed up lumber and sawed it into equal-sized ties between the tracks. When it was all hammered together and the cast-iron wheels and axles arrived, all they needed was to hoist a sailboat onto the iron chassis. Once re-packed with farm produce, the boat was pushed northward along what became nicknamed the "Lake Worth Sawgrass and Jupiter Railroad" until it reached the navigable part of Lake Worth Creek.

One innovation begat another. More tourists were coming down in winters purely to enjoy Lake Worth and scout sites for vacation homes. At the time, Will

Moore had been working as an assistant lighthouse keeper while building a 28-foot, broad boat in his spare time. When it was done, he quit the lighthouse post to launch a charter service for Lake Worth hunters and fishermen.

Along Lake Worth, H. P. Dye couldn't see the sense of each farmer laboring a couple of weeks on the Indian River to take his products to Titusville. He built a much larger boat named the *Gazelle* and announced he was ready to haul people and produce all the way to Jacksonville.

Down in today's Palm Beach, Elisha Newton "Cap" Dimick was tired of raising tomatoes and seeing half his crop spoil. With winter tourists asking where they could stay, he expanded his home into the lake's first resort, the Cocoanut Grove House Hotel.

Fine northern ladies in long white dresses didn't enjoy being hoisted like cargo out of a boat and into the crude carriage on the makeshift wooden "railroad," so Cap Dimick got a better idea. He started a seven-mile mule-drawn hack service from the tip of the lake to the docks at Jupiter. Lurching over a sugar sand trail crisscrossed by lumpy tree roots still wasn't a lady's idea of comfort, but the misery passed more quickly.

In 1885, in a belated effort to increase the number of shipwreck survivors, a government Life Saving Station was built on the beach at Jupiter. Captaining its six-man crew was Armour's former assistant and bosom friend, Charles Carlin. Like the lighthouse, the Life Saving Station was an outpost and not part of a budding settlement's economic underpinning. But Carlin and his wife Mary would soon contribute in a big way. They had just built a large frame home on the river, a mile or so from the Life Saving station, and almost as soon as they'd moved in they were finding strangers on their doorstep. Since Jupiter was the end of the line for passenger boats from Titusville, people would simply get off and wander about wondering where they could get a bite to eat or spend the night. Perhaps with the success of the Cocoanut Grove House Hotel in mind, the Carlins soon opened The Carlin House. Almost instantly it became a thriving little resort and the center of social life in Jupiter.

Meanwhile, the little burst of settlement and economic activity was not lost on the enterprising James Armour. He seemed interested in owning a piece of the area's forthcoming prosperity no matter where it might pop up. According to Charles Pierce, he entered a homestead claim at the south end of Lake Worth in 1875. His land ran from the beach, across a large hammock and over to a marsh on the west side of the lake in what would today be Manalapan.

He "sent two men to clear some land and construct a house," and told them to go to the ever-plentiful beach for the lumber they needed. [3]

Sometime around 1880, Armour also built a large, four-bedroom home on Cocoanut Point on Jupiter Island. It was also the site of the first Hobe Sound post office. According to the *Tropical Sun* (the area's first newspaper) in 1891, Armour's son Will recalled that "Because his father had to spend much of his time at the lighthouse, a man named Allen lived at the Hobe Sound place and tended the post office."

One night, Will Armour relates, his father sailed upriver from the lighthouse and saw the Hobe Sound house in flames. "It was later learned that Allen had taken the ashes out of the stove and placed them in the can on the back porch before he went to bed. They were still hot and set the place afire." [4]

That would no doubt be one Dwight Allen, a happy-go-lucky former sailor who used to make jaws drop open when he climbed to the top of the lighthouse tower and walked around on his hands. The keeper rolls show that Allen's tenure as a lighthouse assistant began June 25, 1885, and ended on April 1, 1886. Under the column that lists the reason for leaving, it reads *"removed."*

Armour's prize acquisition seems to be a 48.25 acre lot abutting the 50-acre lighthouse campus to the west and covering part of today's commercial section of Tequesta. He filed a claim for it in 1884, just after the government opened up the former Fort Jupiter military reservation for private development. It's likely that Armour owned other local land as well. [5]

When did Jupiter officially become a "town?" Although it wouldn't have a mayor or a budget or paved roads until 1925, one could say that Jupiter graduated from merely being home to a lighthouse and a life saving station somewhere between December 23, 1885, and July 4, 1889.

The first date had nothing to do with Jupiter *per* se: it was when the Jacksonville, Tampa and Key West Railroad opened up 41 new miles of track from Sanford to Titusville. It meant that anyone from up north could take a train down the eastern seaboard to Sanford. There they'd change trains for the last twelve-mile leg to Titusville. Waiting for them on the 1,500-foot wharf at Titusville would be a paddlewheeler run by the Indian River Steamboat Company, the railroad's wholly-owned subsidiary. Soon the steamship line was making a dozen stops on its way south, as little riverfront communities sprang up in its path. If passengers took the full 140-mile, 18-hour trip to Jupiter, waiting for them was the steamboat *Chattahoochee*, which had been converted to a floating hotel on the river. Folks could spend a few overnights fishing right off the hotel or exploring Jupiter, then either return on another steamer or take the stagecoach down to Lake Worth.

But that wasn't all. The Indian River Steamboat Company wasn't just aiming to take passengers to tiny Jupiter. It wanted access over land and inland waterway to the growing tourist attractions of Lake Worth and even points south.

So, not long after the new Sanford-Titusville line was completed, the holding company formed another subsidiary, the Jupiter and Lake Worth Railroad, to run a narrow-gauge track over the 7.5 miles that separated Jupiter from the tip of Lake Worth at the hamlet of Juno. Why narrow-gauge? The parent company had recently bought the St. Johns & Halifax Railroad and rebuilt its old narrow-gauge tracks to conform to the rest of its equipment. But instead of scrapping the obsolete narrow-gauge system, why not use seven or so miles worth of it to get people from Jupiter to Juno? After all, it didn't have to connect to another railroad – just to steamboats at either end.

Next problem: how to get the locomotives, passenger cars, tracks and timbers down to Jupiter. Solution: build a barge in Titusville. The *Loxahatchee*, claimed to be the biggest barge ever seen in the Indian River, was just a flat surface with a crane, piledriver and pilot house on top. When the "steam scow," as she was nicknamed, lumbered off southward, a *Florida Star* reporter mused about her capacity to deliver freight on the river when her railroad work was done. "With her long projecting square bow," he wrote, "she can land freight at the shore wherever there is about two feet of water. And gracious, what a load of oranges she would be able to gather at one trip up the river." [6]

Waiting for the *Loxahatchee* in Jupiter, across the river from the lighthouse, workers were building a large wharf, girded with thick timbers so it could support a train backing up to receive passengers and cargo from a steamer. At the same time, the steamboat company brought down the one-time pride of its fleet, the *Rockledge*, to serve as another floating hotel – perhaps for the construction project's supervisors. As the *Jacksonville Times Union* noted: "The large steamboat *Rockledge*, which does excellent duty as a hotel, is moored about a mile from the inlet, and nearly opposite the mouth of Jupiter Sound, as the lower reach of the Indian River is called. From the upper deck of the *Rockledge* there is a good view of the Jupiter Inlet and the far reaches of the Indian River and Hobe Sound to the north." [7]

As a camp full of transient workers hammered on the wharf and scoured the surrounding woods for wood to make cross-ties for the track, the Indian River was enjoying its brief but glorious age of steamboat travel. No less than 25 steamboat companies plied the river, from small freight haulers to 200-foot paddlewheelers with white-gloved stewards and entertaining captains. They called at 25 towns and landings with names like Cocoa, Tropic, Eau Gallie, Melbourne, Sebastian, St. Lucie, and Eden (see page 240).

Let's take a typical steamer trip from Titusville, using the letters and diaries of travelers to supply our imagery. For our vessel we'll insist on the *St. Lucie*, built for $30,000 at Wilmington, Delaware, expressly for use in the shallow, placid inland waters. With a length of 110 feet and a 22-foot beam, she's a trim little passenger and freight boat, recently added to the growing fleet of the Indian River Steamboat Company.

The stern paddlewheeler has three decks. The first one houses two high-pressure engines aft and a boiler towards the stern, with freight piled up in between. We climb a stairs to reach the passenger saloon, which stretches almost the length of the boat. Its forward and after sections are pleasant sitting rooms with rattan settees and antique oak card tables. In the center are the staterooms and a dining hall. All the woodwork is painted white and trimmed with gilt.

The 14 staterooms are only 6 by 6 feet, each with two berths of woven wire springs and soft, comfortable mattresses. Small, to be sure, but you'll want to spend as much time as possible up on the third-level hurricane deck, with its spacious promenade and bright colored awnings.

The company has other boats as commodious as the *St. Lucie*, but there's only one Captain Steve Bravo. Young and gallant, a descendant of the Minorcans who came to farm around New Smyrna a century before, Captain Bravo, they say, has enough stories and legends about the Indian River to regale his guests all the way to Jupiter.

There he is now, checking his passenger list as he stands beside his sternwheeler in the late afternoon at Titusville. Sea gulls and pelicans glide in lazy circles, hoping to mooch some scraps from the cooks. Except for their raucous cries as they maneuver for position, the only other sound is that of the mooring ropes rubbing on the pilings.

Captain Bravo just returned from Jupiter the night before, along with several thousand pineapples and hampers of beans that were quickly unloaded onto the railroad pier for the ride to Jacksonville. In their place went a hundred kegs of nails and several thousand feet of yellow pine lumber, now stacked on the main deck.

Soon the dock becomes alive with voices as passengers arrive, some on foot from Titus House and others by horse and carriage. Stewards take their luggage and they follow up the gangplank onto the decks of the *St. Lucie*.

Now the paddle wheels begin to turn, and startled mullet scurry for safety, their silvery sides reflecting the glint of the sun's low angle. Passengers watch along the railings as Captain Bravo blows the ship's whistle and the paddle wheel begins to move us away from the dock and towards the river's main channel.

Almost at once it's time for a sunset display on the Indian River. One of our lady passengers sits in a wicker settee and pens these notes in her diary:

Sleepy gentians, buttercups, daisies and cattails turn their heavy-laden blossoms toward the drooping sun. As the great orange globe dips beyond the forest treetops, colors flake gloriously in the sky as if a magic fairy wand had lightly touched the great dome of heaven. Clouds of a hundred different shades and colors are seen floating apparently toward one goal. All seem to be slowly dissolving after the sun.

Now, all of the colors have vanished along the river, and darkness has come completely, silently. The moon rises slowly over the rim of the steamer and stands as sentinel over all the land and proclaims that night upon her throne reigns supremely over the Indian River. [8]

It is time for dinner, and it does not disappoint: fresh oysters, fresh greens, and pompano just out of the water. Baked ham, scalloped potatoes, good wines and cherry cobbler. After a leisurely coffee and cordial, we make our way to the hurricane deck where we stroll or lounge in chairs as a chorus of deckhands sing Gospel songs. Then we, too, sing when Captain Steve brings out his guitar and strums old songs we all know. As the curtain of night draws tight, the blanket of stars draws around us so that we can almost touch them. It's now eleven and our berth beckons, but not before having a little of what the stewards call "lunch" to sustain us for the night.

We wake to a thud as day begins to break. The *St. Lucie* is nosing into the wharf at Fort Pierce (opposite Indian River Inlet) where there's a large Indian trading store just behind the dock. Despite the early hour, the Seminoles are ready to invite us in. The women are well clad and even fashionable. But the men make ladies turn their heads and children giggle. They are covered only by light calico shirts, some long but others all too short for a lady's eyes. [9]

It's soon on to Eden Landing at mile 111 on our voyage. At 8 a.m. we dock beside a large pineapple plantation and enjoy a breakfast of eggs, venison steak, sausage, fish and oysters. Then it's once again up to the hurricane deck where we enjoy a sharp contrast to the star-filled sky of the previous evening. The sun sparkles on the water and we see so many ducks that at times they seem to form islands. At mile 118 we pass Waveland and its House of Refuge, where we get a rare glimpse of waves breaking in the ocean.

Around ten in the morning we enter the Jupiter Narrows, an entirely different ecology from the broad Indian River mainstream. Now the river breaks into several channels lined with mangrove islands. The path we take is only a few feet wider than the boat in some places, and so shallow that we sometimes feel the hull grating on the bottom. We stop still several times in the process of negotiating a sharp turn and for the first time Captain Bravo has a rather grim face as we get a glimpse of him in the wheelhouse.

His serious demeanor is understandable, our steward tells us. Most of the paddlewheelers were built for wide rivers and they've already been stuck several times on sandbars in Jupiter Narrows, even though they have average drafts of three feet. Once, the bulky *Cinderella* got stuck in the Narrows for several days, causing the steamboat company to run supply shuttles back and forth and passengers to miss many a connection. Sometimes, the only way off a sandbar is to lighten the load by transferring cargo and passengers to other boats.

But not today. Captain Steve gives a wave and a smile to all as we clear the last of the mangroves and emerge into the broad Loxahatchee. Passengers who plan to be picked up by an ocean steamer for the "outside" trip to Lake Worth or the Caribbean will be deposited on the beach by the inlet, where they will camp until their ship looms into sight and sends out a longboat. The rest of us will pull alongside the moored *Chattahoochee* which, they say, is just as commodious as the *St. Lucie*. Stewards are waiting as we bump alongside. Soon we'll be fishing from its decks and perhaps even catching our next meal! [10]

_____

On July 4, 1889, the last touches had been put on the new Jupiter and Lake Worth Railroad and its parent company went all out to celebrate its achievement with its potential customers on this Independence Day. The

Tropical Sun had just moved its press to Juno and owner-editor Guy Metcalf was on hand in Palm Beach at 8:30 a.m. when the steamer *Lake Worth* boarded 75 locals.

Once they sailed into Juno at the lake's tip, they boarded a train – just one coach and one flat car – and "away we went to Jupiter," gushed Metcalf. In weeks to come, engineer Blus Rice might stop to shoot a large alligator in his path or allow passengers to take their own potshots at deer or turkeys along the way, but on this trip it was all spit and polish.

At 11 a.m. they were met by James Armour and the captain of the *Chattahoochee*, who had brought his steamer-hotel to the wharf. The Lake Worth contingent filed on board and was met by fifty or so of the folks who now lived along the Loxahatchee. Reported Metcalf:

The table was set in the cabin, and…the table not being large enough, the old people and children were served first, after which came the middle aged and young. But no one went away hungry, for there was enough to spare and all kinds of good things…
Visiting the Lighthouse and Signal Station [a newly-built Weather Bureau post on the lighthouse grounds], *strolling on the beach and sailing around the harbor were some of the diversions indulged in by the picnickers to pass away the time. We left for home on the train at 4:15 p.m., being accompanied to the head of the lake by all our Jupiter friends. A little time was spent getting the steamer off the mud, where the falling tide had left her, but we finally bid our Jupiter friends adieu and started down the lake. The trip down was a delightful one and enlivened by our singing patriotic songs.* [11]

They sang "The Battle Hymn of the Republic" and "When Johnny Comes Marching Home," with the old Unionists bellowing just a bit louder than the rest. They sang "Dixie" and "I'm a Good Ole' Rebel," with the Confederate veterans giving it their all. The colored stewards and deck hands sang "Kingdom Coming" and "We Are Coming from the Cotton Fields" to great applause. Then everyone together sang "The Star Spangled Banner" and "My Country 'Tis of Thee."

The modern age had come to South Florida, and editor Metcalf hailed it with his usual exuberance. "Just think of riding on a steamboat and in rail cars in this country – and all in one day!"

But something else had also come to South Florida.

That day, 24 years after so bloody a war, America had become one nation again. South Florida was on its way to becoming America's most cosmopolitan region. And tiny Jupiter had come together for the first time as a *community* — the essential ingredient in becoming a real "town."

Shark hunting/shooting was a favorite weekend sport for locals, often camping on shore near the lighthouse. *(Historical Society of Palm Beach County)*

ABOVE: Assistant keeper Melville Spencer always seemed to be on hand to photograph big or exotic catches. Here it's a giant sawfish, with James Armour at center, right. *(Historical Society of Palm Beach County)*

BELOW: Lake Worth pioneer Benjamin Lainhart (left) poses with Armour and two of the latter's children behind a small whale that wandered into Jupiter Inlet. *(Historical Society of Palm Beach County)*

ABOVE: Hunters who made their way down Indian River invariably topped off their trips with a visit to Jupiter Light. *(Historical Society of Palm Beach County)*

RIGHT: No one enjoyed better hunting and fishing than the keepers. Armour himself bagged this panther on the lighthouse grounds. *(Historical Society of Palm Beach County)*

LEFT: Dwight Allen, a happy-go-lucky assistant keeper, made jaws drop open by walking on his hands atop the lighthouse. *(Historical Society of Palm Beach County)*

BELOW: The wharf built across from the lighthouse in 1889 would transfer passengers and cargo from river steamers to the newly-built, 7.5-mile "Celestial Railroad." *(State of Florida Archives)*

ABOVE: The *Santa Lucia*, another popular steamer, timed its arrivals in Jupiter to drop passengers on the beach just outside the inlet. If all went well, the connecting ocean liner would send a cutter to retrieve the passengers. If it didn't, travelers were expected to camp overnight. *(State of Florida Archives)*

BELOW: The *Rockledge* was a favorite Indian River steamboat. It also served as a floating hotel on the edge of Jupiter Inlet. *(State of Florida Archives)*

ABOVE: Looking west from Jupiter Inlet as a river steamer transfers passengers and cargo at the newly-built railroad wharf. *(State of Florida Archives)*

FAR RIGHT: A ticket on the Tropical Trunk Line, better known as the Celestial Railroad. *(Skip Gladwin Collection)*

1894 | 1895 | 1896 | 1897 | 1898 | 1899 | 1900 | 1901 | 1902 | 1903

20 21 | 22 23 | 24 25 | 26 27 | 28 29 | 30 13 | Nov Dec | Sept Oct | Jul Aug | May Jun | Mar April | Jan Feb

19 | 18 | 17 | 16 | 15 | 14 | 13 | 12 | 11 | 10 | 9 | 8 | 7 | 6 | 5 | 4 | 3 | 2 | 1 DAY

The Tropical Trunk Line.
—GOOD FOR—
ONE FIRST CLASS PASSAGE
JUPITER, FLA.
TO

Lake Worth

WHEN OFFICIALLY STAMPED,

Subject to the following Conditions:

In selling this ticket for passage over other roads, this Company acts only as agent, and assumes no responsibility beyond its own line. The holder hereof in consideration of the reduced rate at which this ticket is sold, agrees with the respective companies over whose roads such holder is to be carried, to use the same **on or before the expiration of date as canceled by punch on the margin of this contract;** and the holder hereof failing to comply with this agreement, either of said Companies may refuse to accept this ticket or any coupons thereof, and demand the full regular fare, which the holder agrees to pay.

If more than one date be canceled, it will not be received for passage by conductors.

None of the companies represented in this ticket will assume any liability on baggage except for wearing apparel, and then only for a sum not exceeding $100.

F. B. Ackerly
Gen'l Passenger Agent.

H. DREW & BRO., PRS., JACKSONVILLE, FLA.

ISSUED BY
THE TROPICAL TRUNK LINE.
ON ACCOUNT OF
Lake Worth Transportation Co.
One First Class Passage
JUNO
TO
Lake Worth

This coupon is not good if detached

Lake Worth

30

B 182-1.

Lake Worth Transportation Co.

RIGHT: One of the most frequent callers at Jupiter was the twin-stacked *St. Augustine*. *(State of Florida Archives)*

BELOW: The Indian River Steamboat Company's popular *St. Lucie* plied the Titusville-to-Jupiter run in the late 1880s, providing white-gloved dining service on the above passenger deck while hauling everything from nail kegs to pineapples on the first level. *(State of Florida Archives)*

ABOVE AND RIGHT: A collage of tickets used on the Celestial Railroad and Indian River Steamboat Company. *(Skip Gladwin Collection)*

RIGHT: The large, broad *Chatahoochee* ran aground so often going through Jupiter Narrows that it proved more useful as a floating hotel at a wharf near the confluence of the Indian and Loxahatchee rivers. Room rates: $3 per day. *(Leonard Dakin photo, Floyd and Marion Rinhart Collection)*

INDIAN RIVER STEAMBOAT CO.

Pass H.L. Hart
F. & Gen'l Mg't
Och. Nav Co
Good During the Year
1893
Unless otherwise ordered.

R.B.Cable.
General Manager

Nº A397

GOOD ON THE
JUPITER & LAKE WORTH RAILWAY.
This Pass is not transferable, and the
person accepting and using it thereby
expressly assumes all risk of accident and
damage to person or baggage

An Indian River Steamboat Cruise

Board the Titusville-Jupiter paddlewheeler in the late 1880s and here are the ports you'd pass (but not necessarily stop at) on your 18-hour journey southward. Names using the possessive (Faber's, Sharp's, etc.) were largely private homes and farms that could summon the steamboat only by signaling from their docks. [12]

Landing	Mile marker		
Titusville	0	Tillman	48
Hardeeville	8	Malabar	50
Courtenay, Merritt Island	11	Micco	57
Faber's	13	Sebastian	62
Sharp's	15	Orchid, Peninsula	69
City Point	16	Enos, Peninsula	72
Merritt, Merritt Island	18	Narrows, Peninsula	75
Cocoa	20	St. Lucie	94
Hardees	21	Fort Pierce	96
Rockledge	22	Ankona	104
Paxton's	24	Eden	111
Magruder's	25	Waveland	118
Georgiana, Merritt Island	27	Jupiter	140
Whitfield's, Merritt Island	29		
Brantley, Merritt Island	33		
Tropic, Merritt Island	37		
Eau Gallie	40		
Melbourne	44		

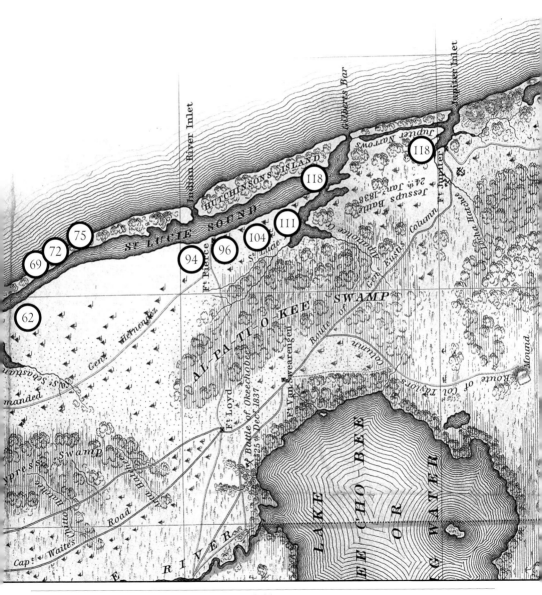

Epilogue

In May 1861 the Lighthouse Service tender *Delaware* was moved to the Second District and renamed the *Wave* for the old tender it replaced. The ship was decommissioned in 1879 after its wooden hull was judged unfit for sea. Perhaps it was the result of all that pounding against the ice in the Delaware River when the ship headed out with its supply of materials for Jupiter Lighthouse.

Hartman Bache, who mentored George Gordon Meade and supervised construction of the Jupiter Lighthouse, was discharged in 1865 after rising to brigadier general in the U.S. Army. He died on October 8, 1872, at the age of 74 and is buried in Woodlands Cemetery, Philadelphia.

In late June of 1862 George Meade was leading his men in the Battle of Glendale (Virginia) when a musket ball tore through his hip, nicked his liver and just missed his spine as it passed through. Meade continued on his horse, exhorting his men, but lost so much blood that he was carried off the field and spent three months in a hospital.

A year later this reserved but resilient man found himself leading the Army of the Potomac against Robert E. Lee in the Battle of Gettysburg. Meade later commanded the Military Division of the Atlantic and, after the war, enjoyed the genteel position of commissioner of Fairmont Park in his beloved Philadelphia. [1]

Meade was feeling in "excellent health" and enjoying a walk with his wife when suddenly stricken with a severe pain in his side – probably an eruption of his war wound. He died five days later on November 6, 1872 at age 57, just a month after his lighthouse mentor and brother-in-law, Hartman Bache, passed away in the same city.

William Franklin Raynolds, who replaced Meade as the Lighthouse Service district engineer in charge of the Jupiter Inlet project, is but another figure in early South Florida history who went on to achieve fame in another capacity. In 1859 he left his district headquarters in Philadelphia to head an expedition mapping the Yellowstone River and other wagon routes to the unsettled West. Although he would later return to serve the Lighthouse Service in the Great Lakes area, he is best known today as the man who first envisioned what is now Yellowstone National Park.

Joseph F. Papy, on whose unlucky watch the Jupiter Lighthouse lighting apparatus was kidnapped (and himself packed off to Key West), understandably seems to have had no interest in another lighthouse assignment. He remained in Key West and was listed in the 1870 census as a grocery clerk living with his 15-year-old daughter Petrona. He married his third wife, Rosario Catala, in 1876, but the 1880 census has him living alone at 75 Duval Street. Papy died in 1905 at the age of 82 and was buried in Key West Cemetery. [2]

Augustus Oswald Lang, the German immigrant who served as assistant lighthouse keeper and helped shut it down in August 1861, met with a cruel fate so common in a lawless frontier. After leaving his lonely hideout on Lake Worth in 1866, he moved up on the St. Lucie River, 12 miles from today's Stuart. With him came Susan Priest, his 15-year-old bride and the daughter of the only other family within miles.

One day in 1873 three scruffy cow catchers, one of them the former lighthouse assistant James Padgett, came to Lang's door, saying their horses had gotten away. They asked if he'd boat them upriver where they thought a path on the other side might lead to the runaways. Once around the bend and out of sight, the men shot their helpful host dead. Hearing shots and fearing the worst, Lang's frantic, pregnant wife ran and stumbled all the way to Fort Pierce for help. A posse of four men, "all that lived in Fort Pierce," returned, but found only the boat with blood and bullet holes in it.

Eventually, one of the killers was shot trying to escape and two were caught. Since Brevard County had no court, the two were tried in neighboring Volusia County, which could at least offer a shed for a makeshift court. Both confessed to stuffing Lang's body in an alligator crawl. Turns out that they wanted to use his cleared property to corral their wild cattle.

They got life imprisonment. A few weeks later, Lang's wife gave birth to a son, Walker Augustus Lang. His father's body was never found. [3]

Earl English, the captain of the Union gunboat *Sagamore*, went on to command ships from Japan to Tripoli. As a rear admiral, he commanded the European station. He retired in 1886 and died in Washington in 1893. [4]

Walter K. Scofield, the young assistant surgeon on the *Sagamore* whose shipboard diary helped illuminate a murky period in South Florida history, served later on the steamer *Union* and then in several naval hospitals. After returning to complete his medical studies at Columbia University, Scofield continued his navy career by being named to a commission that met the czar in St. Petersburg to thank Russia for its assistance to the Union. After seeing duty on four continents, during which he became fluent in six languages, Scofield became a rear admiral and the navy's highest ranking surgeon. Amidst all that, he and his wife Mary Candee raised six children in Stamford, Connecticut.

We last saw John Taylor Wood, John Breckinridge and their four fugitive crewmates leaving Elliot Key in a sunset on their way to freedom in Cuba in 1865. But a serene cruise it wasn't. A terrible summer storm their second day at sea tossed Wood out of the boat (he was quickly rescued) and, in his words, "provided me with the greatest peril in my 19 years experience of the sea." After risking all by pulling alongside an American merchantman and begging for food (the suspicious captain finally tossed down a bag of biscuits), they reached the harbor of Cardenas, Cuba, on June 11. There, the emaciated, dazed arrivals were greeted as heroes, given no rest, outfitted in fine linen suits, and feted in an endless round of parades and parties.

Wood would sail to Halifax, Nova Scotia, become a successful shipping and marine insurance company owner, and one of the town's leading citizens.

John Breckinridge first went to England, then Canada. He returned to Kentucky in 1869 where he quietly practiced law.

Thomas Ferguson, Breckinridge's long-time slave, became violently ill during the storm when approaching Cuba and refused to join Breckinridge on the latter's trip to England. Instead, he accompanied sailors Russell and O'Toole home and returned to his family to restart life as a free man on terra firma.

Henry T. Titus continued to run his hotel and dominate affairs in Titusville, even though he had rheumatism and was confined to a wheelchair in his later years. He died on August 7, 1881, at age 58 and is buried in the cemetery at tiny LaGrange, the town first settled by the Carliles, the family of Almeda Armour. It's possible that his many enemies included the publisher of the *Florida Star* in Titusville, for all it reported on the life and death of a man who gave the town its name was a stingy single line in a column of miscellany. "Titusville has lost an energetic citizen in the death of H. T. Titus," it noted. [5]

Francis R. Stebbins, whose ten winters exploring the Indian River were chronicled in Michigan newspapers, pushed his frontier luck too far in 1888. In early March, as his hired sloop made for the mail stop at St. Lucie, Alanson Worden, an elderly shipmate from Adrian, Michigan, was seized by a "slow approaching paralysis." While his frantic comrades tacked under tight sail towards Melbourne, the only town with a doctor, Alanson lapsed into a coma and died soon after their arrival. Stebbins' feelings of guilt — and the cruel reminder of the primitive conditions of South Florida — kept him from ever returning. He died of heart failure four years later at age 74. [6]

On October 11, 1893, what the Light House Board called a "very serious fire" occurred at Jupiter Lighthouse, endangering all the buildings on the property. A letter of commendation from the Board states that "Mr. J. A. Armour, and the acting second assistant keeper, Mr. J. A. [Joseph] Wells, behaved remarkably well and spent $25 in payment of the services of colored men in putting out the fire." Armour, it adds, "used his own quilts to protect the roof of the storehouse, and three of them, valued at $7.50, were burned." The Board voted that Armour be reimbursed $32.50 and receive its official commendation for the "energy, skill and zeal" he had displayed. [7]

In 1906, as his newspaper obituary reports, James Armour resigned because "upon the death of a sister, Mrs. Thurston of New York, he received a substantial fortune." He had already built "a beautiful home" near the lighthouse. Before his death in 1909, adds the obit, "he passed his remaining days, calmly and peaceably, surrounded by his family of four generations, conversing with friends, tending his garden and flowers, and thinking evil of no man." [8]

As the author was finishing this book, one question nagged at me constantly. Lighthouse lore all over the world is thick with stories of ghosts and unexplainable events in eerie towers. What about Jupiter Lighthouse?

I had never given the matter a thought until one spring day in 2004. I was signing books in a booth at "Riverfest," an annual event held that year on the lighthouse grounds. A man in his early thirties stepped up, and as I was inscribing his copy he said he'd just had "an interesting experience." He said he'd known since childhood that he had psychic talents, but that he'd never been "trained" or tried to make a living at it. "I wasn't even thinking about it," he said, "when I bought a ticket for the regular tour that takes people up the lighthouse. No sooner was I inside the gate when this spirit contacted me. In very forceful terms he told me he was an Indian chief from many centuries ago and he was upset because the lighthouse had been built on or near his grave."

Well, there were others in line and the thought of writing a book on the lighthouse had yet to enter my head. But I wrote down the fellow's name and phone number and stuck it in a file folder at home.

Why? I have no idea. I have no psychic talents that I'm aware of. What I do have are abnormal doses of curiosity and skepticism — the kind of conflicting credentials that lure people into journalism careers. So, as this book wound towards the end, it seemed a shame not to take a stab at answering the question that was, shall we say, haunting me. Namely, if psychics have earned their spurs in the criminal justice system by locating crime scenes and fingering culprits, and if mediums have put so many thousands in touch with departed loved ones (just consult your *TV Guide* to find them on a channel near you), might they not be just as useful in solving historical and archeological riddles?

After Googling "psychic mediums" and finding none nearby except for astrologers and Tarot card readers, I soon found myself on the web site of the Cassadaga Spiritualist Camp in central Florida. There, within a 57-acre, lakeside village, formed in 1894, dwell some forty psychics, mediums and healers. All are "certified" by various peer groups, which distinguish the anointed from the many more fortune tellers who beckon from storefronts just outside the Cassadaga compound.

After asking who might have a bent for contacting ancient Indians, departed lighthouse keepers and the like, I found myself packing my bags and on the way to Cassadaga with an appointment to see Dr. Warren Hoover.

The scene: a Saturday afternoon on the front porch of a quaint, century-old row house. A sign tells me Dr. Hoover is still inside "in consultation," so I sit on the little porch, fidgeting with a Publix bag of lighthouse artifacts – a brick, some shells, a piece of glass. I've been told to bring any objects whose vibrations, or energy output, might serve as "portals" to the spirit world.

After ten minutes the front door opens and a young woman passes by in a hurry. She seems to be mumbling and close to tears. In the doorway beckoning to me is a slight man in his seventies, wearing a blue jogging suit and sizing me up with a bemused smile.

Once inside, we're facing each other almost knee-to-knee across a tiny desk. It's dark and I smell something like incense – not the surroundings to comfort a guy who's never even had his palm read.

First, I learn about ground rules. Dr. Hoover defines himself. He is a *medium*. He doesn't tell fortunes or predict the future. He communicates with spirits through *energy vibrations*. Psychics sense vibrations from energy fields by holding wallets, photos and other solid objects. A medium senses energy vibrations from the spirit world, which are much more difficult to pick up, says Dr. Hoover.

Spirits, he adds, don't enter our dimension unless invited. They don't want to hurt – only to help us. And they don't *haunt* places. They might visit a place periodically because it represents something that was dear to them while in the physical world.

Okay, now for the most important ground rule. Dr. Hoover doesn't want me telling him anything. He's going to tell *me*. But I can take all the notes I want.

This is tough for a reporter. How can you get the proper answer from an interviewee unless you frame your question with proper background information? Secondly, a reporter wants to control the interview, as in "Hey, *I'm* the one asking questions here!"

Dr. Hoover will have none of it. "First, I'm going to tell you some things about yourself," he says.

"No, no," I want to shout. "This is supposed to be about a *lighthouse*." Besides, I've only signed up for forty minutes and I don't want to eat into lighthouse time.

For 15 minutes, Dr. Hoover peppers a man he's never met with amazing insights, including the revelation that I've been a scribe or scribbler in many previous lives going back to ancient Egypt (like maybe I'm starring in my own version of *Groundhog Day*.)

In a daring attempt to break his train of thought, I dip into my grocery bag of lighthouse artifacts and meekly proffer the brick. "Would this help you in answering some of my lighthouse questions?" I ask. Dr. Hoover waves the brick aside. "I have all the information I need just coming from your vibrations," he declares.

"Are there spirits at this lighthouse?" I ask, landing my first solid question.

"There are many spirits who visit the lighthouse from time to time," he answers. "You're talking about an area that's been occupied for centuries going back to around AD 500 to 700. [Remember, he's never been to Jupiter.] Just because the spirits live in the spirit world, they haven't lost interest in what happens here. Even though they can advance to higher realms, they can return to visit places that were special to them."

"Yes, but do you see anyone you can name?" I ask.

Hoover makes me gasp. "I see one man named Papy," he says. "I see another named Augustus who spends a lot of time there."

They, of course, would be Joseph Papy, the deposed Civil War keeper, and Augustus Lang, the assistant keeper who helped do him in.

Almost incidentally, Dr. Hoover mentions a "man with a white mustache standing right behind you," but before I could ask more he's back into ancient Indians. I tell him about the home-grown medium's encounter with the angry chief, and he counters with a story of his own. "I had a call recently from a realtor in Port Orange, Florida," he says. "He had a property he couldn't sell because word got around that strange things were happening there. I went over there and learned that the source of the trouble was the spirit of an ancient Indian. It turns out that the property was located on his burial mound. All he wanted was to let someone know it had been his grave and property. That was all there was to it. He just wanted someone to know."

"What about our lighthouse Indian chief?" I ask.

"Same thing. He just wants people today to know."

I want to know more about our Jupiter chief, but Dr. Hoover dismisses it. "That's it. End of story."

Well, the first thing they teach in journalism school is *get a second source*. I did, only this time it was the next day and I called on a psychic. Unlike the medium Hoover, Nellie Edwards senses a person's energy from photos and other objects. Nellie (her preferred name) had much to say about some key lighthouse characters (to be discussed below), but near the end of my allotted hour she stopped and said, "You know, you really ought to see an associate of mine who is just great on archeological subjects. His name is Albert Bowes."

I didn't meet Albert J. Bowes just then. I could have wrapped up my little postscript then and there, but maybe I was getting hooked on psychics. Back home, in March 2006, I found myself visiting Bowes' web site (he, too, is based in Cassadaga) and being intrigued by the fact that he had been tested by some university archeologists for his ability to hold a strange artifact in his hand and tell the professors its age and purpose. In many cases, the academics had pulled items from dusty shelves that even *they* couldn't identify.

This time I decided to go for broke. I called Bowes and asked if he'd like to visit Jupiter Inlet Lighthouse and poke around. Turns out he was driving to Miami to see a client the next week. After learning he was a kayaker, he agreed to stop off in Jupiter if I'd take him on a paddle up the Loxahatchee before we got down to business.

Late one afternoon a bright red Dodge pickup truck pulled past our gate disgorging a burly, bearded man with a sunny disposition. Before long the ever-curious reporter learned that Bowes had been so dyslexic as a child that the only way he could pass tests was to rely increasingly on a strange ability to summon the answers visually through vibrations. Today he is both a psychic and ordained spiritualist minister who says his only clients "are people for whom I can do good."

After dinner and a good night's sleep, Albert and I were met at the lighthouse by Jamie Stuve, executive director of the Loxahatchee River Historical Society, whom I had persuaded to come along as a witness to whatever would happen. It was Thursday when the lighthouse was closed to visitors, so we had the whole place to ourselves. Like Warren Hoover, Albert asked not to be told anything in advance because the impressions we conveyed might distort the mental images he hoped to pick up. Moreover, I can attest that he had never heard of either Jupiter or its lighthouse when I had called to invite him there.

Jamie was carrying a bagful of artifacts from the lighthouse grounds now in the Society museum. Together we sat on a bench outside the visitor center while Albert rubbed each one in his fingers. We soon had goose-bumps as he gave details about each one. For example, he said a small shark's tooth with a hole in it was used by an ancient shaman as part of a bracelet or necklace of similar teeth to be worn by sick people to promote healing. A piece of ceramics was part of a 1930s plate. Nothing special. It just broke and got tossed out, he said.

A brass, flat coin-like object had been presumed to be a button. Albert said it was an anchor, or snap, for a larger button worn on a military uniform or navy pea-jacket. It had been worn here around 1859 or 1860. Its wearer was a "marine-type person" who had lived his life around guns or canons, and had once fought "savages" in some far-away place like The Philippines. "I see him using a gun with a blade on the end of it."

A round shard, about three inches across, had been found in one of the lighthouse middens by an archeologist and declared to be around 3,500 years old. Albert deemed it to be part of a very large jar, perhaps two feet high that had contained small purplish berries. Albert, who lives in the Florida highlands, didn't know that saw palmetto berries were the staple of Indian life centuries before the pharmaceutical industry found them helpful for reducing prostate growth.

Later, as Jamie was unlocking the gate to the lighthouse pathway, Albert stood for a long time gazing over the fence as if taking in a panoramic view or hesitating to walk inside. "This is a powerful place," he said at last. "Not just the lighthouse, but the whole [fifty-acre] place."

The rest sounds like stream of conscience on my tape recorder. "This was an Indian meeting place. There could be thousands here at a time. Seasonal. They came in summer months to trade, then they went back into the Everglades. I see violent people. Maybe cannibals. I see boats coming from the ocean. Polynesian-like canoes with outriggers on them for stability. They all came to trade. When the first white people came they met with lots of violence. Many artifacts buried here, but many of the mounds were already excavated. One thing

251

I feel is that in the 1920s or '30s people came in here and took out a lot of the mounds to make roadbed. [Indeed they had.] A lot of bones and jewelry went out in those trucks."

We began walking up the hundred or so yard path leading to the mound, or hill, that supports the lighthouse. Almost immediately Albert picks up on something. "I see a man walking right here like we are. I'm feeling guilt, like this man had done something wrong. He had a job to do and he neglected or didn't do it. People are charging him but he's been wrongly accused. He should have been here but he wasn't."

Remember that Albert has never heard of James Armour or any of the keepers. "How do you know it was a man?" I asked, using my superior knowledge as a tease. "Maybe it could have been a little boy who did something wrong."

"No, it was a man associated with the lighthouse. I keep feeling the word 'salvors,' or 'salvaging ships.' People are collecting booty from a shipwreck. People are arguing. They may be pirates or criminals. They didn't have work unless there was a hurricane. They're picking up stuff from the ocean and making a living selling it."

We were now at the base of the lighthouse. I wanted to know about our (supposedly) ancient Indian chief and whether the lighthouse was built on his grave, but I didn't want to taint the question.

"Do you feel anything special about the hill here?" I asked.

"There could be layers here," he said. "I think it was a natural hill that got built higher when the Indians piled up shells and bones."

"Anything else? What about a grave?" I asked, trying to steer Albert where I wanted him to go.

"I see no grave here."

I blurted out the story of the ancient Indian chief.

Again, no grave there. But where Albert *did* see burial places was all along a low ridge that stretched west for more than a hundred yards from the near the lighthouse hill to the river's edge. "This whole series of mounds was much larger then than today," said Albert. "If I were that Indian chief, I'd be angry because some trucks carted off my bones back in the twenties and made them into roadbed."

Albert then turned to face a ridge immediately east of the lighthouse hill. "I see graves over there as well," he said. "I felt an epidemic of some sort that took the lives of six to twelve children. They were buried over there so they could see the sunrise. I see their spirits playing games right there, like they're trying to get my attention."

"Well, what about the lighthouse hill itself?" I asked. "If you had all those Indians gathering around it, what was its purpose?"

"Religious and ceremonial," said Albert. "They climbed it to watch the sunrise."

Well, surely the next location would yield the mother lode. We were now ready to take Albert to the top of the lighthouse tower and into the watchroom where generations of keepers lit the way for history to be made.

But once we climbed, I quickly realized that there were two inter-related problems. The first was simply that so many people had been in the watchroom over such a large period that Albert had trouble knowing where this or that vibration was coming from. The second was that various parts of the works had been replaced over the years — including most of the original Fresnel lens in 1866 — that anything to do with men like Joseph Papy or Augustus Lang was probably long gone. As an example, Albert at one point said he felt that a young Frenchman was longing for a girlfriend or lost love. I laughed because Albert was standing next to the pedestal, which was made by Henri LePaute & Company in Paris. The lovesick Frenchman could have been some apprentice back in the factory.

We walked outside onto the gallery that overlooks Jupiter Inlet and were taking a breather. "What do you see out here," I asked, waving my hand in the general direction of the inlet.

"I pick up a man's name," said Albert. "The name is Titus. The best way to explain him is, there's a character on "The [TV show] Dukes of Hazard named Boss Hogg. He's short and wide — an egomaniac. But this Titus was also a man of vision. When he was older he wanted to dig a canal through the Mosquito Lagoon up around New Smyrna so that you could link up Jacksonville to Jupiter by steamboat. He kept getting grants from the state, but something would always happen to the money.

"This Titus was basically a gangster. During the Civil War he ran guns from places like Nassau and Jamaica. I'd call him a *privateer*. The only difference between a pirate and a privateer is that the privateer works for a government."

Throughout all this Jamie Stuve and I were keeping straight faces, trying to keep our goose-bumps from showing. "Do any other names come to mind?" I said.

"I don't think so."

Albert had told me that prolonged energy divination sapped his own strength after a few hours, so I decided I'd better speed up the detective work if I could.

"What if I gave you an actual name to work with?" I said.

"Okay, I'm pretty good with names. Go ahead."

"James Armour."

Albert bowed his head for several seconds and began his stream of conscience. "He was not a local. He came from up north. He came from a very respectable family. He did something in his youth that made him feel disgraced. Maybe it involved a woman who was much too young for him — something that was considered unacceptable back then but maybe not now.

"In later years he drank a lot. He was alone a lot. He frequented with locals — rough people not as educated as he was — so he had no one to talk to. He looked through a telescope a lot. I feel heaviness in his lungs or chest. He felt very unappreciated. People accused him of things. I think he was the man I picked up on earlier on the pathway. I see a bad storm where he didn't have the strength to come up here [atop the tower]. Or maybe he wasn't here at the time because he thought someone else was supposed to fill in for him.

"Now I see this Titus yelling 'you're a thief' and this and that. But Titus sees him as an educated man who knows things others don't. He could blow the whistle on Titus. So Titus wants to get rid of him, so he tells people he deliberately neglected his work. Titus was not an honorable man."

Interestingly, psychic Nellie Edwards had a lot to say about Armour and Titus before referring me to Albert Bowes. Again, with no prompting on my part, she described James Armour as having come from "a cold, very windy climate" and as a "gentleman" from an "educationally broad background." He was a "fastidious" man who "was the type who would keep all his money in a box in the house."

Nellie, too, saw Armour as "a drinker" who, "around age sixty had developed a problem with his back." She added that "I think he fell" (perhaps referring to the time the gallery stairway broke and nearly toppled Armour over the railing).

But Nellie spent most of the time talking about the acrimony between

Armour and Titus. The latter she described as "a super-aggressive man" who had a "confrontation with Armour when he came to the lighthouse." Armour, she said, told Titus to "mind his own business," but Titus "was a man who would seethe over things. And from that day on he was really down on this man" [Armour].

Without any knowledge about the cotton-laden *Charm* or its capture by Henry Crane and his volunteers in 1863, Nellie zeroed in on a scene in which she said "Titus was the financier." She talked of "intrigue and betrayal" – a "deal behind the scenes" where the capture was pre-arranged, the "ship owner was duped" and the goods sold off at back-alley prices.

I didn't help her with details because I wasn't supposed to. Could Nellie have been saying that Titus tipped off Henry Crane about the *Charm* and its cotton cargo, then arranged to give Titus a cut from their auction proceeds in Key West? Or might Titus have been "tipped" a few bales immediately and allowed to run them to Nassau?

Like Albert Bowes, Nellie talked of the great burden Armour bore at being wrongly accused of neglecting the light so that he could sell plunder from wrecks. Once when the light went out, "he was ill," she said. "I don't see him as ever intentionally causing a wreck," she said. But she also saw Armour "and another man – smaller, younger and with lighter hair – collecting things off the beach from a wreck that was washed up."

That man may have been Assistant Keeper Charles Carlin, the former Irish sailor, who felt the wrath of Henry Titus because he allegedly traded lighthouse duties with Armour while the other languished in Titusville for weeks on end.

After Albert Bowes had come down from the tower in Jupiter, I pulled out one of my previous books from my briefcase and showed him photos of Armour. Albert thought one of the lighthouse keeper in his fifties and another in his sixties portrayed the tortured, wrongly-accused figure he had already described. But when it came to a photo of Armour taken in old age, he saw a different man, "one who had a family support group" and who had "come to be respected in the community."

Finally, what about our mystery man, James A. Yorke? The whole trip into the psychic world had really begun as a last-ditch attempt to uncover something when all conventional research had failed. But Warren Hoover drew a blank. So did Albert Bowes, unless it was Yorke who had dropped the brass button holder from his jacket.

Nellie had an advantage on the others because I gave her copies of Yorke's letters from the construction project. "I feel that he was some type of runaway," she began. "In his early life there was great sorrow. When a woman died, it was a culmination of many sad things in his life. He was never married, or just for a brief time. He left a little girl behind."

Yorke had always lived in or around lighthouses, she said, and it may just have been in being around them that he acquired his array of building skills.

"Can you tell what he looked like?" I asked.

"I see him as always inclined to turn away. I see him with a black cap pulled down over his head. He's trying not to make himself obvious. He had this dark coat that he kept for years. When he put it on he just kind of felt hidden. His face was square with a heavy nose. I see a man who didn't often make eye contact. When he did it was kind of fierce. People didn't challenge him. He was a very strong man."

Nellie saw her Yorke coming to Jupiter Inlet after "being hired by one of the overseers who had known him or his qualifications. He wanted to remain anonymous because he didn't want anyone to locate him."

What happened to Yorke after Jupiter? "He went further away into a world he didn't know," said Nellie. "He lived the rest of his life in a place very foreign."

Where?

"He went to a place with a lot of water around it. A warm climate. Tropical."

And so, we leave Nellie's Edward Yorke living in a place somewhere within half the earth's surface.

I say "Nellie's" Yorke because I now have a problem. The Edward Yorke I envisioned from his letters and deeds is not the man she describes. My Yorke is more like an adult Boy Scout: brave, reverent, thrifty, good-natured, efficient, a leader of men and, presumably, one who would be greeted back in Philadelphia by a loving wife and children who would dote on him until the next assignment called.

So what do we do with this dichotomy? Do you and I, dear readers, insist on our own impressions? If we have just been told all about James Armour, Henry Titus, ancient Indians and their artifacts by people who had absolutely never heard of any of them before being asked, is it prudent or fair to pick and choose what we want to believe about Edward Yorke?

I'm still mulling it over. Meanwhile, I *do* know this:

The steamboats have come and gone.

The Cape Florida light is dark.

The surveyors, soldiers, wreckers, pineapple pioneers, blockade runners and raiders are all gone.

One earthquake, four major fires and countless hurricanes have swept in and out of the Jupiter Lighthouse grounds.

The only living monument to all of them that endures today is the old red lighthouse itself.

Edward Yorke, the man most responsible for building it, must have been an exceptional man. His character and skill speak for themselves in the foundation he built for South Florida.

END NOTES

The endnotes in this section are intended to provide just enough information to send determined researchers to the more complete listing under the "References and Resources" section.

Moreover, so as to not intimidate non-academicians, I have tried to avoid footnotes except in the case of direct quotes, controversial issues and/or newly-discovered information about this period.

One detail: the lighthouse regulatory agency in Washington was officially the Light House Board, even though most everyone else used a single word lighthouse (or hyphenated light-house) when describing the Board's individual installations. Despite the inconsistencies, I've kept the names as used in the nineteenth century.

PART I: A LIGHT

Chapter 1: Nowhere

1. Jacob Rhett Mott, *Journey into Wilderness,* p. 199.
2. Ibid. p. 206.
3. Lieutenant J. C. Ives, "Memoir to Accompany a Military Map of the Peninsula of Florida South of Tampa Bay," April 1, 1856. p. 4.

Chapter 2: Reefs

1. Love Dean, *Lighthouses of the Florida Keys,* p. 23.
2. "The Wrecking Business on the Florida Reef," by Dorothy Dodd, p. 190; "Three Florida Episodes," by John James Audubon, *Tequesta,* 1945, p. 56.
3. "Bradish W. Johnson, Master Wrecker," *Tequesta*, March 1941, p. 31.
4. Ibid. p. 28.
5. Dodd, "The Wrecking Business" p. 187.
6. Ibid. p. 188.
7. Ibid. p. 196.

Chapter 3: Lights!?

1. Dennis L. Noble, *Lighthouses & Keepers,* p. 9.
2. Love Dean, *Lighthouses of the Florida Keys,* p. 38
3. Ibid. p. 39.
4. Quoted in Noble, *Lighthouses & Keepers,* p. 13.
5. Noble, p. 22.
6. Hans Christian Adamson, *Keepers of the Lights,* p. 38.
7. Noble, p. 26.
8. Ibid. p. 16.
9. Ibid. p. 18.
10. Dean, *Lighthouses of the Florida Keys,* p. 39.

Chapter 4: Meade

1. George Meade, *The Life and Letters of George Gordon Meade* (authored by the general's son). p. 11.
2. Ibid. p. 4.
3. Ibid. p. 8.
4. Ibid. p. 9.
5. Ibid. p. 11.
6. Ibid. p. 16.
7. Ibid. p. 19.
8. Quoted in Dean, *Lighthouses of the Florida Keys,* p. 140.
9. Meade, *Life and Letters*, p. 201.
10. Letters: District Seven of the Light House Board, letter from Edmund Hardcastle to Lt. George G. Meade, October 14, 1853.
11. Letters…Light House Board. Thornton Jenkins, naval secretary, to G. G. Meade. Date illegible, but probably May 8, 1854.
12. Jenkins to Meade, August 15, 1854.
13 Jenkins to Meade, August 30, 1854; Hardcastle to Meade, September 12, 1854; John Wilson, Commissioner of the General Land Office, to Meade, November 21, 1854.
14. Excerpt from the Fiscal Year 1855 annual report by the Light House Board to Congress.
15. Ibid.
16. Hill reported his observations to Major J. A. Haskin at Fort Capron in a letter dated January 14, 1855. Ives' comments accompanied his "Map of the Peninsula South of Tampa Bay," published 1856 by the War Department.
17. Ives, "Map of the Peninsula."
18. Kenneth J. Hughes, *A Chronological History of Fort Jupiter*, p. 123. Hughes offers three possibilities as to the man for whom Jones Hill and Jones Creek were named: the surveyor A. H. Jones; an early postmaster named A.S. Jones, and army officer Arnold Elzy Jones. I'm guessing that A. H. Jones got there first as part of a survey did something commendable to get his name on a couple of sites.
19. Hill Letter to Major Haskin, January 14, 1855.
20. Ibid.
21. Letter from Assistant Surgeon A.J. Ford to Captain Joseph Haskins, May 19, 1855.
22. Naval Secretary Jenkins to Meade, October 18, 1855.
23. Letters from George Meade to Light House Board officials, November 1, and November 3, 1855. See also letter of Edmund L. F. Hardcastle, Light House Board, to Meade dated January 19, 1856 and letter of May 8, 1856 from Meade to Colonel J. J. Abert, Corps of Topographical Engineers.
24. Major John Munroe, Fort Brooke, to Colonel S. Cooper, Adjunct General, Washington, D.C., December 8, 1855.
25. John and Mary Lou Missall, *The Seminole Wars,* p. 211.
26. From a report Thompson filed with the Lighthouse Service upon his recovery. My account is distilled from Adamson's *Keepers of the Lights,* pp. 177-79, and Noble's *Lighthouses & Keepers,* pp. 103-05.

Chapter 5: Outpost

1. Letter of Light House Board Engineering Secretary John G. Parke to Lieutenant William F. Raynolds, September 25, 1856.
2. Light House Board Naval Secretary Jenkins to Raynolds, May 9, 1857.
3. Lieutenant Ives, "Memoir to Accompany a Military Map of the Peninsula of Florida," p. 5.
4. Ibid.
5. Captain Joseph Roberts to Captain A. Pleasanton, Adjunct General's staff, Fort Myers, April 1, 1857.
6. Roberts letter to Pleasanton, March 15, 1857.
7. *Chronological History of Fort Jupiter,* p. 129.
8. Captain Oscar Hart to Major Francis Page, November 30, 1857.
9. Ibid.
10. Ibid.
11. Lieutenant Theodore Talbot to his mother in Washington, August 20, 1857. From the Library of Congress collection, "Papers of Theodore Talbot, 1837-67."
12. Ibid.
13. Ibid.
14. A. A. Gannon at Fort Capron to Captain Joseph Roberts at Fort Jupiter, September 10, 1857.
15. Captain Abner Doubleday at Fort Capron to Major L. N. Page in Tampa, February 3, 1858. Also: Doubleday letter of March 11, 1858.
16. Ibid. Some histories have cited these letters as proof that lighthouse construction workers were present at Jupiter Inlet in 1858, that a twenty-man contingent from Fort Capron was stationed there to protect them, and that local citizens were hired to run supplies to Jupiter from Fort Capron. In fact, locals helped supply Fort Jupiter and another garrison at Cape Canaveral Lighthouse. No construction crew occupied Jones Hill in Jupiter until the winter of 1859.

Chapter 6: Progress?

1. Letter from W. B. Franklin, Light House Board, to Raynolds, September 7, 1858. Despite some accounts that work on Jupiter Lighthouse was already underway by this date, Franklin states that the Board wants the project "commenced."
2. Douglas Peterson, *United States Lighthouse Service Tenders: 1840-1939.* p.10.
3. Letters of the Seventh Lighthouse District, Letter Book No. 87, December 2, 1858.
4. W. B. Franklin to Raynolds, February 15, 1859.
5. Raynolds to Colonel J. J. Abert, May 7, 1859.
6. Summary of letter of July 11, 1859 from Seventh District Engineer Hartman Bache to Light House Board reporting arrival of working party from Jupiter Inlet at Philadelphia Navy Yard.
7. B.W. Pickering, Seventh District lighthouse inspector, to Commander Raphael Semmes, naval secretary, Light House Board, November 23, 1859.
8. Major Hartman Bache, engineering secretary of the Fourth, Fifth and Seventh Lighthouse Districts, to Raphael Semmes, November 11, 1859.
9. Raphael Semmes to Hartman Bache, November 12, 1859.
10. Hartman Bache to Raphael Semmes, November 14, 1859.
11. Bache to Captain William F. Smith, engineering secretary, Light House Board, December 3, 1859.

12. Captain Smith to Bache, December 17, 1859.
13. Bache to Captain Smith, December 19, 1859.
14. Bache to Smith, December 20, 1859.
15. Bache to Smith, December 28, 1859.

Chapter 7: Yorke

1. Copy of letter from Edward A. Yorke, clerk of works at Jupiter Inlet, was enclosed with correspondence from Hartman Bache to Captain William Smith on December 30, 1859. Note: during the lighthouse construction period, progress reports were typically sent from Jupiter to the Seventh Lighthouse District in Philadelphia. There, copies of pertinent points were made and forwarded to the Light House Board administrative staff in Washington. Thus, some of the letters from Yorke are "extracts" from the records of the Light House Board.
2. Extract of letter from Edward Yorke to G. Castor Smith, assistant engineer, Seventh District, January 1, 1860. Also: Around January 4, 1860, Yorke sent Hartman Bache of the Seventh District extracts from his personal journal covering the period December 28, 1859 through January 1, 1860.
3. Ibid.
4. Bache to Captain W. F. Smith, Light House Board, January 6, 1860.
5. Yorke to G. Castor Smith, assistant engineer, Seventh District, January 9, 1860.
6. Bache to W. F. Smith, May 22, 1860. Bache appended a list of the tools and materials brought back to Philadelphia on the *Delaware.*
7. Francis R. Stebbins, *The Winter Sailor,* p. 109.
8. Yorke to Bache, January 24, 1860.
9. Ibid.
10. Yorke to Bache, February 7, 1860.
11. Yorke to G. Castor Smith, March 10, 1860.
12. Yorke to Smith, March 20, 1860.
13. Yorke to Smith, March 20, 1860 (a separate letter from the above).
14. G. Castor Smith (in Philadelphia) to Captain William F. Smith, engineering secretary, Light House Board (Washington), on March 22, and March 30, 1860.
15. G. Castor Smith to William F. Smith, March 30, 1860 (a separate letter from the above).
16. G. Castor Smith to Wm. F. Smith, March 30, 1860 (still another letter on the same day as above. With constant courier service between government offices in Washington and Philadelphia, it wasn't unusual to write the same party two or three times a day and to telegraph especially important news).
17. Yorke to Bache, March 31, 1860.
18. Yorke to G. Castor Smith, April 1, 1860.
19. G. Castor Smith to William Smith, April 7, 1860.
20. G. Castor Smith to Yorke, April 10, 1860.
21. G. Castor Smith to William Smith, April 30, 1860.
22. Hartman Bache to William F. Smith, February 20, 1860.
23. Yorke to Bache, April 22, 1860.
24. Yorke to Bache, April 30, 1860.
25. G. Castor Smith, in sending extracts of Yorke's daily journal to William Smith on June 5, 1860.
26. G. Castor Smith to William Smith, May 30, 1860.

PART II: A WAR

Chapter 8: Separation

1. Record of Lights-Keepers' Names, Key West District. The ledger shows names, birthplace, when appointed, and annual salary for years 1866-1908.
2. All notations were extracted from summary sheets of correspondence within the Seventh Lighthouse District. The full letters did not survive the Commerce Department fire of 1920. The summaries did.
3. The *Florida Penninsular* was published in Tampa.
4. John E. Johns, *Florida During the Civil War*, p. 1.
5. Ibid., p. 128.
6. "Blockade Running in the Bahamas During the Civil War," by Thelma Peters. Tequesta, *Journal of the Historical Association of Southern Florida,* Vol. V, January 1946, p. 26.
7. Ibid., p. 25.
8. Ibid. p. 18-19.

Chapter 9: Vigilantes

1. Johns, *Florida During the Civil War*, p. 56.
2. Ibid.
3. Robert Ranson, *East Coast Florida Memoirs*, p. 28.
4. See "Francis A. Ivy/Ivey," by Spessard Stone on www.rootsweb.com.
5. James E. Paine to Christopher G. Memminger, Confederate treasury secretary, October 10, 1861.
6. James Paine to Florida Governor Madison Starke Perry, undated but certainly sometime in August, 1861.
7. Ibid.
8. Ibid.
9. Ibid.
10. Ibid.
11. Ibid.
12. Paine to Memminger, October 10, 1861.
13. Thornton Jenkins, naval secretary, Light House Board, to Secretary of the Treasury Samuel Chase, September 9, 1861.

Chapter 10: Gunboats

1. Johns, *Florida During the Civil War*, p. 24.
2. Ibid.
3. Reports and Letters of the East Gulf Blockading Squadron. *General Order of Acting Rear-Admiral Theodorus Bailey, U.S. Navy, Key West,* January 1, 1863.
4. *Dictionary of American Naval Fighting Ships,* on-line edition, www.history.navy.mil/danfs/s2/sagamore.htm.
5. Johns, *Florida During the Civil War,* p. 72.
6. Ibid. p. 73.
7. Ella Lonn, *Salt as a Factor in the Confederacy*, p. 176.

8. Ibid. p. 178.

9. Walter K. Scofield Collection, Yale University Library. Letter dated "September 1861," written from U.S. Receiving Ship *Ohio* in Boston Harbor.

10. Ibid.

11.East Gulf Blockading Squadron letters: Lieutenant-Commander George A. Bigelow to Gideon Welles, Secretary of the Navy, October 28, 1862.

12. Walter Scofield Collection, journal entry, October 28, 1862.

13. Ibid., November 1, 1862.

14. Logbook of the *U. S. S. Sagamore*, November 1, 1862.

15. Scofield, November 23, 1862.

16. *Sagamore* log, November 28, 1862.

17. Scofield journal, November 27, 1862.

18. Ibid., November 28, 1862.

19. Ibid., December 1, 1862.

20. Ibid., also entry of December 3, 1862.

21. Ibid., December 10, 1862.

Chapter 11: Crane

1. East Gulf Blockading Squadron letters: Rear Admiral Bailey to Naval Secretary Gideon Welles, December 26, 1862.

2. Walter Scofield journals, December 21, 1862.

3. Blockading Squadron letters: Admiral Bailey to Lieutenant-Commander Earl English, January 2, 1863.

4. Blockading Squadron letters: Earl English to Acting Master's Mate Henry Crane, January 3, 1863.

5. "Blockade Runners of the Indian River," by Stuart McIver, *Vero Beach Magazine,* January 2005, p. 166. Although information on Henry Crane is spotty, the National Archives does have records of property he acquired in Mellonville (Sanford), Florida when he served as clerk of the county court there. See Record Group 49, Box 519.

6. Quoted from transcription of Armour obituary, Loxahatchee River Historical Society.

7. Ibid.

8. Copies of Armour's payroll requests and receipts are courtesy, Historical Society of Palm Beach County. Armour's Civil War "enlistment" and desertion are available at www.Ancestry.com.

9. Log of the *Gem of the Sea,* December 30 and 31, 1862; Blockading Squadron letters: Acting Volunteer Lieutenant I. B. Baxter to Navy Secretary Gideon Welles, January 1, 1863.

10. Blockading Squadron letters: Earl English to Admiral Bailey in Key West, January 10, 1863; Scofield journals, January 6, 1863.

11. Blockading Squadron: Earl English to Admiral Bailey, January 10, 1863; Scofield journals, January 9, 1863.

12. Ibid.

13. Scofield, January 13 and 14, 1863.

14. Ibid., January 20, 1863.

15. Blockading Squadron letters: Henry Crane to Admiral Bailey, February 7, 1863.

16. Ibid.

17. Scofield, February 15 and 16, 1863.

18. Ibid., February 19, 1863.

19. Ibid., February 20, 1863. Also: Blockading Squadron letters, Crane to Earl English, March 4, 1863. (The term "concentric wicks" is explained by Ellen Henry, curator of Ponce Inlet Lighthouse. "This referred to the five-concentric wick burner used to illuminate the lens," she says. "The innermost wick was lit first and then the other four, one at a time.").
20. Blockading Squadron letters: Crane to English, March 4, 1863.
21. Ibid.
22. Ibid.
23. Blockading Squadron letters: Earl English to Admiral Bailey, March 4, 1863 (in a cover letter when forwarding Crane's report to the admiral).
24. Ibid., Report of Acting Master's Mate Jeffrey A. Slamm to Earl English, March 2, 1863.
25. Ibid.
26. Scofield journals, March 2 and 3, 1863.

Chapter 12: Breakup

1. East Gulf Blockading Squadron letters: Earl English to Admiral Bailey, March 10, 1863.
2. Transcript from Loxahatchee River Historical Society.
3. Summary of letters in file of District Seven, Light House Board, May 22, 1863.
4. Scofield journals, July 27, 1863.
5. Ibid.
6. *The Schooner Ann and Cargo,* Case No. 228, U.S. District Court for the Southern District of Florida.
7. *The Schooner Charm and Cargo,"* Case No. 421, U.S. District for the Southern District of Florida.
8. Ibid.
9. East Gulf Blockading Squadron letters: report from Acting Master John Sherrill to Naval Secretary Welles, January 12, 1864.
10. Ibid., January 22, 1864.
11. Ibid., February 27, 1864.
12. Ibid., June 30, 1864.
13. Log of the *Roebuck,* July 11, 1864.
14. The entries of January 24, January 26 and March 26 regarding the provisioning of prisoners are all from the log of the *Roebuck,* National Archives.

Chapter 13: Escape

1. Royce Gordon Singleton, *John Taylor Wood: Sea Ghost of the Confederacy,* University of Georgia Press, p. 176.
2. Ibid., p. 177.
3. "Running by Land and by Sea," memoirs of John Taylor Wood as reproduced in *Civil War Times Illustrated,* December 2001.
4. Singleton, *John Taylor Wood,* p. 177.
5. "Running by Land and by Sea," p. 8.
6. Ibid.
7. Ibid.
8. Ibid. p. 9.
9. Ibid., p. 10.
10. Ibid., p. 11.
11. Ibid., p. 12.

PART III: A SETTLEMENT

Chapter 14: Restoration

1. From research compiled by Florida genealogy and history consultant Lynn Lasseter Drake, Jupiter, Florida.
2. Drake genealogies; see also Charles W. Pierce, *Pioneer Life in Southeast Florida,* p. 49, and Mary Collar Linehan and Marjorie Watts Nelson, *Pioneer Days on the Shores of Lake Worth, 1873-1893,* pp. 9-12.
3. *Message of the President of the United States to the Two Houses of Congress at the Commencement of the First Session of the Thirty-Ninth Congress,* 1866. p. 288; also: summaries of letters received by the Seventh District, Light House Board, letter of September 30, 1865.
4. Summaries of Seventh District letters: April 17, May 21, July 12 and 13, 1866.
5. *Pioneers of Southeast Florida,* p. 30.
6. Summaries of Seventh District letters, December 26, 1866, and January 17, March 27 and 31, 1867.
7. Excerpts from a transcript at Loxahatchee River Historical Society.
8. Summaries of Seventh District letters: January 20, 1867; also: *Jupiter Inlet Light Station, Florida,* a research report compiled by the Coast Guard Historical Section in March 1951. Transcript at Loxahatchee River Historical Society.
9. Summaries of Seventh District letters: December 2, 1867 and February 1, 3, 4 and 12, 1868.
10. From a typewritten memoir of Joseph Lark Priest, whose oldest sister had married Augustus Lang. Although not an eye-witness account, Priest and his report are the oldest on record of a story that has evolved into many versions over the years. (Historical Society of Palm Beach County.)
11. From the roster of keepers, Seventh Lighthouse District. Others known to have died on the job are J.P. Collins (sometime in 1878) and Joseph H. Moss (June 10, 1885)

Chapter 15: Armour

1. "Descendants of David Nathaniel Carlile," a genealogy compiled by consultant Lynn Lasseter Drake, Jupiter, Florida. .
2. Bessie Wilson DuBois, *Shipwrecks in the Vicinity of Jupiter Inlet,* p. 7; "Maritime History," *Stuart News,* November 14, 1999 (a chronological list of wrecks compiled from National Archives sources).
3. "Descendants of David Nathaniel Carlile."
4. Henry T. Titus to Light House Board, August 10, 1872.
5. Pierce, *Pioneer Life in Southeast Florida,* p. 32.
6. Ibid., p. 36.
7. Ibid.
8. DuBois, *Shipwrecks in the Vicinity of Jupiter Inlet,* p. 8.
9. Pierce, *Pioneer Life,* pp. 38 and 42.
10. Ibid., p. 40.
11. Henry Titus to Light House Board, sometime in January 1873.
12. "Descendants of David Nathaniel Carlile."

13. Summaries of letters to the Light House Board: two communiqués, both dated March 26, 1873.

14. Pierce, *Pioneer Life,* p. 52.

15. Ibid., p. 43.

16. James A. Henshall, M.D., *Camping and Cruising in Florida,* p. 93. On August 31, 1886, a second earthquake, its epicenter in Charleston, South Carolina, cracked the newly-built tower of Ponce Inlet Lighthouse and reached as far south as a line from Jupiter to Tampa. For more on both events, see the National Earthquake Information Center online at www.earth-quake.usgs.gov.

17. Dubois, *Shipwrecks,* p. 8; Summaries, letters to Light House Board, January 13, 1874; Light House Board reports of inspectors and engineers, Seventh District: W. H. Huer, engineer, Seventh and Eighth Districts, to "Chairman, Light House Board," January 1874.

18. Huer letter to chairman.

19. Ibid.

20. Ibid.

21. Engineer Huer letter to Chairman, Light House Board, April 25, 1883.

22. The Historical Society of Palm Beach County has two sources on the life of Melville Spencer. One is an undated interview from *The Tropical Sun,* published around 1904. The second, entitled "Pioneering in Palm Beach," is an unpublished ten-page memoir written in Spencer's own hand in 1936 when he was 85 years old.

Chapter 16: Settlement

1. Francis R. Stebbins, *The Winter Sailor.*, pp. 23,66,75,79 and 87.

2. From p. 279 of the original typed manuscript of Charles Pierce that was abridged to comprise the book, *Pioneers of Southeast Florida.* The manuscript is at the Historical Society of Palm Beach County.

3. Pierce, *Pioneers of Southeast Florida,* p. 64.

4. Transcript of article from *The Tropical Sun,* May 27, 1891, Loxahatchee River Historical Society.

5. Ibid.

6. Fred A. Hopwood, *Steamboating on the Indian River*, p. 59.

7. Ibid., p. 15.

8. Ibid., p. 61.

9. "A Steamboat Trip on Indian River to Jupiter." Unpublished manuscript with colorful comments by the anonymous author.

10. Ibid. See also: Hopwood, *Steamboating,* p. 62.

11. *The Tropical Sun,* July 7, 1889.

12. Fred A. Hopwood, *Steamboating on the Indian River,* p. 52.

Epilogue

1. Henry F. Beers, "History of Topographical Engineers, 1813-1863." *The Military Engineer,* June, 1942, pp. 287-91.

2. Genealogy compiled by Lynn Lasseter Drake, Jupiter, Florida.

3. Unpublished memoir of Joseph Lark Priest, Historical Society of Palm Beach County; see also, Linehan and Nelson. *Pioneer Days on the Shores of Lake Worth,* p. 9.

4. Ancestry Incorporated, American Biographical Library, 1996.

5. Stamford Historical Society: Civil War Exhibit 2003. Online at
www.stamfordhistory.org/cwsbios.htm.
6. Stebbins, *The Winter Sailor,* p. 154.
7. Light House Board, Inspector & Engineer Reports, Seventh District, 1873-74. Letters dated December 26, 1893 and January 6, 1894.
8. Transcript of obituary at Historical Society of Palm Beach County.

RESOURCES AND REFERENCES
BOOKS AND PAMPHLETS

Adamson, Hans Christian. *Keepers of the Lights*. New York: Greenberg, Publisher, 1955.

Covington, James W. *The Billy Bowlegs War*. Chuluota: The Mickler House Publishers, 1982.

Dean, Love. *Lighthouses of the Florida Keys*. Key West: The Historic Florida Keys Foundation, Inc., 1992.

De Wire, Elinor. *Guardians of the Lights*. Sarasota: Pineapple Press, 1995.

DuBois, Bessie Wilson. *Shipwrecks in the Vicinity of Jupiter Inlet*. Jupiter, Florida: self-published, 1975.

_____. *The History of the Loxahatchee River*. Jupiter, Florida: self-published, 1981.

Hawks, Dr. J. M. *The East Coast of Florida in 1887*. Lynn, MA: Lewis & Winship, 1887.

Henshall, James A. M.D. *Camping and Cruising in Florida*. Cincinnati: Robert Clarke & Co., 1884. Reprinted by Florida Classics Library, Port Salerno, FL, 1991.

Hopwood, Fred A. *Steamboating on the Indian River*. Published privately at New Smyrna Beach, FL, 1985.

Hughes, Kenneth J., *A Chronological History of Fort Jupiter and U.S. Military Operations in the Loxahatchee Region*. Fort Lauderdale: Florida Coast Research and Publishing Co., 1992.

Hutchinson, Janet. *History of Martin County*. Hutchinson Island, FL: Gilbert's

Bar Press, 1975.

Johns, John E. *Florida during the Civil War*. Gainesville, FL: University of Florida Press, 1963.

Keel, James R. *Florida's Trails to History's Treasures*. Fort Lauderdale: Seajay Enterprises, 1981.

Knetsch, Joe. *Florida's Seminole Wars, 1817-1858*. Charleston, S. C.: Arcadia Publishing, 2003.

_____. *Salt and the Civil War in Florida*. Research study presented to the Sons of Confederate Veterans, March 14, 1996, by Dr. Joe Knetsch, Division of State Lands, Florida Department of Environmental Protection.

Linehan, Mary Collar and Marjorie Watts Nelson. *Pioneer Days on the Shores of Lake Worth, 1873-1893*. St. Petersburg, Florida: Southern Heritage Press, 1994.

Lonn, Ella. *Salt as a Factor in the Confederacy*. Tuscaloosa, AL: University of Alabama Press, 1965.

McDonald, Jerry N. and Susan L. Woodward. *Indian Mounds of the Atlantic Coast*. Newark, Ohio: The McDonald and Woodward Publishing Company, 1987.

Meade, George. *The Life and Letters of George Gordon Meade*, Volume I. New York: Charles Scribner's Sons, 1913.

Missall, John and Mary Lou Missall. *The Seminole Wars: America's Longest Indian Conflict*. Gainesville: University of Florida Press, 2004.

Motte, Jacob Rhett. *Journey into the Wilderness*. Gainesville: University of Florida Press, 1953.

Noble, Dennis L. *Lighthouses & Keepers: The U.S. Lighthouse Service and Its Legacy*. . Annapolis: Naval Institute Press, 1997.

Peterson, Douglas. *United States Lighthouse Service Tenders: 1840-1939*. Annapolis, MD: Eastwind Publishing, 2000. R430

Pierce, Charles W. *Pioneer Life in Southeast Florida*. Coral Gables, FL: University of Miami Press, 1970.

Ranson, Robert. *East Coast Florida Memoirs: 1837 to 1886*. Port Salerno, Florida: Florida Classics Library, 1989 (reprint of a booklet first published by the author in 1926).

Rinhart, Floyd and Marion. *Victorian Florida*. Atlanta: Peachtree Publishers Ltd., 1986.

Shingleton, Royce Gordon. *John Taylor Wood: Sea Ghost of the Confederacy*. Athens, GA: University of Georgia Press, 1979.

Snyder, James D. *Black Gold and Silver Sands*. Jupiter, Florida: Pharos Books, 2004.

_____. *Five Thousand Years on the Loxahatchee*. Jupiter, Florida: Pharos Books, 2003.

Stebbins, Francis R. *The Winter Sailor*. Edited by Carolyn Baker Lewis. Tuscaloosa, Alabama: University of Alabama Press, 2004.

Taylor, Thomas W. *The Beacon of Mosquito Inlet: A History of the Ponce de Leon Lighthouse*. Ponce Inlet, FL, 1993. R221

Titus, Leo J. Jr. *Titus: A North American Family History*. Baltimore: Gateway Press, Inc., 2004.

Withington, Chester Merrill. *Jupiter Island at Hobe Sound*. Hobe Sound, FL: The Hobe Sound Company, 1935.

NEWSPAPERS AND PERIODICALS

"The Archeology of Jupiter Inlet and Coastal Palm Beach County." A special issue of *The Florida Anthropologist*, published September-December 2002 by the Florida Anthropological Society, Inc., Tallahassee, Florida.

"Blockade Running in the Bahamas During the Civil War," by Thelma Peters. Tequesta, *Journal of the Historical Association of Southern Florida*, Vol. V, January 1946.

"Bradish W. Johnson, Master Wrecker," by Vincent Gilpin. *Tequesta*, Journal of the Historical Association of Southern Florida, Vol. I, No. I, March 1941.

"Blockade Runners of the Indian River," by Stuart McIver. Vero Beach magazine, January 2005.

Florida Star, the newspaper of Titusville (later the *Star Advocate*). Several articles and advertisements have been quoted from issues during 1880 and 1881, including the nearly ignored death of town founder Henry Titus. Copies of the newspaper are on microfilm at the central Brevard County Public Library, located in Cocoa, Florida.

"History of Topographical Engineers, 1813-1863," by Henry F. Beers, *The Military Engineer*, official magazine of the Society of American Military Engineers, Alexandria, Virginia. Issue of June, 1942, pp. 287-91.

"History of Wrecking," by Jerry Wilkinson. *South Florida History*, Vol. 32, No. I, 2004.

"Pre-Flagler Influences on the Lower Florida East Coast," by George E. Merrick. *Tequesta*, Journal of the Historical Association of Southern Florida, Vol. I, No. I, March 1941.

"Running by Land and by Sea," Part I, by John Taylor Wood. A personal memoir of his daring escape down the coast of Florida, published in *Civil War Times*

Illustrated, December 2001, Vol. 40, Issue 6, p. 22.

"Three Floridian Episodes," by John James Audubon. *Tequesta*, the Journal of the Historical Association of Southern Florida, 1945, Number V., p. 52.

"Watchman, What of the Night?" Editorial in the *Florida* (Tampa) *Peninsular*, November 17, 1860. Microfilm Collection at Miami-Dade Public Library System.

"The Wrecking Business on the Florida Reef, 1822-1860," by Dorothy Dodd, *The Florida Historical Quarterly*, Vol. XXII, April 1944, No. 4.

"Yellow Fever Treatment." *The Florida* (Tampa) *Peninsular*, August 25, 1855. Microfilm Collection at Miami-Dade Public Library System.

REPORTS, LETTERS, UNPUBLISHED WORKS

From the author: most of the new insights about this era have come from government records largely un-mined until now. It seemed to me that instead of being lost in a blizzard of individual citations, future researchers would benefit more from an informal narrative on what information various sources contain and where to look for it. Please note also: the initials NARA after so many references indicates the Washington, D.C. headquarters building of the National Archives and Records Administration.

Seminole Indian Wars and Occupation of Fort Jupiter

Fort Jupiter: Second Seminole War, 1838-1842. Letters of March 15, 19, 22 and May 1, 1838 from Fort Jupiter. The March 22 letter lists all Indians, their horses and other property being transferred to western reservations. NARA, Record Group 94, MC 567/167. Many other letters are referenced in *A Chronological History of Fort Jupiter*, (see Books).

Fort Jupiter: 1855. Letter of January 14 from A. P. Hill to his commanding officer at Fort Capron describes his explorations around Jupiter leading to a decision to establish a new fort there. Muster Report for February 1855 describes troop strength after first month at new Fort Jupiter. June 5 letter describes illness and malnutrition among troops. Letter of December 8 discusses plans to transfer all troops to Caloosahatchee River. NARA, Record Group 363, Letters Sent, Register of Letters Received by Headquarters, Department of Florida, 1850-1858, Racks 9 and 10.

Fort Jupiter: 1957-1858: 14 letters, from March 15, 1857 through April 1, 1858, include muster reports, scouting reports, attempt to cut through Jupiter Inlet, dealings with Jupiter's probable first settler, David Stone, and enduring widespread illness. NARA, Record Group 363, Letters Sent, Register of Letters Received by Headquarters, Department of Florida, 1850-1858, Racks 9 and 10.

Ives, Lt. J. C., Topographical Engineer. "Memoirs to Accompany a Military Map of Peninsula of Florida South of Tampa Bay, War Department, April 1856." Describes the terrain and military trails from Fort Capron to Fort Dallas (Miami). NARA and Historical Society of Palm Beach County.

Talbot, Theodore. The letters and drawings of Lieutenant Theodore Talbot from Fort Jupiter dated August 20 and 29, 1857. Library of Congress, Card catalogue: Talbot, Theodore, 1825-1862, Papers, 1837-1867, 200 items.

Lighthouse Construction Work in Jupiter and South Florida.

Fresnel, Augustin Jean. More on the life of the French inventor of the revolutionary lens for lighthouses can be found online at www-groups.dcs.st-and.ac.uk/~history/Mathematicians/Fresnel.html.

Jupiter Lighthouse: Summaries of correspondence, Seventh District, Light House Board. Contains brief descriptions of dispatches received by the Board staff from its engineers, inspectors, ship captains and others in the field. For the period July 20, 1853 through July 11, 1861, the file contains 168 letter summaries involving the Jupiter Inlet project. They are found in Record Group 26E38, Light House Board Letter Books from No. 11 through 133, NARA.

Jupiter Lighthouse: Letters from the Journal of the Light House Board, October 1852-August 1854. Fifteen letters from various Board engineering supervisors to George Meade from October 14, 1853 to May 6, 1854. They describe the authorization of the project at Jupiter Inlet and efforts to site a specific location. NARA.

Jupiter Lighthouse: Meade letter on even of Indian hostilities. On January 7, 1856 Lieutenant George G. Meade wrote Major William H. Chase of the Topographical Engineers (both were in Key West) requesting arms for a work crew of twenty men. Instead of referring to Jupiter Inlet, it's highly likely that Meade had in mind another lighthouse work party closer to the main Seminole camp in Big Cypress Swamp. NARA and Historical Society of Palm Beach County.

Jupiter Lighthouse: Records of Letters to Seventh District Inspectors, December 18, 1852 to July 7, 1873. Twenty-one letters from Light House Board officials to Seventh District engineers from August 30, 1854 to December 17, 1859. Describes the many false starts and delays at Jupiter and provides ample evidence that the project was not begun in earnest until 1859. NARA.

Jupiter Lighthouse: Letters of the Light House Board, Inspector, Seventh District, July 1859-June 1860. This invaluable volume contains 144 letters involving the problems that nearly killed the Jupiter Lighthouse project, the eventual provisioning of the work crews and all of the on-site reports from Clerk of Works Edward A. Yorke. NARA, Letterbox 105.

Jupiter Lighthouse: Letters Received by the Topographical Bureau (Army Corps of Topographical Engineers). Twenty three letters from June 20, 1855 to March 1, 1861. Nearly all are required reports from successive Seventh District Engineers George Meade, William Raynolds and Hartman Bache routinely keeping headquarters in Washington up to date with their status. On microfilm at NARA (M66, Volume 6).

Jupiter Lighthouse: Special report: "Jupiter Inlet Light Station Florida," by a "Mr. Eldridge" of the Coast Guard Historical Station in March 1951. The nine-page report, perhaps made at the request of Jupiter historian Bessie Dubois, highlights construction activities at Jupiter Inlet based on abstracts from annual reports of the Light House Board. It also summarizes all appropriations for the project, which totaled $61,923 upon completion. Copies at NARA and Loxahatchee River Historical Society.

"The Nation Builders." A history of the Army Bureau of Topographical Engineers, online at www.topogs.org.

South Florida in The Civil War

Anaconda Plan. A succinct description of the Union's strategy for containing the South can be found online at www.civilwarhome.com/anaconda.htm.

Crane, Henry Abijah Roberts. Some of this Union swashbuckler's pre-war background in Mellonville, FL (Sanford) can be gleaned from NARA records showing his claim to various properties after Congress passed the Armed Occupation Act in a bid to encourage settlement at a time when unfriendly Indians posed a barrier. See NARA, Record Group 49, Box 519, Land Entry Files, St. Augustine.

Letter from James Paine to Florida Governor Perry, dated only "August 1861," announcing extinguishment of Jupiter Light by Confederate volunteers. Printed copy at Loxahatchee River Historical Society.

Handwritten letter from James Paine to C. G. Memminger, Confederate Secretary of the Treasury, dated October 10, 1861. Historical Society of Palm Beach County.

Letter from the Secretary of the Treasury to Thornton Jenkins, naval secretary, U. S. Light House Board, September 9, 1861. Acknowledges notice that the light at Jupiter was extinguished by "a band of lawless persons on the 23rd August [1861]. From "Letters Received by the Light House Service, 1829-1900," NARA, Vol. 126, Box 69, Entry 36.

Letter from James Paine to Thomas Martin, Chief, Confederate Light House Bureau, dated June 17, 1863, lamenting the re-capture of lighthouse materials by gunboat crews on the Indian River. Typed copy at Loxahatchee River Historical Society.

Descriptions of many Union vessels can be found in the on-line edition *Dictionary of American Naval Fighting Ships*, www.history.nevy.mil/danfs. For more, visit the Naval Historical Center, Department of the Navy, Washington Navy Yard, Washington, D.C.

Earl English: details on the life of the *Sagamore* skipper are available from the American Biographical Library, Salt Lake City, Utah, and online at www.arlingtoncemetery.net/eenglish.

Letters of the East Gulf Blockading Squadron in this book cover from September 23 through May 22, 1865. They involve 43 orders, capture reports, and other exchanges between the Key West command post and various blockade ships from Key Biscayne to New Smyrna. NARA. Some reports are available online from Cornell University Library's "Making of America" collection at www.cdl.library.cprnell.edu/cgi-bin/moa.

Auctions of captured ships: Cases of adjudication of prize Confederate ships in Key West are available on microfilm at the main Miami-Dade Public Library. The two highlighted in this register are: The Schooner *Ann* and Cargo, Case No. 228, February 19, 1864; and The Schooner *Charm* and Cargo, Case No. 121, February 26, 1864. Also illustrative of how the legal process worked is The Schooner *Diana* and Cargo, Case No. 93, January 22, 1864.

Ships Logs of Union gunboats have been preserved for the *Beauregard*, *Gem of the Sea*, *Roebuck*, *Sagamore* and *Union*. Request them through the naval history office at NARA.

Scofield, Walter Keeler. For a thumbnail biography, see the Stamford Historical Society website at www.stamfordhistory.org/cw sbios.htm. Scofield's journals and letters are preserved in the Yale University Library, Manuscripts and Archives Department, Boxes 1, 2 and 3.

Edward A. Yorke. Attempts to learn more beyond his brief period at Jupiter Inlet have been fruitless except for a leads turned up by the Historical Society of Pennsylvania and Jupiter history researcher Lynn Lasseter Drake. An historical society search of Philadelphia directories covering a twenty-year period yielded three successive addresses for an Edward Yorke on South 5th Street, which is near the navy yard. Lynn Drake unearthed a page from the 1860 U.S. Census, Philadelphia, Ward 1, Precinct 4, p. 181, Roll M653_1151 showing a 46-year-old Edward A. Yorke listed as a "ship's carpenter, U.S.N." Also in the household were a Sarah, aged 58, and an Elizabeth Miles, 83.

Jupiter Inlet Lighthouse in the Post-War Era

"Report of the President of the Light House Board" to the U.S. Senate, January 12, 1866. Describes plans to re-establish operations at Jupiter and other damaged lighthouses in south Florida. Misc. Document No. 34, NARA and Library of Congress. The same plans are described in the president's annual Message to Congress, March 1866, p. 288.

"Record of Lights-Keepers" Names," Seventh District, U. S. Light House Board.
A roster of keepers at Jupiter Inlet through October 1, 1906. Shows name, rank, salary, date of appointment, date leaving service, and reasons for leaving. Letterbook 343, NARA.

Summaries of correspondence, Seventh District, Light House Board. Contains brief descriptions of dispatches received by the Board staff from its engineers, inspectors, tender captains and others in the field. For the period September 30, 1865 to January 6, 1894, there are 208 summaries involving Jupiter and South Florida. Due to a major fire in the Commerce Department storage facility in 1920, only 62 of the complete letters have survived. The summaries are in Record Group 26E38, Light House Board letterbooks 177 through 1024, NARA.

Letters of the Light House Board, Inspector & Engineer, Seventh District, 1873-1874. Twenty-eight of the 62 complete letters referred to in the above paragraph are in Letterbook 343, NARA.

Settlement in the Fort Jupiter Military Reservation. Private ownership in the 9,077-acre reserve was allowed only after 1884. Background on claims filers can be gleaned from a 10-page Letter from the Secretary of the Interior to the U.S. Senate Committee on Public Lands, December 13, 1894, Executive Document No. 13.

Thompson, John W. B., Charleston, South Carolina, letter to the U. S. Lighthouse Inspector, 1837, Record Group 26, NARA.

Southeast Florida Settlers in the Post-Civil War Era

Armour, James Arango. Descendant Kathy Legal has provided the Loxahatchee River Historical Society with copies of Armour's family genealogy dating back to 1545 and including the family's prominent involvement in the affairs of New Amsterdam (New York) in the Revolutionary War period. The Society also has several Armour family photos and a typewritten copy of an obituary appearing shortly after his death on July 8, 1910.

The Historical Society of Palm Beach County has a different typed transcript of an Armour obituary as well as copies of pay requests and receipts when Armour served as a river pilot (and perhaps carpenter) at Fort Capron.

Lynn Lasseter Drake, a Jupiter genealogist and historical researcher, has compiled a lengthy genealogy of the James-Almeda Armour offspring and of Almeda's family in La Grange, entitled "Descendants of David Nathaniel Carlile." Drake also compiled records of Armour's service record in the Confederate army.

Armour's heroic role in quelling the fire at Jupiter Lighthouse is described in a letter of commendation to the Secretary of the Treasury from the Light House Board dated January 6, 1894. Letters of the Light House Board, Letter Box 1024, NARA.

Lang, Augustus Oswald. One of the "kidnappers" of Jupiter Light and first settler of Lake Worth, the German immigrant has been profiled in several latter-day feature articles on file at the Historical Society of Palm Beach County. Lang's family genealogy and Confederate army records have been compiled by Lynn Lasseter Drake of Jupiter, Florida. The account of his post-Lake Worth life on the St. Lucie River and his murder in December 1873 was typed or dictated by brother-in-law Joseph Lark Priest in the early 1900s and is at the Historical Society of Palm Beach County.

Spencer, Melville Evans. The Historical Society of Palm Beach County has a 12-page handwritten manuscript by the one-time assistant lighthouse keeper and pioneer photographer of early Jupiter-Lake Worth, dictated January 4, 1936 at age eighty five. Also at HSPBC: an undated interview with Spencer by *The Tropical Sun* and an anonymous, three-page "M. E. Spencer Biography."

Titus, Henry T. In addition to the family biography by Leo Titus, Jr. (see Books), the founder of Titusville and James Armour nemesis is profiled by the Historical Society of North Brevard, Inc. online at www.nbbd.com/godo/history.html. The three letters from Henry T. Titus to the Light House Board, accusing lighthouse keeper James Armour of malfeasance, are dated August 10, 1872, September 23, 1872 and January (day missing) 1873. See Letterbook 315, Letters to Light House Board, Seventh District, NARA.

Note: the author has relied principally on records furnished by Jupiter-based genealogist Lynn Lasseter Drake for several of the persons mentioned in this book. In addition to the references already listed, they include William B. Davis, Francis A. Ivey, Allen Padgett, Judge James E. Paine, Francisco José Papy and David Stone. Drake can be reached at 561-575-7925 and jupiter-history@aol.com.

INDEX

I

Indian Removal Act 5
Indian River:
  Civil War 148,172-174
  Life on 142,221
  Steamboat travel 226-229
  Transport 62,88-92

Indian River Inlet 41,42,69,102,127,134-
136,139,146,153-165,173,196
Indian River Narrows 149,150
Indian River Steamboat Company 225-230
Ives, Joseph C. 42,56
Ivey, Francis A. 117-119

J

Jacksonville, Tampa and Key West Railroad
225
Jacksonville Times Union (newspaper) 226
James (ship) 12
Jansen, Cornelius Otto 19
Jenkins, Thornton A. 40,56
Jesup, Thomas S. 3
J. L. Davis (ship) 130
J. L. Pusey (ship)
Joe Hagger (ship) 84
John F. Starr (ship) 82
Johns, John E. (quoted) 105
Jones, Alfred H 43
Jones Creek 43,57,58
Jones Hill 40,43,70,71
Johnson, Bradish W. ("Hog") 10
Jones, Sam (chief) 64
Julia (ship) 145
Jupiter and Lake Worth (Celestial) Railroad
226,230
Jupiter Inlet 3,6,59-60,73,133,164,165
Jupiter Island 40
Jupiter Narrows 42,*66-67*,133,174,194,229
Jupiter Inlet Lighthouse
  Strategic location 7
  Construction 51,53,55,73-76
  Role in Civil War 127,134-
136,158,164,165,191
  Postwar era 192-197, *198*,201-215

Jupiter River (Loxahatchee) 58-
64,193,229,230

K

Kantz, Albert 211,214
Katie (boat) 64
Kearsarge (ship) 74
Key Biscayne (see Cape Florida)
Key West
  Lighthouse 37
  Map *112-113*
  Navy base 47,123,132
  "Prize ship" adjudication 124,158
  Wrecking center 12-13
Kingfisher (ship) 131

L

Lake Worth 56,57,193,212,222-230
Lang, Augustus Oswald 117-120,
121,192,244
Lang, Susan Priest 244
Lang, Walker Augustus 244
Las Islas de los Martires 8
Last Resort (ship) 164
Lee, Robert E. 29,162,243
Lenox (ship) 73-76,81-92
Lewis, William Penn 22,
Lewis, Winslow 20-22,*25*
Light House Board
  Creation 23,24
  George Meade relationship 33,39
  Jupiter project 40,41,69,73-76
  Postwar reorganization 191
Lincoln, Abraham 74,103,10,171
Loxahatchee (river barge) 226
Loxahatchee River (Jupiter River) 58-
64,193,229,230
Lucinda (ship) 145

M

Madison Shoe Factory 106
Magnolia (ship) 139
Martin, Thomas 147,158
Marvin, William (judge) 11

FRONT COVER: RON PARVU

The half-built Jupiter Lighthouse on the cover is the folk art creation of Ron Parvu, one of South Florida's most accomplished and versatile painters. As this was written, Tequesta-based Parvu was deep into a series of folk art paintings of historical sites around Jupiter Inlet and the Loxahatchee River. But it's just the latest avenue of exploration for an artist who has already excelled at watercolors, portraits, miniatures and nature scenes.

Ron Parvu was born in Akron, Ohio in 1942 and had climbed the corporate career ladder as a graphics designer when, in 1983, he moved to Florida and began painting full-time. Many Parvu clients appreciate the striking similarity of his style to Andrew Wyeth's. But just when you think of type-casting him, Parvu shows you another side of his creativity. In the case of folk art, he was "inspired," he says "by Grandma Moses, her great-grandson Will Moses and the late Charles Wysocki."

Adds Parvu: "You have to learn to see the drama in the ordinary. Things that might be commonplace, you have to dig deep to find out what's interesting about it." In the case of the cover, the artist has painted in several sub-plots unfolding. Did you notice the man who spilled his load of bricks? The bricklayer goofing off on the scaffold? And, how many of the sixty birds and animals can you count?

BOOK DESIGN : JIM JOHNSTON

With over thirty years experience in illustrative design and prepress – Jim Johnston's company *ImageBlast Inc.*, has one passion: image building. Whether it is design, animation, image detailing or photo preservation, the desire is to build "visual eloquence" into every project.

Jim Johnston has lived in Palm Beach County since 1969, beginning his career as a news illustrator for the *Palm Beach Post* in 1973. He and his family now live and work in Tequesta, Florida.

AUTHOR: JAMES D. SNYDER

Jim Snyder lives in Jupiter, Florida and enjoys volunteering as a lighthouse docent for the Loxahatchee River Historical Society.

Snyder was raised in Evanston, Illinois and graduated from Northwestern University's Medill School of Journalism. He spent 35 years as a Washington correspondent and publisher of business magazines before deciding to combine his love of writing and history into a new calling. In addition to *A Light in the Wilderness*, Snyder has written the following books:

All God's Children, How the First Christians Challenged the Roman World and Shaped the Next 2000 Years. An historical novel about the intertwined fates of the Romans, Christians and Jews in the first century. (2000, 680 pp., ISBN 09675200-02)

Life and Death on the Loxahatchee. The story of Trapper Nelson, a real-life Tarzan who fascinated a generation in South Florida. Runner-up for best book on Florida history, Florida Publishers Association, 2002. (2002, 160 pp., ISBN 09675200-6-1)

The Faith and the Power. A chronological history of the early Christians in the turbulent forty years after the crucifixion and how they confronted the Roman Empire in the darkest days of its debauchery. Winner of the Benjamin Franklin Silver Award for best book on religion, 2002. (2002, 416 pp., ISBN 09675200-2-9)

Five Thousand Years on the Loxahatchee: a Pictorial History of Jupiter-Tequesta, Florida. Over 200 photos and maps illuminate a rich history from the days of the Jeaga Indians to modern times. (2003, 217 pp., ISBN 09675200-4-5)

Black Gold and Silver Sands, a Pictorial History of Agriculture in Palm Beach County. With 250 photos, the dramatic story of a county's emergence from the unsettled swampland to modern and abundant farm production in a just few short generations. (2004, 224 pp., ISBN 09675200-5-3)

PHAROS BOOKS

8657 SE Merritt Way, Jupiter, FL 33458-1007
Phone: 561-575-3430